327.09

LASKI H.J.
The dilemma of our times.

HO/68/09445

THE DILEMMA OF
OUR TIMES

THE DILEMMA OF OUR TIMES

AN HISTORICAL ESSAY

Harold J. Laski

FRANK CASS & CO. LTD.

1968

Published by
FRANK CASS AND COMPANY LIMITED
67 Great Russell Street, London WC1
by arrangement with George Allen & Unwin Ltd.

First edition   1952
New impression   1968

Printed in Holland by
N.V. Grafische Industrie Haarlem

FOREWORD

I n 1943 Harold Laski wrote and in 1944 published what he called an 'essay in historical analysis' under the title of *Faith, Reason and Civilisation*.[1] The date is important. It was written amid the heavy duties of his war-time activities, governmental, party and professorial, largely, one feels, to clear his own mind on the issues confronting the world as a result first of the war then fiercely raging and second of the victory in which he was confident. That year saw what appeared to be to many a real closing of the breach between Russia and the West which, always open, though in the heyday of the united opposition of national majorities to Hitler proved capable of being narrowed, had been violently widened to the verge of virtual completeness by the Russo-Nazi treaty of 1939 whereby the Bolshevik revolution to the consternation of all its friends and not a few of its enemies ranged itself on the side of wanton and brutal aggression and of the plan to dominate the free world, and sealed the bargain in the classic manner by the unforgivable re-partition of Poland.

That the assassins of Poland would eventually fall out was apparent to even the dullest but honest student of politics, but it remained a matter of anguished speculation whether it would come soon enough to save the free world which in 1940 and the early part of 1941 was never quite free from the apprehension, justified now by the latest diplomatic revelations, that it might yet have to meet the Red Army in the field. The sudden attack on Russia by Hitler in 1941 virtually ended for the war period at least that particular apprehension, but still left the future of Western-Russian relations a matter of doubt, for the permanent alliance between them on which a durable and profitable peace was held to depend, an alliance of states differing in aim and ideology and having these differences openly or secretly actively at work within the body politic of each of them, in turn depended on internal changes and mental readjustments, all of which were bound to encounter fierce opposition even if

[1] London, Gollancz.

political ambitions could be reconciled and political fears removed.

With others who held themselves to be friends, if critical ones, of Russia and her revolution, Laski had gone through the emotions of the pre-war period when the union of the anti-Nazi forces appeared the only guarantee of peace, and suffered the deep disillusion when Mr. Stalin renounced that union in favour of close alliance with what was considered the common enemy. But by 1943 all alike had been fused in the excitement of having Russia as an ally of the West and of receiving at least indications that alliance would be interpreted as necessitating a move in Russia itself away from imperialism and towards democratic freedom.

In that atmosphere much of the past had to be discarded and the new situation analysed as a point of departure towards what was called 'the revolution of our times'. The purpose of the essay was to study the historical background, and from it glean at once the possibilities of such a development and the lines on which those who wished reconciliation in a new and united free world should best go. It was obvious that from the material point of view victory would leave Russia and the United States incomparably the strongest states; they would also be able to exercise the greatest political and spiritual influence, and it was the effects of that exercise which troubled so much of the old world now dethroned from its pride of place. To both nations Laski was deeply attached. In Russia he saw a process at work creating a new form of society and with it new values; in the United States he saw a nation still like Russia in the stage of becoming which had not indeed broken with the historic past as Russia had done but was capable of a similar creation. In their reconciliation Laski saw at once the hope and the peril of the future but without in the least minimising the historic obstacles which were placed in the way of both and in the way of all other states which would assuredly in their weakness be attracted to one or other.

The question was whether the world would follow their united lead or which it would follow should they not remain united, in which case the tendencies in each most calculated to annoy the other would be developed. Laski therefore made of the essay a searching examination of the moral, intellectual

6

and political crisis of the time. It was written with the same precipitation as that of the thoughts which crowded into his mind in his scanty 'leisure hours'. It was not definitive; it could not be in a time of violent change of unforeseeable extent. It examined and stated problems rather than solved them. It did not prophesy the future which was being at the moment decided in the first instance on the battlefields. It sought mainly to indicate the consequences to that future of not solving the right problems in what he believed to be the right way. It contained strong even violent criticisms of men and policies since criticisms alone could warn the readers of the dangers involved in certain evolutions which had been tacitly accepted, a warning addressed mainly as always to younger readers, who had found in actual war or in war work a respite alike from crisis and the urgency of solution.

It was emphatically a book of the day and it was inevitable that he should think in terms of revision and addition to fit it better to the days which had succeeded. It was in these days that victory instead of lessening the crisis had deepened it and the evolution of events begun to disappoint the optimists and confirm the pessimists. Laski believed that the 1943 analysis being sound was still of value, but it required in the cant phrase to be 'brought up to date'; the field must not be left to the pessimist even if optimism had begun to wilt. He therefore in what were to be the last months of his life began to write a supplementary chapter.

These months were even busier than the war months, the strain of which had begun to tell upon him and was not relieved by post-war events at home and abroad. He wrote as always in a torrent of words and ideas with the result that the supplementary chapter developed into virtually a new work roughly equal in length to the book to which it was to be but a supplement. Much of the earlier argument was repeated though often more fully and always in different form but there were subtractions and there were additions made in the light of the latest developments of which the chief feature was the 'cold war'; there is much that is quite new, some of it contradicting rather than supplementing the original essay. Whether he would have abandoned the idea of a supplement and ended by writing a comprehensive new book, or whether he would have pruned

7

both and reconciled one with the other equally to form a new book we do not know. The MS was left unfinished, and there is no obvious indication that it was near its completion; in what remains the argument is certainly by no means exhausted. The problem before his literary executors was that of deciding for or against publication. It was clear, first, that in the form in which it was left it could hardly be added as a supplementary chapter to a reprint of the 1943 essay, and, second, that no other hand could, with any prospect of producing the work he had designed, seek to undertake its completion. The alternatives then were to allow the MS to remain unpublished, thus leaving the 1943 essay as it were in the air, or to publish it in its incomplete form as his last but unfinished work in the belief that his readers and his students in many lands, warned alike of the circumstances in which it was written and the lack of revision by the author would rather have it as a last gift even in its present state than not have it at all. With this latter view Mrs. Laski was in full agreement and it is now published.

The work of its editor, if he may claim such a title, has been severely kept within the bounds which he believes Laski himself would have set. Nothing has been changed in the text except in the way of correction of those obvious slips in fact or in grammar which are the inevitable features of first drafts, and the appending of an index, and as what was done in similar fashion on earlier work earned Laski's approval, so it is hoped that what has been done now would equally have been approved. There has been nothing in the way of editorial change either in style or opinion even where it is obvious that Laski himself would have made modifications, for a study of new publications and the turning of the 'cold war' into a 'shooting war' in Korea, the sort of development which he feared but confidently hoped would be averted, would necessarily have compelled him to draw deductions other than those which he did make for a situation which by the rapidity of its changes, though in some cases it reinforced his views, does also seriously 'date' them in others. Lacking his own final revision of what was itself a revision, it cannot be taken as a final political will and testament. None the less it is the last word of one who for thirty years and more was listened to on precisely this topic of civilisation's survival through change in agreement or disagree-
8

ment by an audience which was far wider than that which falls as a rule to a university professor. As such there is reason to believe that it will be welcomed.

This is emphatically not the place for either appreciation or biography. There is nothing of substance which the present editor can add to the appreciations already published by such a diversity of persons or offer to the biography which is now in the capable and kindly hands of Mr. Kingsley Martin. Yet it would seem excusable if, on what is as it were the occasion of taking professional leave of him, one thing personal were to be said by one who rarely agreed with him in politics, or indeed in any other sphere, yet received from him a constant and almost embarrassing kindness. He was in fact by nature the kindest person I ever met.

1951.   R.T.C.

CONTENTS

CHAPTER I

THE years after the cessation of hostilities with victory have not brought us peace; rather, on the contrary, they have made us aware how long and hard the road is which separates us from its realisation. For not merely do the former partners in the European war against Nazi Germany and Fascist Italy now stand divided into two great groups which confront one another like gladiators poised for the stroke by which battle is joined, not merely is there no major agreement upon the future of Germany or of Japan, but a great tidal wave of nationalism and revolution now sweeps the world from Malaya to China and South East Asia; and there are deep stirrings in the Africa both of the Arab and of the Negro peoples which threaten the white settlers of that continent with problems quite different in profundity from any which they have previously confronted. There is hardly yet any sign that we have found the kind of equilibrium, political or economic or social, which gives men that sense of ease and security out of which they gain confidence in themselves and faith in the goodwill of their neighbours. It is, indeed, one of the major sources of doubt and fear that, in the age when the aeroplane may carry an atomic bomb across practically the whole world, neighbourhood begins to lose much of its meaning, and goodwill becomes an empty gesture save where it is backed by an armed potential capable of being mobilised overnight.

Complexity has been added to our issues by the overwhelming power of the United States on one side and of Soviet Russia on the other. Never has so much of the world's productive power been concentrated under the control of a single government as that which the American government controls today; never, either, have its technological standards so far outdistanced that of any possible rival. Soviet Russia has larger manpower, and, it may be, productive resources which, when developed, will rival, perhaps surpass, those of the United States. But it is hardly excessive to say that, despite the immense Russian progress since 1917, there is a major element in the technology of production in which the government in Moscow could not hope even to rival the present American standards; and there is no inherent reason to suppose that, a generation from now, the difference will not be at least as great as it is at the present time. For Soviet Russia has not only to complete the psychological process of adjusting all its peoples to the tempo of life and to the discipline that the machine demands; it has to do so over a vast area in which fantastic devastation was caused by war, while the United States remained not merely unscathed, but was able to increase in a remarkable degree the productive power of which it can dispose. While Soviet Russia, moreover, can give substantial aid to its allies in food and in some important raw materials, it is itself in need of capital goods like machinery, and hardly likely, for a long time to come, to be able to assist its allies in that process of industrialisation upon which all of them have embarked. The United States, on the other hand, is not only able to feed its allies on a generous scale, but it is also in a position to export to them both capital and consumer goods upon a scale which, in Western Europe, has unquestionably prevented a catastrophic fall in the standard of living. And even if it be true, as the Russians claim, that Western Europe has purchased American aid in recovery at the cost of adjusting much of its policy, especially its international policy, to a pattern which, in its ultimate outlines, is set by the government of the United States, it is far more true to say that the allies of Russia in Central and South-Eastern Europe have been compelled to adjust both their internal and external policies to Russian requirements in return for little more aid than moral support from Russia. Their Communist-controlled governments, indeed, have been maintained in power as much by the knowledge that they are assured of Russian support as by the free choice of their own peoples; and the relations between the Yugoslavia of Marshal Tito and the Cominform make it fairly obvious that it may well be a dangerous adventure for the government of any of Russia's allies to fail in its search to satisfy the policy approved by its masters in the Kremlin.

It is, practically all over the world, an era of insecurity and confusion. No one doubts that vast revolutionary forces have been unleashed, and that it is impossible even to guess when

14

their energy will have spent itself. No one doubts, either, that the unleashing of these forces has bred a fear and indignation which six years of war have increased rather than diminished in volume. There is no government which has not, directly or indirectly, sought to take steps to limit the influence of ideas it holds to be hostile to the way of life which it approves. The American Government has built a massive bureaucracy to prevent Communist infiltration into its services; and it has created an atmosphere of hostility to Communists outside the sector it directly controls so that there are trade unions, for example, the major energies of which are almost as fully employed in attacking Communists as in seeking to protect and to improve their members' standard of life. The Russian Government, in its turn, has almost sealed off its people from contact with the outside world; the prohibition issued to the Russian women who married British airmen during the war against joining their husbands abroad is not more remarkable than the unending insistence of its propagandists that the Russian Government and people won the war without the benefit of aid from its allies. The spirit of repression, moreover, is not confined to the United States and Russia; in greater or less degree, its instruments are active in every country in the world. In one group of nations it is the Communist who lives almost daily on the verge of danger; in the other group the citizen who finds the Communist way of life inacceptable may well be risking imprisonment or even death.

But the intellectual and moral confusion does not stop here. Communists outside Russia are emphatic in their insistence, not only that it is democratically governed, but that its institutions represent a higher form of democracy than those of nations which do not accept the Russian way of life. For the most part, they find no difficulty in believing that, alike in Russia and in the territories of its allies, their citizens enjoy the fullest freedom, but, also that those put on trial for treason or lesser offences by their governments are judged with an objectivity of view which cannot with fairness be called into question. They find the habits of those governments far more directly related to the well-being of their citizens than those of the governments under which they live; and they explain the normally complete absence of organised opposition to their policies as due, not to repression, or to fear, but as the expression of a satisfaction that is well-nigh universal. If they are asked to explain why, granted the reality of this satisfaction, the operations of the secret police are upon so massive a scale, they are content to affirm that these are merely precautions against the danger of conspiracy encouraged from abroad. I have myself heard an Anglican clergyman affirm publicly in Moscow that the Russian Church enjoys a freedom far beyond any freedom for which the Church of England might permit itself to hope. The control of literature, of music, of the theatre and of related arts has resulted in warnings to some of the most eminent names in Soviet cultural achievement of their failure to produce work which satisfies the criteria of the Politbureau of the Communist Party. The controversy in genetics, in which Lysenko triumphed over his critics by securing the support of the Politbureau, is remarkable not only for the way in which the critics of his views hastened to abandon their opposition and observed in silence both the purging of institutes of research of geneticists who had been obstinate in their opposition, as well as the decision to rewrite textbooks of genetics in order to remove from them the defence of theories which Lysenko rejected; it is also notable for the fact that when eminent foreign members of the Academy of Sciences, like H. J. Muller and Sir Henry Dale, resigned from it in protest against the methods by which Lysenko imposed his doctrine as orthodox, their resignations were refused in order that the Academy might reserve to itself the privilege of expelling them from its ranks.

Given the monolithic structure of Soviet Russia, as well as the almost neurotic obsession with conspiracy so deep-rooted in its history, this compulsion to intellectual conformity is explicable, even if its range and intensity are tragic. But the mental climate in the United States, though far less stormy than that of Russia, has been none the less deeply disturbing in the post-war years. It is easy to dismiss the work of the 'Un-American Activities Committee' of Congress as untypical. But the fact is that it has begotten similar committees in a number of American states. It has resulted in the purge of a large number of civil servants, many of whom have not known the nature of the charges which led to their dismissal. It has led to something which it is difficult not to call a witch-hunt in a number of universities, as well as in industries like the 'movies'. It has made the profession of Communist opinions the source of grave economic insecurity to a large number of persons, and even made it a dangerous adventure for men and women of liberal opinions to be associated not merely in public organisations— the attempt of Mr. Henry Wallace, for instance, to form a third political party—but even in the relations of private life. Any- one who has enquired into the methods by which the Federal Bureau of Investigation 'screens' an official about whose ortho- doxy doubts have arisen will be tempted to think that he has had a real insight into the significance of Tacitus's description of the temper in Rome during the reigns of Tiberius and his successors. It is, no doubt, a healthy thing that this witch-hunt- ing causes as deep an indignation among Americans themselves as it does among foreign observers who obtain a close view of its operation; but what it is difficult to explain is the fact that the institutions of repressive activity seem to be able to survive all protest against their modes of behaviour, and that there is seldom any redress for their victims, even when it is a matter of common knowledge that they have not an atom of reason for the wild charges they do not hesitate to fling at those they are eager to destroy. And it is not seldom true that notorious journalists devote their main energies to wilful attacks upon the characters of eminent men and women, knowing not only that these attacks are wholly devoid of foundation, but, also, that the more slanderous their character, the wider is the audience they are likely to reach. There are few techniques which Dr. Goebbels practised in Nazi Germany which are not now commonplace methods among some of the best-known purveyors of gossip-columns in American newspapers.

It is, of course, easy to say that Americans have always been mostly extraverts, and that reticence has never been a charac- teristic of the American press. It is easy, also, to insist that what is now almost officially known as 'smear tactics' has been a weapon in political warfare ever since the time when General Washington took over the presidency of the new federation in 1789. That was how Jefferson was treated when he was elected president even by men so well known as Timothy Divigat; and the bitterness of the attacks on Andrew Jackson and his wife may well have hastened the death of Mrs. Jackson. The same ruthless indecency was heaped upon Abraham Lincoln during his lifetime; the enemies of Franklin Roosevelt have not ceased their bitter malignity even after his death. It is often argued that there is no reason to suppose that 'smear tactics' are more bitter in their character, or more dangerous in their results than they were; and we are asked to remember the habits of *Le Gringoire* and of Charles Maurras in France, of Northcliffe and Rothermere in England, to realise that the climate of American invective is not a special phenomenon, but merely a species of a genus which is as widespread as social organisation. Any history of the press reveals the inevitability of its use of fear and of hate as weapons wherewith to reach the ends which those who control its different organs are anxious to obtain. Were the newspapers and journals to confine themselves to rational argument as their means of persuasion they would rarely win an audience large enough to enable them to meet their costs of production. Even the religious press, it has often been pointed out, displays a rancorous hostility to those who attack the outlook of the particular church whose interest each of its organs is written to promote, no different in character than that of the secular press. The treatment of non-believers like Paine and Bradlaugh sufficiently illustrates this habit of mind.

I do not doubt that, taken by itself, the denial of any deterioration in the standards of the press has much evidence upon its side; indeed, I should go further and say that, save in those countries where a single pattern of uniform information and comment is imposed alike on the press, and upon all other means of communication, with serious penalties for all who are discovered evading the pattern imposed, there is less possibility to-day that the press can determine the climate of opinion than at any time since the close of the Napoleonic Wars. What makes the appeal to fear and hatred, and the use of 'smear tactics' in the press to-day a matter of exceptional importance is that it is associated with an atmosphere of general insecurity over most of the world in which all the old values are challenged, all the old criteria seem doubtful, and the sense of common purpose both within and between nations is probably weaker than at any time since 1848. We are not only experiencing the strain of a revolutionary age; we are in the midst of an

18

international civil war in which, more and more, men are taking sides, and the governments in the various national societies are erecting barriers as solid as they can make them against the intrusion of ideas which threaten their existence. We have far less ability to be tolerant in 1949 than we had in 1899, even, perhaps, than in 1849. We can no longer take for granted most of the popular aspirations of the nineteenth century. We are no longer certain that democratic government, based on universal suffrage, is a legitimate ideal. We no longer urge, as John Stuart Mill urged, that 'the boundaries of nations ought, in general, to be coincident with the boundaries of states'. We have no longer any confidence in the inevitability of progress. We no longer find it easy to insist that there are areas of life into which no government can legitimately enter. We have lost a good deal of the ardour which went into the struggle for freedom of speech and freedom of association. We mostly regard the effort to realise racial equality between the white man and the coloured man, especially if the coloured man be black, as far more complicated than seemed possible to the proponents of racial equality in the nineteenth century. We are not even certain that we owe the gratitude which before 1914 was almost a commonplace, to the men whose scientific achievements had done so much to enable us to conquer space and disease, and penetrate the secrets of so vast an area of what was previously unknown territory for which we often lacked even the instruments of exploration. We regard with a wry smile those who think that the power of reason over man is growing, or that the development of education on a much wider scale will solve all our major problems. Even great words like 'equality' and 'fraternity' have fallen from their high estate; and the concept of freedom undergoes a spectacular change when it crosses frontiers.

There is an important sense in which the observer of the post-war scene finds the temptation to describe its habits in terms of the famous account in Thucydides of the Corcyrean revolution an almost irresistible one. The scene, no doubt, is more complex, its problems far larger in scale; but there are the same cult of the extreme, the same almost unbearable social tensions, the same abuse of words so that argument is almost impossible, the same poisonous confusion of ends and means,

19

the same tendency to treat the critic as an enemy, the same suspicion of anyone who remains enfolded in the categories of private life as either anti-social or else escapist—in both cases a public danger. But these resemblances all shrink before the fundamental distinction between the classical world of Greece and Rome and our own world. For, in theory, at least, we insist that there is a dignity in the human person as such which forbids his permament relegation to the condition of a slave. We have gone on record as denying that the major basis of the social structure must consist of men and women who perform, and can be compelled to perform, duties which debar them from access to those qualities which, in their intricate combination, we call civilised living. It is indeed important that, despite all the humane qualifications which both philosophers and practical men sought to use to mitigate the general horror of a slave-owning system, the inevitable dependence of civilised life on slavery was taken for granted by the classical world. There may have been a sense of unease about its validity, as in the Stoic lawyers, for example. Here and there, an occasional figure like Cicero may have been genuinely anxious to treat his slaves with kindness and with understanding. But one of the central facts of that world was the acceptance of slavery as a necessary element in the fabric of civilisation. The merciless treatment of slave-revolts is evidence enough of the inability of that world to think of civilisation as compatible with universal freedom of the person as the premise upon which social life is organised.

It would not, of course, be true to say that, even in the fifteen hundred years since the fall of Rome we have succeeded in abolishing slavery. Our achievement is the lesser, but still important one, of insisting upon the invalidity of its central principle, of emphasising the dignity of the human being as the criterion by which to judge the adequacy of the rights he is entitled to enjoy. There has been an effort, always wavering, seldom profound, never continuous, to give to the principles of freedom and equality a universal status unthinkable to the ancient world. It has been an effort, often consciously and still more often unconsciously, denied on one ground or another, of colour or race, of religion or of nationality, of birth or of wealth. But the denial has usually, above all since the Reforma-

20

tion, been on the defensive; its exponents have been increasingly aware that their attitude is in contradiction to what, increasingly also, becomes accepted as the conscience of mankind. The influences which lead to the ever wider perception of this contradiction are, in their basic expression, economic; they spring from the growing power of man over nature, and the change in his productive relations which is the outcome of his effort to utilise as fully as he can the new resources made accessible to him by that growing power. It is particularly notable that the scientific revolutions which are so overwhelming both in the seventeenth century, and in the hundred years from the great discoveries of Faraday and Clerk-Maxwell, should in both cases give special sharpness to the idea of the rights of man, and thus register an exceptional depth of dissatisfaction with modes of behaviour and organisation which appear to involve a denial of those rights. They move, in some fifteen hundred years, from the protest of exclamatory challenge, sometimes bitter and indignant, sometimes wistful and tragic, to the protest of a formulated ethic which may move by steps so massive that we can actually describe in detail the men and the movements they involve, to a demand for specific legal changes which touch directly the central notions of property in a given society. The abolition of the slave trade in 1807, and the conference of freedom upon all slaves in British territory in 1833 are the obvious outcome of a formulated ethic which gathered perceptible momentum over some three hundred years, until its translation into political action by the use of the state power became virtually irresistible.

It is usual to say that this recognition of the dignity of the human person is the result of the impact of Christianity upon the habits of mankind. But this generalisation has no more validity than innumerable similar claims to other great insights by some other religion or people. For what was important to primitive Christianity was not the external status, with its associated rights or their absence, in the relatively simple pastoral society in which its first apostles announced their message; what was important to it was that acceptance of the Christian faith, whether by bond or free, brought salvation to the believer in a world the end of which was at hand. It was concerned with an inner state of mind which rose above the dispositions of an

21

earthly order which was so shortly to give place to the Kingdom of God. When this expectation failed, Christianity had no more difficulty than other religious systems in adapting the practical expression of its doctrines to the demands of the society in which its votaries lived; and after its acceptance as the official religion of the Empire by Constantine, it would be nothing more than simple historical fact to describe it as an influence essentially hostile to progress, embodied in a Church which, in Western Europe, acquired a strong vested interest in preventing social change. Throughout the period up to the Reformation the values to which it lent the sanction of its authority were overwhelmingly values which implied a partnership with men and institutions whose acquisition of power and privilege naturally created a desire to prevent changes which might challenge their right to continued possession of them.

The mediaeval Church, this is to say, was given its character by the framework within which it worked; as an organisation, despite particular movements among its members, it never sought to transcend the character stamped upon it by each phase in the history of that framework during more than a thousand years. That is why we had a Reformation which was not merely a revolt against Rome and against what was evil in the behaviour of its officials but, even more, a drive to attain the recognition that new values were justifiable, the expression of which in terms of behaviour made for relations of production more likely to facilitate access to new wealth whose acquisition was hindered by the Church's refusal to sanction the values necessary to make those relations socially acceptable. The speed with which the Protestant Churches achieved the revaluation required by the rise of the new middle class against the feudal system is only just more remarkable than the swiftness with which the Roman Church made similar adjustments lest delay should result in a disastrous sacrifice of its power. The success of the Counter-Reformation in France and Italy, in Spain and in Belgium is fascinating proof of how old forms can be given new content when their survival is in question. Nor is it less significant to note that, within a century of Luther's death, the major Protestant Churches had effected their own compromise with those who possessed the state-power in the political societies where their rebellion against

22

Rome had been successful. They, too, in much the same way as Rome itself, became instruments, if not directly of repression, at least instruments assisting secular authority to secure obedience from the masses to the relations of production it enforced. Where a religious organisation calls into question the values of the new social order, it will be found, almost invariably, to be a small sect of poor men, low in social status, and often so harried by the law that it is either broken by persecution, or compelled to live a life a large part of which is hidden from the public view as though it were a conspiracy. And if it is to be agreed that the Society of Friends is an exception to this rule, the answer is the important one that within a generation of its origin, George Fox himself had effected brilliantly that kind of compromise with worldly power which leaves the latter content that the preachers of the new gospel seek only individual salvation and have no social innovations to promote which might threaten the basis of the new social order. On the contrary, the Society soon made it manifest that its special field was a passport to the kind of success which breeds acquiescence in, rather than revolt against, the demands of secular power. Since the death of James Naylor, there has been no tendency in Quakerism to find allies among the men and women who organise active resistance to policies they deem evil.

We may, this is to say, argue with some confidence that the intellectual pattern of an age is shaped by the character of its economic organisation, by the possibilities these reveal, and the adaptation of its institutions to the task of exploiting fully those possibilities. It is, of course, true that the intellectual pattern has its effect upon the economic organisation in turn. But the degree to which ideas can, by themselves, change the character of productive relations is, relatively, of a secondary order. This can be seen, for example, in the history of religious toleration. The case for its desirability on both moral and intellectual grounds had been made out long before the ruling classes of most countries had seen that it was an important economic imperative for any of them which sought material advance; and the countries which refused to accept this view suffered, like France after the Revolution, grave economic loss to their more perceptive competitors. It is illuminating to note how obvious to English opinion was the argument of Locke's

Letter concerning Toleration, of 1690, though, in itself, it was nothing more than a masterly restatement of ideas which had been persuasively urged by a long succession of writers for almost a century and a half. Not less illuminating is the fact that within a decade of Locke's *Letter,* the great river of controversial pamphlets which, throughout the seventeenth century, had flowed with almost torrential force, had diminished to a tiny stream. Within a generation, the partisan tactics of the Anglican Church over the Whig views of Bishop Hoadley resulted in its convocation being closed by the writ of the Crown, and the enforcement of silence upon its collective voice from 1717 until 1854.

It is not difficult, in short, to show that the customary basis of all significant institutions in Western Europe and the United States was, until the outbreak of the First World War, given by the needs of that middle class which from the end of the fifteenth century was thrusting its way to power. As it rose, it broke in pieces the productive relations of feudalism, defeated the feudal nobility in alliance with the Crown, and then accepting a large number of its former enemies as friends, reshaped the authority of the Crown to suit its needs, and used the state-power it held thus re-shaped to discipline the great mass of the population to the acceptance of conceptions of law, imposed, if necessary, by coercion, which maximised the privileges it enjoyed as a result of the re-definition of productive relations. The middle class in England, during the first half of the nineteenth century, had given the state-power new objectives to reach which had taken some two centuries fully to define. In defining those objectives, it had evoked a new economics, a new·political philosophy, even a new metaphysic to effect this purpose. It had profoundly changed the historic relation of church and state; it had begun to give the man of science and the technician a different place in society. The world it built changed both the form and the content of literature, as it changed the form and the content of the plastic arts. Anyone who compares the typical costume of the men and women whom Reynolds and Romney and Lawrence painted with the clothes of the men and women who patronised the fashionable artists of half a century later can see how startling is the change produced by the almost universal recognition that power has been transferred to the great bankers and manufacturers and merchants. Though the highest positions in the executive and the legislature were still, over a large part of the nineteenth century, occupied by the nobility and its connections, names like Jenkinson, Huskisson, Wilson Croker, before 1830, and Peel and Gladstone, Cobden and Bright, after it, show that the *novi homines* are able to elevate themselves, or their children, to the most influential places in politics. Few things are more significant in Parliament than that, after Peel's defeat in 1846, the Tory party, the symbol of the 'gentlemen of England', should have turned, even if with doubt and difficulty, to an exotic Jew like Disraeli for their salvation, and that, within a few brief years, the mysterious magic of his personality should have captivated both his party and the Queen and her consort. That achievement is hardly surpassed if, indeed, it is surpassed, by the recognition, after 1848, that government by a heterogeneous body of more or less benevolent amateurs in Westminster must be flanked by an efficient bureaucracy in Whitehall. By 1870, when Gladstone established open competition as the normal mode of entry to the Civil Service, only the Foreign Office remained able, in any serious degree, to stand up to the powerful claims of the solid middle class to a well-nigh universal supremacy. Anyone who compares the Oxford and Cambridge of Whately and Copleston, or even of the young Mark Pattison, with their temper and habits after Jowett had become Master of Balliol, and Clerk-Maxwell had begun to give the Cavendish Laboratory at Cambridge a world reputation, cannot but be aware that the men who won scholarships there from schools like the Rugby of Thomas Arnold, would give a very different account of their ideals and accomplishments than could be found, in the eighteenth century, in the stinging sarcasm of Gibbon and Adam Smith. Nor must it be forgotten that, between 1770 and 1850, both legal eminence and legal reform were wholly the work of self-made men who rose to the height of their achievement with no advantage but their own talents and a remarkable capacity for unbroken continuity of intellectual effort.

What, however, is striking is the fact that at the very moment when the ardent economic individualism of the successful middle class appeared to have reached an unquestioned supremacy, it began to be challenged successfully on the very ground it appeared to have made permanently its own. It had not only to face the emerging competition of growing industrialism in France and Germany and the United States, the need for adaptation to which the very size of its own triumph had made it slow to understand. Its doctrines, in their internal expression, were challenged from three very different quarters. They were attacked by the able group of early English socialists, of whom Thompson and Bray and Bronterre O'Brien were the main theorists, and Charles Dickens, Mrs. Gaskell, and, in his way, Thomas Carlyle, were the chief expositors; they were attacked by the massive reports of great civil servants like Edwin Chadwick and John Simon, who set out in remorseless detail the terrible cost of economic individualism to the health and responsibility of the workers; and their basic questions were being given very different answers from any they could approve, not only half-consciously by John Stuart Mill with increasing vigour after 1848, but by Fitzjames Stephen and Sir Henry Maine, after the 'fifties, who were saying quite openly that the economic individualism and the political democracy with which they were so content was a temporary historic phenomenon due to special circumstances which had not arisen before, and were unlikely to continue for any period of time. Economic individualism might take temporary comfort in the skill with which, after the late 'sixties, Stanley Jevons had appeared to find a means of repelling the socialist attack on the classic theory of value. It might even find it in the strong defence of its cause worked out by Henry Fawcett and Walter Bagehot, and, a little later and with all sorts of careful precautions, by Alfred Marshall and Sir Robert Gitten, who came to look to that generation as effectively persuasive as Ricardo and Nassau Senior had been to the generation after the Napoleonic wars, which was glad to have at its disposal writers who compensated it somewhat for the passionate denunciations of Byron and Shelley, of Cobbett and that new press which seemed to lack all reverence for the solid achievement of escape from national danger and a power to trade all over the world. It liked the solid achievement of the Utilitarians who insisted that good had an attractive materialism about it—that it meant good to eat and to wear, and a condition where confidence could be placed in self-reliance and that attitude to the Common Law which Lord Abinger had so persuasively expressed in *Priestley* v. *Fowler*. It agreed that England was not like other nations; its Chartist Movement ended in no explosion like the revolutions on the Continent, and, apart from minor disturbances in Ireland and Canada, it was evident that the colonies were bound to England by hoops of steel. It regretted the defection from the Church of England of picturesque figures like J. H. Newman, and brilliant organisers like Henry Manning. But, by the end of the 'fifties, most of its representatives thought they had made a bargain with fate which future history was unlikely to re-open; and few of them saw any reason to suppose that the foundations of their social philosophy was being rapidly undermined. In particular, they congratulated themselves on the extraordinary hold Mr. Gladstone had obtained on the allegiance of the working class. Given peace, retrenchment, and reform, either party might well secure political power, without any disturbance of the superb equilibrium in which everything pointed to the skill with which, in answering the problem of freedom, they had solved for eras to come the delicate question of their right to moral authority in the community.

CHAPTER II

THEIR satisfaction was short-lived. In the moment of its triumph, the validity of the victory economic individualism had won was challenged in the name of those masses of the population whose labour was to be the instrument of its consolidation. The historic structure of society in which a small, but relatively wealthy minority lived by the labour of a large majority only a small proportion of whom had security or comfort, began quickly to seem no more unjust in principle under capitalism than it had seemed to the new rulers themselves when they had been seeking the overthrow of feudalism. Passionately as the victorious minority desired to maintain a stable society, it had lost the power to control the dynamic of its routine. Until the era of capitalism, change had always been slow, and conditions from one generation to another had altered but little; a peasant in the age of Diocletian would have recognised the forms of the agricultural technique by which his successor, over fifteen hundred years later, sought to scratch a meagre living from the soil. A Phoenician merchant would not have been greatly surprised by the methods whereby an English merchant of the eighteenth century carried on his traffic in goods in the Near East or India or China. All the social philosophy of the middle class from 1780 to 1850 assumes relations of production that are broadly fixed and certain. The striking feature of social life after the French Revolution is the immense increase in the pace of social change. All the circumstances in which the principles of its economics and politics had been formulated by Adam Smith and his successors were wholly different a hundred years later. Science had, over vast areas, changed the conditions of living so enormously that the categories of thought which suited the period from 1750 to 1850 were in large part an anachronism. The new technology exacted a new philosophy for the simple reason that it opened up new and immense horizons which the old philosophy had not been able to foresee. The contours of the forces of production were already, in the closing years of

29

the nineteenth century, making obsolete the relations of production upon the stability of which the successful middle class had relied. And the greater the degree in which they sought to deny the fact of that obsolescence, the more profound were the difficulties, internal and external, by which they were confronted. They could neither appease the masses nor could they defeat them. Even by the outbreak of the First World War, it was becoming clear that their self-confidence in Europe was disturbed; by the end of that war, the issue of its restoration was the main preoccupation of statesmen. And though this self-confidence lasted for another decade in the United States, it was undermined, as though by a tornado, in the last months of 1929. With the outbreak of the Second World War, some ten years later still, it was obvious that there also the basic philosophy of life upon which the business world relied could not create that new vision of the world without which society drifts rapidly towards catastrophe. For it is legitimate to doubt whether any ruling class was more fearful than the Americans of the need so to define the nature of that new vision that it would give the people ruled the sense of hope, the conviction that life is worth while, the ardour for great adventure. It is only when the philosophy of a ruling class makes its dominant ideas seem universally acceptable that a society can avoid the danger of breakdown through conflict.

It is by the uneasy sense that breakdown is one of the foreseeable risks by which our civilisation is faced that the life of the world has been haunted ever since the second decade of the twentieth century when blind leaders began, perhaps only half-consciously, to drag their peoples into the abyss of devastating war. There was a number of reasons why they lost the power to maintain the peace. In the capitalist democracies, foresight should have made obvious the need for immense social reforms; what was offered was always too little, and, invariably, it came too late. Their standard of life, moreover, as with Great Britain and France, Belgium and Holland, depended upon their possession of vast and wealthy colonial territories the resources of which they were able to exploit to their own special advantage; and to maintain that advantage they had maintained a doctrine of white supremacy which quite naturally bred what was, first, a sullen and secret, and then a fierce and active, nationalism,

30

among the native peoples over whom they dominated. The life of all Europe, moreover, was poisoned by two things. The first was the determination of the ruling class in Germany—an intricate partnership between feudal landlords, big business based on an outstanding use of science and technology, and a military caste which dominated both its allies—to compensate for its late achievement of national unity by bullying its rivals into according to it a full share in those spoils of imperialism by means of which they also hoped to be able to offer the concessions to their own people by which it is possible to delay a shift in the structure of class-power. From the epoch of Bismarck onwards, his policy of 'blood and iron' was an inescapable feature of the European scene. There was no difficulty which the German leaders were not eager to exploit; and there was no brief interval of peace that they did not transform into a blow against their prestige for which they were insistent upon their right to compensation. The inferiority complex of Germany for two whole generations produced a pathological nationalism, which must have ended in revolution or in war. That it produced the second result and not the first was mainly because the socialist parties in Germany were far more committed to the achievement of national prestige than they were to the revolutionary overthrow of the partnership which—and even in defeat—they had an inner conviction alone possessed the capacity for victorious advance.

The second reason why peace could not be maintained was the character of Tsarist Russia. Half Europeanised since the time of Peter the Great, maintaining an uneasy equilibrium by its unresting expansionism, a cruel autocracy supported by a corrupt and inefficient bureaucracy, the Russia of the Tsars had that inner disease which only the surgeon's knife could cure. Though capitalism had made considerable strides in Russia in the half-century before 1914, it had never gone far enough to develop a middle class with the power to insist on replacing a fantastic and foolish despot, with a real faith in the validity of the Caesaropapism which was the doctrinal justification of his rule, by an effective system of constitutional government. With all its territorial ambitions, Russia had shown that it was no match for Japan, and its obvious weakness and internal divisions made its rich farming land in the Ukraine an obvious possibility for German conquest. To safeguard itself, the Russian Government had to seek an alliance with France, which, later, was joined by Great Britain. The Russian Government displayed, also, a strong tendency to regard itself both as the historic protector of the other Slav peoples in Eastern Europe—which made it the contingent enemy of the Austro-Hungarian empire—and it maintained its long expressed demand for the expulsion of Turkey from Europe, and its right to the inheritance of Constantinople. Were this right to be recognised, two important consequences would follow. By getting astride the Dardanelles, Russia would gain, for the first time, direct access to the Aegean, the Adriatic, and the Mediterranean; and it would be in a position at least to challenge, and possibly to thwart, the German ambition of controlling the rich territories of the Middle East, with their vast oil-fields, the exploitation of which in 1914 was only in its infancy. Victory in war was, in 1914, of immense importance to Russia. It would restore the prestige which the Tsarist régime had lost after the defeat by Japan; and it would check the growth of that revolutionary temper which had already staged an exciting dress-rehearsal in 1905, and was again becoming dangerous to the established order as it began to recover from the grim repression which had followed the defeat of the revolutionary parties. What was obvious, after 1906, was that Russia could not stay still. Either it must develop its industries through foreign investment—which involved the growth of a middle class and a large urban working class—or it must rely upon the technique of terror to root out the grave discontent by which the government was faced. In 1914, the circumstances must have suggested to the rulers of Russia that war was a legitimate gamble in which success offered them relief from overwhelming difficulties.

The third reason why peace was impossible was the special position of Great Britain. Its rulers could not afford to be neutral. That might well mean the eclipse of France, the control, if not the actual conquest, of Holland and Belgium by Germany, whose naval power—of threatening magnitude in any case—might then be based on Antwerp, and make British control of the Channel and the Atlantic a matter of grave difficulty. The defeat of France, moreover, would make the control

32.

of the Mediterranean a heavy liability on the British taxpayer; and though the attitude of Italy in 1914 was uncertain, its government was bound by treaty to Germany and Austro-Hungary, and, if France was defeated, an Italy so allied would obviously seek to inherit its Mediterranean influence. Since Italy, moreover, was already a colonial power in Africa, its government was at least likely to ask in the event of France's defeat for its due share of the French empire there. As the British Cabinet surveyed the scene in those anxious days after the assassination of the Archduke Franz Ferdinand at Serajevo, it must have looked to its members as though a large-scale departure from the contemporary balance of power would jeopardise its interests all over the world. Belgium, no doubt, gave the occasion for a British declaration of war; but the chances were obviously overwhelming, that if Great Britain remained neutral and France were defeated, Germany would not only dominate Europe, but control, directly and indirectly, the gateway to the Middle East and India.

It was the fear of German victory in the First World War which brought the United States into the conflict. Though President Wilson did not avow it, it had become clear by 1917 that a Germany which dominated Europe would be an expanding Germany, certain to dominate the Atlantic, and able, in alliance with Japan, to control the Pacific as well. Had Great Britain and France been beaten in the West, and Russia in the East, the Germany of William II would have presented the same challenge to the United States as did Hitler and Japan during the Second World War. It is, indeed, at least a real possibility that it was the failure of Woodrow Wilson to clarify to himself, and, thereby, to the American people, the fact that the strategic security of the United States was bound up with the defeat of the Kaiser's Germany which led to American isolationism after 1918, and thence to a body of measures like the Neutrality Act, the Arms Embargo, the acceptance of passive defence, the refusal to embark on 'entangling alliances', the financial assistance rendered to Mussolini, the sale of scrap iron to Japan, the association with the fatal policy of non-intervention in the Spanish Civil War. I do not think it is excessive to say that the American refusal to reflect upon the fundamental conditions for the strategic security of the United

33

States was as basic a factor as any in organising the conditions which made possible the aggressions of Hitler and Mussolini in Europe, and of Japan in Asia. Even Jefferson, who had coined the historic phrase about the danger of 'entangling alliances' saw clearly that, were Napoleon to conquer Russia, he would be the master of Europe, and that this would lead to a situation in which every prospect of American independence would be jeopardised; that this was not again effectively understood until the famous 'Quarantine' speech of Franklin Roosevelt in 1937 provided the Fascist dictators with their opportunity to gamble on the prospect of world-power. They came very near to success; and it was, so to say, only by inches that the forces of civilisation were able to overcome the forces of barbarism.

The lesson of the inter-war years is painfully clear. It is a period in which the nations, least of all the Great Powers, have no common purpose and no clarity of vision. The external confusion was matched by deep internal schisms in almost every country. There was fear at the periphery of each national life, fear also at its centre. Economic contraction led to the unemployment of millions, and sharpened to the point of danger the contrast between rich and poor all over the world. We can sense a growing tenseness in the atmosphere as economic security diminishes, and see how the tenseness is heightened as, after 1932, the shadow of war begins to brood over the minds of men. It is an age in which the onset of disaster is never really absent; after the re-occupation of the Rhineland by Hitlerite Germany in 1936, it is not excessive to say that each year made the world increasingly conscious that the barbarian stood at the gate poised for the assault. Even the 'appeasers' must have learned after Munich the folly of paying ransom to men who regarded each surrender as merely a basis upon which to formulate new demands. It was an epoch which made peace of mind impossible to any who saw the depth of the threat to civilisation. That is why it was not an age either of great literature or of great art, why, also, the rationalism of philosophic analysis made in terms of logic seemed cold and unsatisfying beside the irrationalism of ardent emotion which demands belief in terms of a blind faith insisting on the surrender of the right to think freely, on the annihilation of individuality, on
34

the duty of the citizen to obey instinctively commands which he is not permitted to understa'nd.

In a period of this character, we find what we expect always to find when a civilisation is faced by a revolution adaptation to which is angrily refused by the greater part of those who have political power in their hands. They are compelled to safeguard their authority by what is in fact the cult of unreason, the retreat from the known to the unknown, the encouragement of strange cults which profess to offer some secret source to the initiated whence comfort and security may be derived. New mysticisms, the foundation of new cults as various as those of which Dr. Buchman is one prophet and Mr. F. H. Alexander another, arise to kindle an enthusiasm which stifles the craving for thought by emphasising the limits of its power to confer understanding. Anyone who examines with care the evolution of a new pagan religion in Nazi Germany will see how the pathology of crisis comes at length simply to stop the effort of the mind to master the material environment about it. Tolerance becomes a crime because it may leave freedom to ideas which call the authority of these escapisms into question. When toleration goes, justice goes too; the criteria of behaviour are set by the rulers' determination to equate morality with obedience. Thereby they can drive the diversity which civilised living requires into a uniformity which enables 'mass-man' to obey, even to find emotional satisfaction as he obeys, and to regard the dissenter as a danger to the community in which he speaks. Thence it is but a step to glorify power for the sake of power, to develop the cult of violence, to make success the test of right. The result was the wholly natural one that the life of the spirit declined, and the world became obsessed with the imminence of calamity. We can almost find the mental climate of those years in the moving letter of Sidonius to his bishop. 'If', wrote Sidonius, 'you can hold out no help in our extremity, then seek to obtain of Heaven by your unceasing prayers that, though our liberty be doomed, our race at least may live. Provide a land for the exile, prepare a ransom for the prisoner, make ready to welcome the refugee.' Here, indeed, is that haunting fear which seeks to avoid catastrophe by embracing a world in which he is conscious that the lights have gone out, and that the new masters will have no use for the gracious life he had known in his country villa near Clermont. Not least important is his insistence on the urgency of silence. 'Do not expect me to speak out,' he wrote to a friend. 'Your own fears, akin to mine, explain the need for silence.'

There is a special interest for us in the letters of Sidonius because he describes with such charm the life of the privileged class in Gaul near the beginning of the fifth century, rich, cultured, living a life of grace and luxury. The comparison with conditions in eighteenth century France as we read of the daily experience of Madame de Geoffrin, or the Maréchale de Luxembourg, or of M. Necker and his wife, is obvious enough; so, too, is the resemblance to what we know of Chatswood and Holland House during the years of the French Revolution and of the Napoleonic wars. The privileged classes of France and England performed their elegant minuet in the knowledge that catastrophe was always round the corner; like Sidonius, they knew it, even when they shut out the nightmare and tried to live in the faith that things, in the end, are bound to come out right, that the forces of progress are, in some mysterious way, bound to triumph over the forces of defeat and of decay. What is striking in each of the three societies, despite the thirteen hundred years which separate Sidonius from the Augustan Age in France and England, is the way in which they ignore the unprivileged classes, their inability to interest themselves in the ideas and the emotions which were penetrating the unprivileged, and making them ready to follow the men who called upon them to overthrow a social order which had no interest in their grievances, and treated them, for the most part, as though they belonged to a lower species of the human race.

When catastrophe came, it brought with it to the age of Sidonius a devastation that made havoc of civilisation for many hundred years. If the ruin of the conflict with which the eighteenth century closed was more rapidly repaired, it nevertheless left behind it a profound spiritual disintegration which reached its climax in the Second World War. We hardly dare to admit to ourselves the volume and intensity of pain involved in the terrible passions it aroused; still less have we the courage to examine the depth of the hatred and the schisms which are its legacy. It has perverted science, broken into pieces the great international community of organised knowledge, made justice

36

everywhere the slave of political belief, broken the hope that we can rapidly recover the level of economic well-being which permits the growth of ease of mind, and out of hope, creates the conditions in which we can re-discover high common purposes the very search for which is an instrument of spiritual regeneration. So powerful indeed are the centrifugal forces in the world to-day that reciprocal communication and ease of movement are, despite the immense advances in technique, more difficult than they were more than fifty years ago. Whole nations cut themselves off by deliberate will from contact with other nations whose pattern of ideas they are unwilling not merely to accept, but even to examine. We have, no doubt, the expectation that, under certain conditions, we can hope for the emergence of compassion and pity. But those conditions are rare in their emergence, and they do not often last long enough to make a durable impression on social behaviour. It is a fair guess that the young aviator in a bombing plane over a great city is more moved to-day by his sense of power than by a longing to be merciful to its crowded inhabitants fifteen or twenty thousand feet below. It is a guess even more probable that few of those with the capacity to dominate the markets in meat or rice or wheat feel that they can afford even to take the time to reflect upon the suffering they exact when they are able to compel their customers to pay the prices they impose. Self-pity for one's own agony as a nation may come to act, as it has largely acted in Germany, to wipe out the memory of the insane and limitless cruelties inflicted, from 1933 to 1945, upon millions of men, women and children, most of whom had either no knowledge of what was happening around them, or asked nothing more than to be obscured in the categories of private life. The rulers of Soviet Russia dismiss as enemies of the public good all foreigners who are sceptical of even the least of their passionately held dogmas. The rulers of the United States are driven by a wild hysteria to denounce and to persecute those among their citizens who think that there may be something of social import in the dogmas to which Soviet Russia pins its faith.

'Our victory will be thrown away,' I wrote in 1942,[1] 'unless it is devoted to great ends.' It cannot be so devoted while a

[1] *Faith, Reason and Civilisation*, p. 11.

'cold war' is being waged by two great combinations of nation-states each of which devotes such ruthless energy to the organisation of witch hunts against the supporters of the other. Fantastic as is the effort of the Central Committee of the Russian Communist Party to control the 'line' to be followed by artists, musicians, writers, biologists, and evil as are the penalties visited upon those of their number who fail to follow the 'line', it is hardly more fantastic than the work of the Un-American Activities Committee in Washington, or of its progeny in the different American states, the evil mysteries which surround the activities of the ex-Communists who, as the remarkable trial of Alger Hiss makes evident, have begun to make the process of delation a kind of occupational disease, or of the important college presidents, in the list of whom one regretfully notes the name of General Eisenhower, who announce that, in their view, no Communist ought to be employed in academic work. Nor is it less than painful to see the speed with which the Federal Bureau of Investigation extends, year by year, the area of its jurisdiction, and the ugliness of the methods it is permitted to use in its operations. The attack on the actors and screen writers in Hollywood, even more, perhaps, the character of the evidence so eagerly admitted against them, reminds one of nothing so much as of the activity of the informers in a reign like that of Claudius, or of the White Terror after the return of the Bourbons in 1815. And, in its ultimate implications, the attempt by Senator Hickenlooper and his supporters to traduce Mr. David Lilienthal, and his colleagues of the American Atomic Energy Commission as inefficient is perhaps as sinister as any of these evil things, since its real objective is to secure for the professional forces the control not only of the supreme weapon of warfare so far known to man, but also, by such a transfer, to subordinate the civilian prospects of development in atomic research to military aims the mere discussion of which has done much already to poison the prospect of friendly international relations.

I do not think it is an answer to the condemnation of these American developments to say that much of what has happened in Russia and among its satellite allies is by far more evil than anything that has occurred in the United States, still less to argue that, if Russia and its allies had been more co-operative, much of this American fantasia would not have occurred. The over-simple view, constantly affirmed both by President Truman and Mr. Ernest Bevin, and supported with all the power of his flashing oratory by Mr. Winston Churchill, that Russia is solely responsible for the present world-crisis, and especially, for its magnitude, could not be honestly accepted by any serious and detached observer. It is, no doubt, true that the Russians have broken important agreements, some made at Yalta and some at Potsdam. But France has done the same. So did the United States in May, 1946, when it prevented the continuance of reparation payments. If Russia has done injury to the United Nations by its constant use of the veto, I believe that America has injured it at least equally by the policy it has pursued in Greece and Turkey and China, and in a somewhat less degree, in Italy also, in each case without even the pretence of consulting the United Nations. The responsibility of the Government of Great Britain for the tragic history of Greece and Palestine in the post-war period is a very heavy one; and, in each case, the Government has pursued policies in which brutality, lies, malice, and evasion have been elements of major importance. When British and American statesmen accuse Russia of destroying democratic régimes in all the countries under its influence, the fact, of course, is that, in the Anglo-American sense, only Finland and Czechoslovakia possessed democratic régimes. There was no democracy, before 1939, in Hungary or Bulgaria, Rumania or Yugoslavia, they were stagnant, predominantly peasant states, dominated by anachronistic feudal aristocracies which ruthlessly exploited the masses. Nor had there been anything democratic about the Poland which was brought into being in 1919; on the contrary, right down to Hitler's declaration of war against it in 1939, its chief industries were expansionism, and an anti-semitic virulence only surpassed by that of Nazi Germany. Nor must we forget, when we speak of Russia as having attacked or destroyed the independence of all these states, as well as that of Iran and of Turkey, that all them, in fact, have been client states ever since the First World War, and that, since 1945, most states in Western Europe have been client states of the

39

power-bloc which the Governments of Great Britain and the United States have been so carefully building.

We really gain nothing by denouncing, with President Truman, Russia's 'ruthless course of action and the clear design to extend it to the remaining free nations of Europe', as having 'brought about the critical situation in Europe to-day.' That is a comforting simplification which enables the enemies of Russia to insist that Stalin has merely replaced Hitler as the enemy of mankind, and that we have entered upon the 'cold war' to prevent Russia from conquering the world, just as we entered the war of 1939 to prevent Hitlerite Germany from conquering the world. That may enable the governments of the Western Powers to embark upon a programme which, in varying degrees, is a threat to civil freedom and a basis for demanding large-scale rearmament, and universal military service. But it does not prove that President Truman or Mr. Bevin, or their supporters have accurately diagnosed the motives of Russian policy. All that the strongest case against Russia has so far proved is that its leaders are cynical, obstructive, fearful, not without cause, of attack from the West, and determined to use the present ugly condition of the world to minimise the possible impact of such an attack by extending its sphere of influence as far as it can. But that is the case Russia makes against the governments to which it is opposed; and when it sees the activities of British and American statesmen in Greece and Spain and the Middle East, and to some extent, also, in Scandinavia, it can draw up an indictment against them which is strong enough to make the more sober of its critics seek for more careful diagnosis and understanding instead of for the chance to indulge in wild and furious invective.

I argued in 1942 that both the World Wars and the immense events in Russia in 1917, are part of a revolutionary process as profound as the Reformation or the great French drama of 1789. This process has three unmistakable aspects. There is the unmistakable technological revolution, which has not only made the whole world move interdependent than ever before, but has also created demographic problems which we cannot solve without the peace and disarmament which are now the necessary conditions of economic well-being. But, alongside this technological aspect, there is also a revolutionary change

40

in the distribution of social and economic power. All over Europe, the middle class which mainly dominated its life finds its very existence jeopardised by depression, by currency depreciation, by the inability to renew productive power by new capital formations, by expropriation, and by the tragic compulsion to exile. Over a large part of Asia, also, the traditional semi-feudal ruling class is visibly disintegrating. The position of China and India illustrates the parlous condition of that age-long exploitation of backward peoples we call imperialism. To this must be added the grave fact that the devastation caused by the war of 1939 has struck an immense blow at the productive possibilities of Europe and the Far East. Much of its machinery has been destroyed, or has become obsolete; its agricultural losses have been immense. It has suffered from the diminution of its technical and managerial skills—already inadequate in 1939—on an immense, even overwhelming scale. Those who have to live by manual labour are inevitably suffering from the malaise, physical and psychological, which comes from the fatigue and frustration of six years of total war. The example of Russia shows clearly how hard a task it is to school a new ruling class to the creation of the behaviour and the evocation of the ability which enable a revised social order to ascend from devastation to the point where it can utilise the implications of the technological revolution in which it is involved.

The third aspect is one which gives our present situation its dramatic tensity. It is the fact that the United States and Russia stand on a level of power far beyond that with which any other nation-state is likely to be able to compete in the next generation. The result of that pre-eminence, linked as it is with profoundly antagonistic ways of life, has been twofold. It has made each of them a centre of attraction, drawing to itself as many lesser nation-states as it can; and it has made each group, as formed, watch every move of the other with suspicion and fear, so that, in the insecurity of all, the world has already begun to rearm on a scale which no nation can seriously afford. And that insecurity is immensely deepened by the knowledge that if fear did lead to war, atomic weapons certainly, and bacteriological weapons possibly, would be used with catastrophic effects, the scale of which no one can attempt to measure. Whatever else is in doubt, it is at least certain that the organisation a third world war would render necessary is of a kind that could not be reconciled with the maintenance of democratic institutions. If we cannot avoid war, whatever survives when hostilities are concluded will necessarily be shaped by power that must assume totalitarian forms.

It is this fear of war, which broods like a vulture over all mankind, that has put civilisation into jeopardy. What we call the 'cold war', indeed, is not a new thing, for it was long ago described by Hobbes in a famous passage of the *Leviathan*. 'War consisteth not in battle only, or the act of fighting,' he wrote, 'but in a tract of time wherein the will to contend by battle is sufficiently known; and therefore the nature of time is to be considered in the nature of war; as it is in the nature of weather. For as the nature of foul weather lieth not in a shower or two of rain, but in an inclination thereto of many days together : so the nature of war consisteth not in actual fighting, but in the known disposition thereto, during all the time there is no assurance to the contrary . . . In such condition there is no place for industry because the fruit thereof is uncertain; and consequently no culture of the earth, no navigation, nor use of the commodities that may be imported by sea; no commodious building . . . no arts, no letters, no society and, which is worst of all, continual fear and danger of violent death. And the life of man solitary, poor, nasty, brutish and short.' There are large areas of the world in which Hobbes's description closely resembles the facts; there are other areas in which the misery he describes is only held back by an immense effort of peoples whose fatigue is unmistakable—the kind of fatigue, I add, which has always been the occasion which enables malignant interests to attempt, at least, the arrest of inevitable change. For in all critical times there have always been traditionalists whose main purpose is to prevent the development of innovation beyond that point where its obvious outcome is the building up of a new social order; and those traditionalists have rarely failed to phrase their purposes in terms which seek to convey the conviction that the changes demanded are bound to result in disaster and that only by reliance upon the basic principles of the past can the boundaries of freedom be enlarged.

42

The outstanding traditionalist of this type in the world to-day is, regrettably enough, Mr. Winston Churchill. To affirm that this is so is not to diminish by an iota the recognition of the debt the whole world owes to him as one of the three supreme architects of the victory over Fascism and Nazism. But it is now apparent that all his genius and courage as a leader in war had no essential relevance to either the issues over which the war was fought or to the problems it has left us still to solve. Mr. Churchill, from the outset, was concerned with the preservation of what he called 'traditional Britain' merely; if he expressed his willingness to agree to what he described himself as 'a few measures of practical reconstruction', that was only to make it easier to preserve 'traditional Britain'. Granted the magnificent sense of expediency which made him instantly accept Soviet Russia as an ally on June 22, 1941, we can see now that it was with the reservation that he regarded Soviet Russia as simply a war-time friend, the forces of which were part of the insurance he sought against the destruction of 'traditional Britain'. The skilful and persistent effort he brought to the great task of enlisting American aid no doubt was the outcome of more complicated motives. He rightly valued American productive power as the 'arsenal of democracy'. He assessed with imaginative insight the impact upon our enemies that the mobilisation of American manpower would make to the actual waging of war. Not least, by any means, he inspired the British people by his own inflexible will, expressed in memorable phrases, with the courage never to submit or yield. But, fairly clearly, some considerable time before the Yalta Conference. and very certainly after it, two things were clear in his mind. The first was that, if he could, he would take no step 'to liquidate the British Empire'; the second was that he wished the future of Europe to be decided by the Atlantic Powers, including the United States, that he saw no reason for the advance of Russia in Europe, and the third was that he was determined to build, in the post-war world, a great European union, guaranteed by America, to keep the Russians behind the line of the Vistula. His enthusiasm for his special brand of European Union, whose function, when all the decorative rhetoric was swept away, was at all costs to keep Russia from entrance into the Middle East and Europe; his glowing enthusiasm for the monarchical systems of Europe, before and after 1945, proved how little he had really learned from the experience of Europe. He was for the return of the reactionary monarchies, which showed how little he was able to understand their obsolescence. His conduct of the British election campaign of 1945 was evidence and to spare that he regarded as moderate a socialism as any in Europe as in essence nothing more than episodic and comparable only to the 'Kerensky episode' when moderate socialism took the path which led inexorably to Lenin. His fanatic opposition to Mr. Attlee's proposals to liberate India and Pakistan and Ceylon and Burma was the outlook of a man who would stake his all upon the gambler's throw that their primary allegiance was to Great Britain and not to their own citizens. His speeches at Fulton, Missouri, in 1946 and at the Massachusetts Institute of Technology in the spring of 1949, made it obvious that he regarded himself, in essence, as the man whose destiny it was to form the great coalition which Russia would not dare to meet in deadly combat; and that his zeal for European Union was, more than anything, a plea for West German rebuilding so that it could, if necessary, stand, with the aid of the United States, firm and unified against what, after Yalta, he came more and more to regard as the Russian enemy. Indeed, it is not too much to say that, after 1946, preoccupation with putting limits to Russia's destiny, 'bringing', as he put it, 'things to a head', was the spinal column of all his thinking. He carried Mr. Truman with him; no one has a better claim to be regarded as the real author of the 'Truman doctrine'. Still more remarkable, he carried Mr. Ernest Bevin with him; and from the time he left office, it is not unfair to say that no Labour Minister, if any, was more influential in the shaping of British foreign policy. Palestine apart, he caught Mr. Bevin on the horns of the masterly dilemma that the Labour Foreign Secretary had either to accept the principles of traditionalist foreign policy, or to embark upon risks and adventures about which he could not be certain. Despite all his noisy thunder, foreign policy was a realm in which, to Mr. Bevin, Mr. Churchill's word was law. The outcome was his choice of a full-blooded alliance with America, the essential plans for which Mr. Churchill drew, and the implementation of which Mr. Churchill really superintended.

The Atlantic Security Pact was signed by Mr. Bevin; but Mr. Churchill's was the hand which guided his pen. Despite all Mr. Bevin's claims, the Pact was, in its real roots, above all a threat to Russia to keep out of the West or risk a head-on collision with America and its allies. If anyone invented the policy of 'containing' Russia, it was Mr. Churchill's traditionalism which was the vital parent of the idea.

In the post-war world, in short, Mr. Churchill was the pivotal figure. The world was doubtful, strained, hesitant. On the Western side, he alone was certain what he wanted to do. Mr. Bevin paid to virtue the price that one pays to hypocrisy; disliking the Russian pattern he fell back, if with retarded effect, on what Mr. Churchill wanted passionately. So did the four Secretaries of the United States who in his time presided over the State Department. So did the majority of the Foreign Ministers in Western Europe. None of them saw that what, in truth, they were doing was returning with Mr. Churchill to his ideas of 1919-20, except, perhaps, the Foreign Minister of Sweden. Few of them recognised that, in accepting Mr. Churchill's ideas, they were, in fact, accepting principles which he had been unable successfully to operate a generation ago. They felt that he really knew his mind when they were doubtful of the next step they should take; and they accepted the authority of his conscience as though it were their own. There was some discomfort in France; there was an acrimonious debate in Sweden; there was a sigh of hesitation in Norway. But the immense prestige of Mr. Churchill was sufficient to override all doubts; and just as, after 1933, he was slowly able to build the grand coalition against Hitlerism, so in the years after 1949 he was able to build the grand coalition against Stalinism. In both cases he spoke as a private member of the House of Commons, but in both cases, he secured a submission to an irrational authority which was more than anything a 'pseudo-rational vision' which he succeeded in getting accepted as faith in a rational validity based on the experience of the war years. He succeeded, like Nietzsche, by the immense emphasis he laid on the statesman's capacity to promise that which he hopes he may not be called upon to perform. He spoke ardently of man's dignity and power; but he emphasised that which all of them were aware of only too keenly, the

45

danger of man's powerlessness before the might of Russia. He insisted that national independence was merely pride, and he made hate seem rational because it conferred upon the governments which felt it not only the feeling of emotional relief, but the pleasure of hating an enemy who called for the asceticism of selflessness and sacrifice. His skill, moreover, lay in the immense reputation he brought to the service of a destructiveness in which his supporters found immense self-comfort—the potential fatality of the atomic bomb.

What, in fact, Mr. Churchill has achieved is what he failed to do in 1919-20. He has organised the counter-revolution, and brought in to its support the might of American power. There were glimpses of his purpose during the war years; we now know that beneath a very real admiration of Russian heroism in battle, there was always a steadfast determination, if he could, to keep Russia and its revolutionary doctrine out of Europe. When this failed, as it had already by the time of the Yalta Conference in 1944, Mr. Churchill devoted his energies to an attempt to confine Russia to Eastern Europe. He hoped to preside over this effort by a sweeping victory in Great Britain in the general election of 1945; and it is notable not only that he sought to rally the nation to his side by the insistence that a socialist victory would mean political and economic slavery, but that he has steadily re-affirmed this insistence ever since he was overwhelmingly defeated at the polls. His energies in opposition have been devoted to the creation of a union of the West European states for whose resistance to Russian influence he has continually pleaded for American patronage. Partially, at least, he has had his way; and it is not the least significant aspect of his effort that he has obtained throughout the co-operation, sometimes closely, sometimes more loosely, of the Labour Government, and especially of its first Foreign Secretary, Mr. Ernest Bevin. His argument has always been the determination of Soviet Russia to communise Europe, and the warning that its rulers have only been prevented from doing so by fear of the American monopoly of the atomic bomb. He has been urgent that the Russians should be driven to a showdown while the American monopoly remains, the inference obviously being that a refusal on their part to come to satisfactory terms would then justify a preventive war against

46

them, the minimum outcome of which would be the compulsory abandonment by Russia of any ambition to penetrate the West, in which, for reasons of strategy, he includes both Greece and Turkey. In a real sense this is to say that Mr. Churchill's notorious Fulton speech in 1946 may be regarded as the foundation upon which the Truman doctrine, in all its immense perspective, has been built.

Alongside Mr. Churchill's international policy, it is important to bear in mind the perspective which determines his criticism of the Labour Government's domestic measures, since, here, he has been profoundly hostile to it. He has pinned his faith to the view that socialist planning is indefensible. It chokes enterprise, it offers no incentive to men with the spirit of adventure, it is inefficient, and it transforms a society of free men into the dispirited dependents of a fantastic bureaucracy. He compares the poverty of Great Britain with the wealth of the United States, and concludes that the difference is the outcome of the inherent inferiority of socialist planning to the capitalist reliance upon the free play of the price-system in a market economy. He taunts the Labour Government for its dependence upon American aid to maintain the standard of living in Great Britain; and he pledges the party he leads, if it is returned to power, to liberate the people from controls, to stop the process of nationalisation in industry, to lower taxation, and broadly speaking, to go back to the relatively 'free economy' of the pre-war period. To this end, as he has explained, while he proposed to maintain 'necessary' controls, lest the people suffer in the process of restoring the 'free economy', he will require a 'doctor's mandate' to undo the grave damage inherent in what has already been revealed by the movement of the Labour Government towards socialist planning.

It is clear that Mr. Churchill's approach to the problems of our time rests upon four major principles. In the international field, it requires a United Europe, firmly united with America for military purposes, to stop any Russian advance into the West, and the transformation of the European Union he desires into some kind of economic federation capable of learning the lesson inherent in the results of the great free trade area upon the American continent. In the domestic field, it requires the

47

limitation of government action in industry and commerce to the narrowest possible area, and reliance upon private enterprise as the best way of increasing the national standard of life. Mr. Churchill, indeed, does not propose to return the coal industry or the railroads or the electric power industry to private hands. But he will denationalise road transport; he will leave the iron and steel industry to its present owners; he will trust to the private builder for the provision of houses, and he will indulge in no further programme of nationalisation. By freeing private enterprise from control by Whitehall, he will make possible the return of that free competition which enables the most efficient producers to survive by proving their capacity to satisfy the effective demands of the market. Like the United States, consumers' sovereignty will be the governing principle of the national effort.

I cannot discuss here with any fullness the principles of which Mr. Churchill is the proponent. Their dangers, on the domestic side, are clear. The proposed return to 'free enterprise' means the return to an economy in which, in the pre-war years, there were never less than one million unemployed, and most of the major industries were dominated by cartels and price-rings which made the notion that the system was genuinely competitive in considerable part a hollow mockery. In the pre-war years, moreover, there was no prospect of solving the housing problem, quite inadequate expenditure on education at every level, grave neglect of scientific and technical research—the one basis upon which, in any circumstances, we can maintain our economic position—and a distribution of wealth so unequal that social relationships were poisoned by class-differences. Preventive medicine occupied a minor place in our system of public health; and the nutrition of a family depended wholly upon the income which came into the household. There were grave inequalities of opportunity; and, for the overwhelming majority of the population, the chance of an advance in life was a small one. Most people remained in the class into which they were born, and there existed a large reservoir of talent which was never afforded a chance to flow forward. That is the Great Britain to which Mr. Churchill proposes to return, at a moment when its overseas investments have been lost, its war devastation only partly repaired, the

48

renewal of its capital equipment only in its first stage, and the prospect of the complete cessation of American economic aid. His comparison of the British economy with the American takes, of course, no account of the fact that the first is that of a small and thickly-populated island, deeply scarred by war, and the second that of a vast continent with immensely greater resources, a modernised technological equipment, and a territory unscathed by the experience of war; nor does he dwell upon the fact that even this wealthy nation was caught in 1929, in the grip of a depression from the horrors of which it was only saved by the intervention of the Federal Government in its economic life. Mr. Churchill, too, is silent about the fears in the United States lest it enter, in the near future, into a second depression of a magnitude comparable with that of 1929. He is, in short, asking the British people to gamble upon the consequences of a return to the economic system which was responsible for most of its sufferings between 1919 and 1939. He demands a return to a society the relations of production in which were geared to the protection of the privileges of a minority; and he represents that return as the restoration of freedom for the whole community.

On the international side of his policy, there is more that must necessarily be said. No one can doubt that the post-war diplomacy of Soviet Russia has, combined with its ruthless indifference to freedom, done great harm to its moral status in the Western World. Directly or indirectly, it has forcibly destroyed not only the reactionary parties of the Right, but flourishing social democratic parties, in all its satellite allies, and it has turned all of them into police-states subordinate to its own purposes. It has shown hardly a sign of any willingness to give strength and direction to the United Nations. It has done all that it lies in human power to do to impose a grim uniformity of outlook upon all its own citizens, and to isolate them from any contact with the outside world. Whereas, moreover, the Russian Revolution of 1917 was the expression of a great popular upsurge of which Lenin and the Bolsheviks took charge, and to which they gave direction and purpose, the post-1945 revolutions in Russia's satellite states have been imposed from above, at the orders of the Politburo in Moscow, and are maintained by continuous purges even of Communist

49

leaders who show signs of refusing to follow the line that Moscow has laid down; nothing here is more significant than the massive offensive of the Cominform against Tito, and the dismissal of men like Gomulka in Poland, of Kostov in Bulgaria, and of Rajk in Hungary. The forcible destruction, moreover, of the Social Democratic Party in Soviet Germany was not only an unconvincing spectacle at the time, but was shown to be unconvincing when the free elections there, in the summer of 1949, showed that forty per cent of the population desired to express their opposition to Russian methods of government even when they could see no time-limit to their application. There was a savagery in the Russians' relations both with their satellites and their former partners in victory the unpopularity of which gave Mr. Churchill enormous assistance in building up the forces of counter-revolution.

It was, no doubt, of high importance that the war left Russia the strongest Power in Europe; but that strength is, for many years to come, offset by America's abandonment of isolationism, and its decision to regard Northern and Western Europe as its own Atlantic frontiers. Since, moreover, American interest in Middle Eastern oil made it the partner, with Great Britain, in protecting all that area, inclusive of Turkey, and in denying Russia access to the Mediterranean, it followed that Russia could not attempt to invade the Anglo-American sphere of influence, in an endeavour to extend the area of its revolutionary influence, without war. Even in Germany, the harshness of its policy weakened its authority; and fear of its expansionism led America and Great Britain, with a somewhat frightened support from France, to abandon the idea of restoring German unity, and move to the creation of a West German state the industrial potential of which it was their purpose to integrate into what may be called the Atlantic economy. That left Russia with the difficult problem of restoring its own huge losses from war partly by demanding further sacrifices from its own people, and partly by using the productive power of its satellites to nourish its own development—a method of which one outcome was the schism in the Cominform caused by the immediate emergence of Yugoslav nationalism. And once the Russian leaders refused, both for themselves and for their satellites, to take advantage of the Marshall offer of American

50

economic aid, they were obviously bound not only to prevent the large-scale development of East-West trade in Europe—an important condition of European recovery—but to do all they could to prevent the success of Marshall aid by using Communist parties in Western Europe to hamper the effort there at the economic rehabilitation which American aid sought to achieve. Granted, further, the dependence of West European economy on American aid, at least until 1952, the real hope of Russian victory in the 'cold war' had necessarily to be built on the hope of an American depression.

Yet, in that Russian hope, there lay the gravest threat to the peace which Russia itself required at least as much as any of the Western Powers. By far the easiest way out of a depression for any industrial nation is an immense increase in its armaments programme; I do not need to emphasise the significance of this in the atomic age. It is sufficient to affirm that an America in an economic crisis from which it seeks to emerge through rearmament would compel Russia to precautionary measures fatal to its own effort at recovery. That is, I think, the fatal period when a system founded upon the principles of social revolution cannot peacefully co-exist with a system which denies those principles. One will challenge the other simply because, in such circumstances, there is no room for the survival of both. The world will be plunged a third time into the maelstrom of totalitarian war. And this war will be the more horrible in that few of the participants will be able to avoid the coincidence of foreign war with civil war on their own territories. There will be large-scale sabotage, dangerous mutinies within the armed forces, the swift abandonment everywhere of all democratic institutions and all tolerance of mind and heart. Every state will become at once a quasi-military dictatorship in which the only virtue will be obedience, and the overwhelming nightmare the uncertainty in each citizen about which authority he ought to obey. It will be a world of terror the more horrible because in such a war even victory is defeat, and the scale of devastation will be so extensive as largely to nullify the dignity of human nature. The civilisation we know will undergo a long and agonising eclipse. Many years of bitter anguish will pass before an endless winter of the spirit begins anew to show some almost pitiful sign enabling man to think in terms of the coming of a new spring.

51

CHAPTER III

I T is not, surely, surprising that in a period like ours of insecurity, of violence, and of deep distrust, the prevalent mood everywhere should be one of sombre pessimism and of bitterness. Even in the United States where, since the close of hostilities, there has been more wealth and a higher standard of living than any nation has ever known, the prevailing undertone of policy is that of fear. There is fear of communism, fear of war, fear of depression, fear of a growth of doubt about the values inherent in the American way of life. Even the possession of the atomic bomb bred fear lest its secret be discovered. The world of American science is afraid lest its freedom be destroyed by subordination to military authority. The academic world is afraid lest unconventional thought should bring its institutions under the suspicion of 'Un-American' activities. Fear pokes long fingers into the glamour-world of Hollywood. The witch-hunt is so wide and so hysterical that men and women seek to atone for a radical past not only by a loud confession of sin, but, even more, by wild accusations against strangers, and even friends, with a violence that reminds us of the terror in imperial Rome when the Augustan peace had ended. Perhaps nothing illustrates quite so vividly the sense among Americans of a danger which threatens the foundations of their social order as the vast extension Congress has given to the size and authority of what is, in fact, a secret police, and the agreement that its members shall test the loyalty of federal officials without the need to formulate charges against the men and women whose good faith they call into question. And when the witch-hunt is conducted as though it were a gladiators' show, with the different interests raucously applauding their respective champions, it is difficult not to feel that sense of despair which recognises the impossibility of removing profound evils from a social order without a violent transformation of its central principles of coherence and continuity.

The fear which pervades the foundations of American society is, of course, characteristic of the rest of the world also. Our traditional values are in doubt because, over wide areas, the experience of the masses lags so far behind the hopes they have come to deem legitimate. They are less willing to endure the frustration of purposes which have moved rapidly from the periphery to the centre of their lives. That is why so many of the customary routines which gave the social order its stability have ceased to evoke their acquiescence. They have a sense of frustration which makes them deeply dissatisfied with the methods of co-ordination by which the inherited pattern of our communal life could be peacefully adapted to a changing environment by slow steps none of which involved crisis or even strain. We are dealing, moreover, with problems which deeply involve whole peoples whose experience has largely lain outside the presuppositions, both political and economic, of the central stream of sociological observation from which great thinkers had wrested the generalisations which are the assumptions upon which statesmen act. The largest of these assumptions was the belief that the main categories of a society are a privileged minority and an under-privileged mass subdued, in one way or another, to acquiescence in the privileges of that minority as, for the period it is possible to foresee, the necessary shape of the social order. Since the weapons both of persuasion and of force belonged to that minority in the hands of which rested the power of the state, it was able, in all normal circumstances, to meet and overcome any challenge it might encounter.

The outstanding feature of this age is the swift breakdown of the presuppositions of which I have spoken, and the widespread refusal of privileged minorities to accept the necessity of their revision. That is why ours is an age of violence in which values once deemed permanent by reason of the powerful institutions which protected them are angrily rejected because their protective institutions have lost their power. We shall not re-establish those values without an alteration of their content upon a scale far greater than we are yet prepared to admit. Certainly we shall not re-establish them by war. We sought to do so in the six years' struggle against Nazism and Fascism; yet the overwhelming defeat of these has only altered the directions from which the challenge comes to their simple constitution. We may, of course, be foolish enough to make the attempt to overthrow the new challenge by force; if we do, my own guess is that we shall merely move from an age of fear and violence to one of greater fear and greater violence. We need, in fact, if our civilisation is to survive, to admit that we have reached one of those points in history when, as Edmund Burke, himself no lover of change, insisted that 'they who persist in opposing that mighty current will appear rather, to resist the decrees of Providence itself than the mere designs of men'.

Let us quote Burke once more as the starting-point of a more positive approach. He had quoted with approval the great saying of Sully that popular violence is always the outcome of popular suffering. He had told the House of Commons, in his speech on the East India Bill, that 'my observation has furnished me with nothing that is to be found in any habits of life as education, which tends wholly to disqualify men for the functions of government'. Even in the first months of that French Revolution which he came to hate so furiously, he preserved the insight to pronounce that 'in all disputes between the people and their rulers, the presumption is at least upon a par in favour of the people'. To that we may add that nothing is so likely to avoid violence in a community than popular participation in power, and much more likely than popular exclusion from it. Since our civilisation is built upon the pre-supposition that the personality of ordinary citizens is entitled to respect, it clearly becomes our duty to find the institutional means for its expression, and to admit that where their interests are considered only in the context of a minority's privilege, the whole society becomes morally degraded in the outcome. That is one of the secrets of Russian power over its neighbours. Just as in Russia itself, the violent overthrow of Tsar and landlord and manufacturer and even Kulak aroused no sense of pity among the urban artisans or the endless millions of poor peasants in the rural areas, so the immense reforms which swept away the large land-owners of Poland and Hungary, the rich and exploiting manufacturers of Warsaw and Lodz, of Budapest and Szeged, of Bucharest and Jassy, left no sense of remorse, no admission that evil deeds had been committed. The popular poetry and the folksongs of these peoples are a long record of enduring anger and of painful resentment. So, too, in Czechoslovakia, when the Sudeten Germans were driven out, however cruel their fate, their suffering seemed to most Czechs little more than poetic justice. We shall miss altogether the emotion produced by the sweeping agrarian changes as well as the large-scale industrial nationalisation introduced under Russian patronage unless we realise that they appeared to the overwhelming majority as liberation from an ancient servitude, and that those who were hostile to the magnitude of the changes the Russians encouraged appeared to the masses in each satellite country as men who sought ways and means to transform an emerging freedom back into an obsolete slavery.

There is an important sense, too, in which this was true of Italy, both agrarian and industrial, and even of urban France. In the former, poverty was normal on the land, especially in Sicily, and, in the cities, for over twenty years, the great manufacturers had not hesitated to give their support to Mussolini becaust he safeguarded their power from the pressure of the trade unions which he had reduced to impotence. Even in France, the urban worker was aware that no government, not even under the Fourth Republic, had the courage to force the farmers to pay their due share of taxation, and that prices were high because a fantastic tariff gave them undue protection against cheap wheat and other cereals imported from abroad. They knew, too, that the *haute bourgeoisie* enjoyed a conventional immunity from the power of the tax-collector, and that even the parties of MM. Herriot and Léon Blum lacked the courage to enquire too closely into the legal validity of these arrangements. The curious *moeurs* of *la république des camarades* was expounded to them not merely in the special terminology of Communist propagandists, but in the admirable French of conservative royalists like Charles Maurras, and conservative Republicans like M. de Jouvenel. One myth, at least, they were tutored to accept : the technical competence of the French General Staff. When this was broken, in June, 1940, by the pitiful surrender of Pétain and Weygand to the historic enemy at the same Compiègne where, a generation earlier, Foch had received the surrender of the German representatives, it is not really surprising that the average Frenchman either lost all faith in bourgeois institutions, or like the great historian Marc Bloch, found an emotionally satisfying death

56

in a guerilla warfare in which Communists inspired by Moscow played, if not a pre-eminent, at least a persistently heroic part. To the ordinary Frenchman, after liberation, the acceptance of the Communist idea, whatever it meant to Thorez and Duclos, represented the conviction that there was at least one group in France eager to cleanse his country from that taint of which the Vichyisme of Laval and Darlan was the ugliest expression. To citizens such as these, a quarter of the French people, General de Gaulle was little more than a renovated and egocentric Boulanger, trying, with scant success, to double the rôles of Joan of Arc and Clémenceau, and, in any case, inadequate to his proposed function because he massed behind him the doubtful ranks of the clerical power.

It is important for us to realise that the idea of the Russian Revolution has increased, and not diminished, in influence a generation after the Bolsheviks assumed power. From the angle of most of Western Europe, it is, of course, easy to point out the immense evils in its record. Its leaders bear the responsibility for the execution and imprisonment of some millions of men. I know of no account of its labour camps which does not suggest a brutal disregard for the fate of their inhabitants. None of the apologias seem to me to justify that 'disease of orthodoxy', as the Webbs termed it, which is as virulent to-day as it was before 1939. A large amount of Soviet propaganda is at least as raucous and untruthful as the worst of the hostile propaganda of which the Russian Government makes such angry and constant complaint. No one can deny with any honesty that the one-party state transforms opposition, and even criticism, into treason whenever it is the decision of the rulers so to regard it. Outside a relatively small group of political leaders, intellectuals, industrial experts and managers, the officers of the Red Army and the upper grades of the bureaucracy, it is difficult to see and feel in the climate of government opinion much regard to the need to respect the dignity of ordinary people. It is still grimly true that most Russians must look over their shoulder for fear of the secret police; and no one can have been a week in Moscow without realising not only that it has been driven into the people that the foreigner is the enemy, but also that this attitude has been forcibly imposed by a fantastically suspicious government upon men and women whose natural disposition is friendly. To this must be added the ugly way in which the great hero of to-day becomes the foul enemy of to-morrow, the incredible genuflexion before Stalin, who, like the Caesars of the Roman empire, has achieved the status of a god in his own lifetime, and the deliberate falsification of history to suit the purpose of the men in power. There must now be few scholars and scientists still in high repute who have not been compelled, at one time or another, to choose between subscription to doctrines they knew to be false, and the sudden termination of an eminent or a promising career. There is an irretrievable ugliness in the treatment of scholars like Pokrovsky and Rydzanov and scientists like Vavilov, the geneticist, which will remain an ugly stain upon Russian history.

It is nevertheless fatal to stop at the point where what is evil in Russia becomes so oppressive to one's mind that one ceases to think of it as the source of new and creative values in our civilisation. We gain nothing by dismissing Soviet leaders as a handful of quasi-oriental barbarians who have imposed on their people the most efficient of modern tyrannies, achieving in their communist outlook the fear Herzen expressed when he thought it possible that Russian communism might turn out to be Tsarism upside down. For when Herzen expressed that doubt, he said specifically that its condition was the danger that the Russia born after a revolution might not be understood by Europe and America. That danger has been amply realised, and this is so because the criteria we apply to what is essential in Soviet Russia are derived from an historical evolution which has resulted in a system which it is the central purpose of the Revolution to deny. We are overwhelmed by features of Russian life which are only different from our own because they operate in areas of behaviour where we do not expect them to occur. We denounce the absence of qualities we take for granted among ourselves without examining whether those same qualities do not exist in forms different from those to which we are accustomed. We are puzzled, for example, at the overwhelming confessions in the treason trials of the 'thirties; but confessions of a similar character are not only exacted by the Roman Catholic Church from those whom it charges with heresy, but have been the commonplace of most religious
58

revivals of which we have any serious knowledge. We exclaim at the lack of individuality in Russia; but we do so in an epoch when the mechanisation of life in Europe and America is doing more, for the most part impersonally, to secure that than at any time since the American Revolution; individuality is scarcely fostered by the ideal of 'keeping up with the Joneses'. We rightly praise the spacious character of American hospitality, its effort to break down the conventional formalism of Anglo-American and French receptivity. The dislike of that formalism is, after all, one of the most striking features of Russian behaviour and literature from Pushkin to Maxim Gorki. Indeed, if I had to put my finger on one of the central features in the Russian literature of the last hundred years, I should emphasise its marvellous gallery of eccentrics in contrast, for example, to the set pattern of conduct of the character in Western literature. The qualities the Russians call *sbornst* are present in far more characters in the classics of Russia than in the literature of the West. We may translate it as that spirit of community in which the individual conscience discovers its proper place.

I suspect that more of this spirit is found in Russian life than in any other nation of our time. It does not require the annihilation of individuality; it rather requires a collectivism which refuses to make formal submission to any collective authority which the world creates in the way of an organised and imposed collectivism. It is always seeking a humanism which is at once persuasive and dignified. It is hostile, indeed, to the individualism of the *bourgeois;* it proclaims the infinite worth of human dignity, and not only denies the passive acceptance of one's lot in the West, but replaces it by a voluntary co-operation with the community which seeks to bring out the best in both. In the habits of Bolshevism itself there is implied, after all, the exaltation of the individual will which, at certain moments, exalts personal spontaneity at the expense of communal power, even when that spontaneity transcends the obvious implications of orthodox Marxism. There is, in brief, an irrepressible anarchism in the Russian mind that we neglect at our peril. For what Russia has done, paradoxical as it may seem in a community dominated by a dictatorship, is to throw new light on the nature of that freedom which alone gives dignity to the human person. It is true, and, of course, it is important that the Russian has no say in the choice of those who govern him. It is true, also, that the price of opposing their decisions is heavy and cruel. It is true, further, that there surrounds him, on every side, the ugly shadow of the political police. I do not want, for one moment, to offer any plea in mitigation of these evils; I would, indeed, emphasise that their presence after the war of 1939 is far less defensible than it was before it.

But he has important compensations over which we should do well to ponder. He does not suffer from the omnipresent sense of a permanently superior social stratum. None of his fellow-citizens can exercise power over him simply because of wealth or power. No barrier stands in the way of his right to self-improvement except his capacity and character. The values of his community are not set by the small number who accumulate property by reason of skill in the market, or who have been born into a class which still enjoys the right to privilege by reason of a rank no longer associated with a socially valuable function. He works in the knowledge that labour itself is regarded as honourable, and that by putting his mind and heart into his work he can win respect, and hardly less important, achieve self-respect. No doubt he lives in a world where privacy is difficult to attain, and where every known agency of propaganda is used to condition his mind to acceptance of the assumptions upon which his rulers are seeking to rebuild the community they dominate. No doubt it is true also—and it is certainly of the first importance—that the men in the Kremlin have taken the immense risk of subduing that anarchic spontaneity which, historically, has been the main condition of intellectual and artistic creation, to all the perils to which it is chained by official reorganisation. Yet behind all this does seem to lie the passionate conviction of the need to regenerate man. There is in the effort a vision that it is difficult not to call messianic. Behind all the dogmas and the orthodoxies, the cruelties and the fanaticism, there is an elasticity, a power of sweeping adjustment, a capacity to admit error, an experimental audacity, which have in them something that is essential to freedom. There is a conscious effort to make man the master of his own fate, a deep respect for the cultural heritage,

60

a recognition of the need for cultural diversity as the safeguard against the implications of technological uniformity. We are witnessing the gigantic spectacle of a whole community plunged, as it were, into the mould of a new pattern whence it is to emerge having overcome the vast contradiction which Dostoievsky's Grand Inquisitor affirmed between happiness and freedom. I do not know that they have any decisive assurance of success. I do know that behind the effort there are a resolution and imagination that have quite certainly given a new perspective to the adventure of man.

CHAPTER IV

I SHOULD accept at once the argument that what has happened in Russia, though Marxist in some of its most fundamental aspects, has a uniqueness of its own precisely because it is Russian, and that its influence is likely to be swifter among peoples where the development of capitalism has been relatively small, as in the Balkans, or India, or China, than where, as in Western civilisation, an advanced capitalism has not only created a strong middle class, but permeated all parts of society with the spirit of bourgeois individualism. Quite clearly, that spirit resists the Russian emphasis on the identity of society with the state; the totalitarian insistence on unifying the man with the citizen, and on conveying authority to the state of which he is a part is bound to seem hypocritical to anyone with the experience of constitutional government. Western Europe and America, as well as Australia and New Zealand, have found in parliamentary democracy what has seemed to their citizens an alternative road to freedom which by-passes all the evils they regard as inherent in the social philosophy for which Soviet Russia stands sponsor. They are aware of the great triumphs it has won over a despotic Crown and a privileged aristocracy, and that, under its aegis, there have been achieved great reforms, political, economic and social, in which the mass of the community has shared. They see in the method of parliamentary democracy a means of settling by rational discussion what the method of Soviet communism settles by violent revolution followed by a dictatorship to which there is no perceptible end. They point out the value of government under the rule of law compared to government by the arbitrary discretion of the small oligarchy in whose hands, as in Russia, the state-power is effectively concentrated. Their peoples enjoy far more tolerance, political and social freedoms unknown to communist societies, and a standard of material well-being which, if it is still inadequate, tends steadily to increase, especially for the workers. With universal suffrage, universal education, a freedom of speech and association such as no communist state would dare to permit, the democrat of the West, whether conservative or socialist, is convinced that majority-rule offers advantages, both spiritual and material, which permit far greater freedom and freedom more solidly based than can be offered by the communist alternative.

There are different aspects of these affirmations which require more careful analysis than they usually receive. Bourgeois society has bred, generally, two types, the conservative and the radical. The first type has accepted a way of life in which the framework of society is set by values inherent in the market-economy. A man may live to all outward appearance in conformity with the demands of the church or synagogue or mosque to the creed which he announces his adherence. But his real concern is power through the possession of property, and this concern makes him not only insist that the criterion of value is success, but also insist that success is the outcome of the peculiar qualities required by those who survive the battle to sell their commodities at the highest price obtainable in the market. From the time when they first undermined, and then overthrew, the feudal society in which they developed, those who have survived in the battle involved in production for the market have adapted all institutions to the preservation of its stability; and the main principles of their creed are built upon the conscious separation of ethics and economics. Bourgeois society, in its conservative aspect, has always been wanting in the elements of a true community. It has used its growing power over nature to adjust all social purposes to an economic end— the getting of wealth for a minority regardless of the consequences to the majority whose lives are harnessed to the fulfilment of that end. No doubt from time to time, concessions have been made to the protests of that majority against its exploitation; no doubt, also, there have been occasions when the conservative bourgeois has allowed humanitarianism to outweigh the possibilities open to him by ruthless efficiency in the market. But, in general, it cannot be gainsaid that, as the middle class fought its way to supremacy, it imposed everywhere the principle that the individual fulfils himself at his best by his skill in attaining wealth, and that the state-power shall be so organised as to create the social conditions under which this supreme objective is least hampered by barriers which

64

seek to protect the weak against the strong. Bourgeois capitalism has, of course, had immense, even dramatic, triumphs, and it is difficult not to admire the great qualities which have distinguished its technological triumphs. It is still necessary to remember that, behind those triumphs, is the same bitter tragedy, no doubt differently named, which not even the highest achievements of Greek civilisation are able to conceal. That is why Lord Keynes, by so much the most eminent economist of our time, could write that 'modern capitalism is absolutely irreligious, without internal union, without much public spirit, often, though not always, a mere congeries of possessors and pursuers'. If the ancient world seems at its ugliest when it uses all the coercive machinery of government brutally to sustain its foundation in personal slavery, the modern world is at its ugliest too when all its defences are mobilised to defend by argument or, if necessary, by coercion, its system of wage slavery. The simple fact is that bourgeois capitalism, above all in its conservative form, has dehumanised man; and the revolt against its principles is, above all, an attempt to strike from the vast majority chains which do not bind them less closely because they are described by their defenders in the language of freedom.

The radical bourgeois differs in degree, but not in kind, from the conservative bourgeois. He has a sense of dismay and unhappiness as he sees the logical consequences of capitalism at work. His anxiety, therefore, is to temper its operation by mercy, to insist that the power of democracy shall be used to limit the injustices it can perpetrate. He seeks to penetrate behind the class struggle to an objective social harmony which reason can discover and translate into the relations of production by the acceptance of democratic principles. He argues that the acceptance of majority-rule, through which a political party is given authority by the electorate to make its purposes the law after debate in a parliament, offers a means of by-passing the violence of catastrophic revolution in which Marx and Engels saw the main method of social change. The aid of the radical bourgeois is, to put it briefly, to transform capitalist democracy into socialist democracy by peaceful means. He argues that in societies where there is profound technological maturity, not only does there develop a politically mature electorate, but, as an expression of its maturity, a willingness on the part of a defeated minority to accept the verdict of the majority, thus making possible large-scale change through constitutional means. Admittedly, says the radical bourgeois, the pace of change will be slower than the communist would demand. But the gains are consolidated; the capitalists are not shocked into violent attack by the rapid and profound change in the relations of production; and we avoid the period of dictatorial power, with its barbarities and injustices, and, above all, its enforced uniformity of mind. The change is made by persuasion, and not by force; and the value of this approach lies in its ability to maintain the habits of civilised behaviour during an epoch of fundamental transformation.

The assumptions which lie behind the optimism of the radical bourgeois are, of course, of overwhelming importance in the assessment of its validity. They assume that, as the relations of production change in a political democracy, the values of the class which has, hitherto, owned the instruments of production with all the power that goes with this ownership, will change also. Thus far in history, all the evidence is against this assumption. In every country where feudalism gave place to capitalism, there were long years of struggle, culminating in revolutionary civil war, before the old order yielded to the new. It is only in a fundamental crisis of this kind that we learn how differently men think who live differently in the degree to which they accept or reject the values of capital. It is only then that we become aware how systems of ownership give birth to ideas which penetrate and colour all the institutions of a community. Churches, educational bodies, the armed forces, the art-forms, the clothes people wear, even the entertainments they seek, are shaped by the economic order and its consequences. So is the legal system, its judges and its doctrines alike. So, also, is the administrative apparatus of the society For while it is easy to say that, in a capitalist democracy, the political leaders of the party that forms the government give orders which the officials execute, that is, of course, a simplified abstraction which has only a formal relationship to the concrete reality it claims to summarise. It is taken for granted that an official who believes that his political chief is embarking upon a disastrous policy will, nevertheless, after suitable

66

representations, wholeheartedly carry out the orders he receives if he is unable to persuade the Minister that he is wrong. It argues that a government engaged in the task of fundamental social reconstruction can count upon the impartial loyalty of the armed forces and of the police; and it argues, still further, that the owners of the instruments of production which are late priorities in the process of social transformation will, in the period before their industries are taken over by the government in the name of the community, work with all the necessary zest and efficiency to keep the economic life of the society at the highest possible level.

All these are very large assumptions, how large were clearly set out by the Labour Government in Great Britain in its *Economic Survey for 1947*. 'The task of directing by democratic methods an economic system as large and complex as ours', said the *Economic Survey*, 'is far beyond the power of any Governmental machine working by itself, no matter how efficient it may be . . . Events can be directed in the way that is desired in the national interest only if the Government, both sides of industry, and the people accept the objectives and then work together to achieve the end.' What, of course, is central to this is the common acceptance of the objective. We know that there is no such common objective in Great Britain, that, if a Conservative Government were to succeed the Labour Government first elected in 1945, it would not only use its power to pursue other objectives—its leaders have indeed said so—but that it would also seek to repeal some, at least, of the basic legislation passed since 1945 as part of the process of peacefully changing a capitalist, into a socialist, democracy. Presumably, if that Conservative Government were subsequently to be defeated at a new general election by the Labour Party, then the process of transformation, begun in 1945, would be resumed. It seems obvious that no industrial system would possess the requisite stability and self-confidence if it were subject to such recurrent changes in governmental objectives. Capital investment would halt; industrial disputes would be constant and bitter; and the impact on the national economy would be frustrating from whichever side it was regarded. Either objective, in fact, requires a long term of power for the political party that promotes it, as well as genuine acquiescence in the objective by the Opposition party and its supporters. How far is this likely? Is it not more true to say, as Lord Balfour said, that our parliamentary system presupposes two parties so fundamentally at one on matters of major import that they can afford, in his phrase, to 'bicker' about incidentals. But if they are not fundamentally at one, is the parliamentary form of government held in such high esteem by both parties, that there is no reason to suppose that either would transgress the boundaries of constitutional opposition? Each would, that is to say, accept defeat for the time being, and work for victory against the other at the next general election.

We have had no revolutionary experience in Great Britain since 1689, so that there is no means of answering these questions with any confidence. We know, indeed, that had the Duke of Wellington not given way in 1832, there would have been a revolutionary outbreak over parliamentary reform in that year; and we know, also, that had the Home Rule Act of 1914 been imposed upon Ulster against its will, the Unionist leaders in Ulster would have fought against the Act, and that they would have been officially supported in doing so by the Conservative Party in the House of Commons; indeed, a preliminary movement of troops as a precautionary measure led to a mutiny of officers at the Curragh Camp in Ulster, in the spring of 1914, and this was organised with the connivance of the Conservative leaders at Westminster who pledged themselves, through Lord Milner, to reinstate any officers who might be dismissed on this account, if and when the Conservative party came back to power. We know, too, that, in almost fifty years, no British Government has felt able to establish a national system of education in England in which the Church of England has not had a major position, in large part paid for out of general rates and taxation. We know that, in France, the political outlook of the Army chiefs, as shown both in the Dreyfus case, and in the débacle of 1940, had immense influence in deciding the limits within which, on both occasions, the government of the day was prepared to move. We know, further, that, in the early days of the Weimar Republic, the agreements come to between the first President, Friedrich Ebert, and his colleagues Schiedemann and Noske, not only prevented a left turn on the part of the government,

68

but enabled the German General Staff to recover all the ground it had lost after its defeat in the war of 1914-18, and become the master, rather than the servant, of its political allies, with the ultimate ability to persuade President Hindenburg to hamstring the authority of the Reichstag by putting in Adolf Hitler as Chancellor, and so enabling him, though in a minority of electoral votes, to establish himself as a dictator over the whole German nation, so that he nearly became the master of all Europe. Nor must we forget that when Franklin Roosevelt took America into the war of 1939, after the Japanese attack at Pearl Harbour in December, 1941, he had to win the co-operation of big business by suspending the progress of his New Deal principles until his death, with victory in sight. If it be said that his successor, President Truman, attempted, in the spring and summer of 1948-9 to resume the policies of Franklin Roosevelt, I think it is a sufficient answer to insist that his effort was made in large degree abortive by the fact that, though the elections of 1948 had given his party a majority in both chambers of the legislature, he was only in a position to advise the two parties, and not to command them to carry out his will. Nor is it insignificant in this context, that the foreign policy of the Labour Government in England was broadly the same as that of its predecessor, the government over which Mr. Churchill presided, and that, from the moment Mr. Truman took office, on Mr. Roosevelt's death, he accepted a bi-partisan policy worked out by his supporters and opponents alike, in which the word of his opponents may fairly be regarded as carrying at least as much—possibly more—weight as that of his supporters. Mr. Churchill, in England, may have loathed most of Mr. Bevin's domestic alignments, but, Palestine apart, he was the enthusiastic supporter of the general lines of his foreign policy.

And all this depends upon the argument that each state is free to arrive at its own conclusions in matters of policy without heed to the line that other states are following. This is, of course, very far from being the case. It needs no elaborate discussion to-day to prove that the interdependence of states is one of the major factors in their relations both economic and political, and that not even giant powers like the United States and Soviet Russia could aim at self-sufficiency without grave risk to the standard of life of their peoples. It is the fact of this interdependence which makes it so urgent to find terms of a common life in our civilisation which safeguards us against war as an instrument of state-policy. It is not only that war breeds war. Fear leads to an expenditure upon national defence which may well be ruinous to the individual's standard of life by the taxation it involves and thence, by its scale, to greater fears lest one government become able to overwhelm another by the size of its armaments; and this leads to a competition in armaments which merely continues the vicious circle. Before 1939, we had learned by grim experience that, at a given stage of its development, the need of capitalism for larger markets than those afforded by domestic consumption led to imperialism, and that imperialism in its turn led to war. Now we have the additional complication that capitalist societies are challenged by socialist societies, and that their antithetic ideologies intensify the strain upon peaceful relations between them. It is hardly excessive to say that the 'cold war' now being waged by the United States and its allies, on the one hand, and Soviet Russia and its allies, on the other, bears all the marks of a creed war such as those waged between different churches after the Reformation. The tenseness this gives to external relations is reflected in growing intolerance within each national society; and the outcome becomes a threat to internal freedom which may become gravely destructive of human personality.

The most passionate argument, indeed, that bourgeois defenders of capitalism deploy against the defenders of a socialist order is that such an order is incompatible with freedom. Socialism implies ownership by the community of all the major instruments of production, and this results in the planning of its economic life. It is then urged that this means not only the control of citizens as consumers, but also the control of the citizen's choice of occupation. There is painted a terrifying picture of the ordinary citizen at the mercy of a horde of bureaucrats who, in their turn, depend upon the decision of a small group of dictators who lay down the final imperatives of the society. If there is planned production, it is said, there cannot be free demand, and the citizen as consumer has no choice about the way in which he will spend his income.

70

Once the citizen has no choice of occupation and no choice in spending, it becomes rapidly obvious that a planned economy such as that upon which socialism is based is bound to destroy the foundations of liberty.

It is important to be clear at the outset that the bourgeois conception of freedom is itself a function of the market-economy, and in that market economic freedom is necessarily a function of effective demand. Historically, it is obvious that the vast majority of any population in a capitalist society do not enjoy access to this effective demand. Though their rights are formally universal, their right to utilise them is set by the need to make profit-making primary, and all other rights are necessarily subordinate to it. No doubt it is true that the ordinary man can be an artist or a manager, a poet or a business director; but his ability to be any one of these things depends upon the effective demand for his services in the particular sphere he chooses. If his wishes are not welcome to the economy of the market, he is no more free to choose than he is under any other system. No one, for example, who examines the position of the negro or of the Jew in the United States would seriously claim that, in their case, the problem of freedom is any more simple than it is in Soviet Russia. 'The historical mission of capitalism,' wrote Lenin, 'consists in the development of the productive society's productive forces; but its structure inhibits the useful application of these technical advances for the benefit of the masses of the people.' The rise of a ruling class depends exactly on its power to profit from limiting any freedom to the few, and from the subordination of the many to the discipline which this limitation involves. And the more the many resent this discipline, the more likely, as Hilferding saw, is the ruling class to narrow the opportunities of freedom. Liberty is never likely to flourish where the price of its enlargement is internal strain and external excitement. Yet that is the impasse to which we have been brought by the crisis in the struggle between different modes of capitalist production. Its power to produce has immensely increased; but the ruling class its extension has rendered superfluous insists, not only upon remaining on the historic scene, but, in claiming its right to maintain the formal universality of choice, it claims to be the mainspring in all forms of social freedom. The nearer, in fact, we approach to anarchy in the realm of government, the more real is the freedom we are likely to enjoy.

Freedom, in fact, is not the abstract negation that the bourgeois era urged that it was. That view of freedom suited the type of civilisation which the capitalist relations brought with them as they rose to power. As their authority declined, so, also, their conception of freedom began to prove less imposing and effective than it had seemed to be. Its sponsors had claimed for it the merits, first, that it reduced the interference of government with individual choice to a minimum; and they claimed, secondly, that this reduction of interference meant the absence of barriers to advance so that any citizen of capacity found the career open to his talent. It is not necessary to deny that from some such period as the middle of the eighteenth century this was true in a number of industrial occupations as in a number of the professions. But it is clear enough not only that the price paid by those who were unsuccessful in the race for wealth was high, but that, by 1900, it was increasingly difficult even for men of ability to find either the chance or the scale of success that had been frequent fifty years before. No doubt there were dramatic exceptions, like Henry Ford in the United States or Lord Nuffield in England. But even they tended to illustrate the important characteristic of highly developed capitalism; they arrived at the front in a new industry in which, as yet, it was possible to organise innovations in technique upon a large scale. Once maturity comes, the pioneer who dares to adventure is dramatically exceptional, for were he to appear with any frequency he would destroy the stability of the market-economy upon which a bourgeois society has come to depend. The truth, in fact, is that in a bourgeois civilisation, freedom means that the owners of the instrument of production are secure in their ownership, and that the privileges they enjoy are not invaded by changes in the complex of social institutions which are naturally geared to the working of the market. That is why any control of the market is regarded by them as a restriction upon their freedom. It is, indeed, rare to find that they approve governmental policies which aim at the more equal distribution of freedom. They oppose the regulation of prices. They suspect

72

the increase of safeguards against unemployment, or poverty, or ill-health. They have persuaded themselves that freedom means a citizen's own power to build his own contractual relations, without seeing that this power means effective demand for commodities in the market. Since those in possession of this power are not responsible for the poverty or the unemployment, the bad housing, or the ill-health, since, moreover, he can pay for what he wants, the citizen regards the invasion of the market-economy by the state-power as, in fact, the invasion of his freedom. He has become so accustomed to regard his unfettered market-activity as freedom, that he has ceased, mostly, to be aware that it was itself the result of a long process of deliberate planning, which, at practically every stage, has involved not only government interference, but the sanction, sometimes violently exercised, of its coercive power against those who argued that capitalist's freedom was worker's slavery. That is why they were appalled at the growth of collectivist legislation. They seriously felt that it was a violation of the order of nature. They were, indeed, so anxious to prevent that violation that they urged the need to restore the freedom of the market by a mass of legislation and regulations to prevent any interference with its operations.

The market economy has carried with it its own ethic, the elaboration of which has been the work of almost four centuries. It is not unfair to summarise it by saying that poverty has been to the economist very much what hell has been to the Christian theologian—the just reward of sin. This view has been put with remarkable force by the famous French publicist, Charles Dunoyer. 'Poverty,' he wrote, 'like inequality is, in some degree, an inevitable thing, and like inequality, an element in social progress. If it is said that poverty is incompatible with civilisation, the answer is that it is inseparable from it. If it is urged that it is a hideous evil, the answer is that it is a necessary evil. The more humanity, in its development, has to fear the effect of certain vices, the more it was essential that these should result in evils capable of turning men away from them. It is good to have in a community low categories into which a family may fall when it behaves badly, and out of which it can rise only by a change to good behaviour. Poverty is just such a hell as men and women fear. It is an inescapable

73

abyss destined for the insane, the dissipated, the debauched, for all types, indeed, of evil men; it receives them and punishes them if they have not known how to practise self-restraint. Only poverty, perhaps, and the healthy horrors which accompany it, can lead us to that intelligence and that exercise of morality which are necessary to the progress and steady development of man. If poverty makes no impression on nature inherently vicious, or on character inherently vile, it still is a salutary spectacle to that part of the less fortunate classes in which signs of health remain. Poverty fills them with a healthy fear. It urges them to a morality which, if difficult to attain, is necessary to permit them to climb upwards. It makes possible, it even makes easy, for them, patience, moderation, courage, economy. Above all, poverty urges them to that restraint which is the most necessary of all—their power, by limiting their fertility, to refrain from bringing to life a more numerous generation than they have the room or the means to bring up in a decent way."[1]

This is a classic expression of the bourgeois interpretation of the market-economy, and it is important to be clear about all its implication. But before we do so, it is worth adding to Dunoyer's sombre view of the poor, the attitude to the rich of his contemporary, Thiers, whom the liberal historian, the late Herbert Fisher, regarded as perhaps the greatest political figure of the nineteenth century. 'It is the rich man,' wrote Thiers, 'who helps to form that educated public for whom the humble and poor scholar does his work. He builds the great libraries. He reads Sophocles, Dante, Galileo, Descartes, Bossuet, Moliere, Racine, Montesquieu, Voltaire. And if he does not study them himself, it is in the circle round him that they are read and enjoyed and appreciated. He makes possible that enlightened and polite society, with a taste at once trained and exquisite, for whom men of genius write and sing and paint. Sometimes the wealthy man is himself one of that distinguished band who do not limit themselves merely to the appreciation of works of genius, but themselves produce striking achievements in this realm. Sallust was a rich man, as were Seneca and Montaigne, Buffon and Lavoisier. Nor must

[1] Charles Dunoyer, *De la Liberté du Travail* (Paris, 1845) Vol. 1, p. 457.

74

we forget that the wealthy man is the eminent statesman who presides over the destiny of his country.' The conclusion can hardly be better stated than in the incisive words of Paul Leroy-Beaulieu, the wealthy and learned son of a wealthy and learned father. 'The working-class,' he wrote,[1] 'has something better to do than to fight against the bourgeoisie. It ought to follow the example of the bourgeoisie by adopting its habit of order and of regularity, of discipline and of foresight.' Clearly, in the view of Thiers and Leroy-Beaulieu, monetary success entitles those who attain it to regard themselves as the real sponsors of moral excellence and civilised living. It is by emulating their virtues that the poor can escape those habits which make them, as Louis Napoleon said in 1851, the inevitable enemy of religion, morality, and society itself. It is this frame of mind, perhaps, which explains why, in the February Revolution of 1848, Victor Cousin could insist to Charles Remusat when they chanced to meet on the Quai Voltaire, that only by a swift acceptance of the Church's direction was there any hope that France might still be saved.[2]

No one can examine the attitude of men like Dunoyer without seeing that, for them, capitalism has become a genuine religious creed in which salvation belongs to the successful, while the poor are urged to recognise that their poverty is the outcome of sin. No doubt, he put his hell in this world, and not in the next; and, no doubt also, he offered the prospect of escape from its agonies by assuring those who practised the bourgeois virtues that, in the degree to which they do so, material success may be theirs. He even thought that the picture he painted was the outcome of an experience of 'natural law'; poverty resulted in death, and death was the great instrument by which an equilibrium between population and the demand for labour was achieved. He accepted as final the pessimism of Ricardo with its view that if the current wage-level was above the 'natural' wage-level, nothing could prevent the workers' fate from being a deplorable one. Were the state to intervene to alter the wage-level above what it attained through the operation of natural law, it would destroy the very foundations of

[1] *La Question ouvrière au XIXme Siècle* (Paris, 1872) p. 294.
[2] P. de la Gorce, *Histoire de la Seconde République Française.* Vol. II, p. 276.

the social order. That was why, during the Revolution of 1848, Tocqueville insisted that the outstanding characteristic of all schools of socialist thought was 'an energetic and persistent appeal to the material passions of man'; the February Revolution, he thought, could only maintain the great traditions of 1789 by accepting the idea of a classless society, and this acceptance involved abandoning the futile pretension to create a social power which would substitute the dubious wisdom of government for the practical and direct wisdom of each citizen. Governments did their duty, Tocqueville thought, when they gave to their citizens enlightenment and freedom.[1]

All this is worth recalling since it is the expression of what the theorists of capitalism believed in its era of triumph. In the hundred years that have passed, the evidence suggests that, in a broad way, the approach of Dunoyer is still the main basis of their speculation. It may be expressed with more sophistication or with less; it may consider a period of actual warfare one in which it is legitimate to suspend the claims of the 'natural' economy of the market. It may even recognise that the development of competition is imperfect, even that the danger of monopoly is great enough to justify the use of the state-power to enforce by law the restoration of competitive conditions. That of which it remains convinced is that central planning is not only bound to be less efficient than an economic order which leaves choice to what Tocqueville called the 'practical and direct wisdom of each citizen', but, even more, that if central planning is substituted for individual discretion, the freedom of the citizen is bound to be destroyed. It is the view of capitalist theory to-day, as it was a century ago, that socialism is 'an energetic and persistent appeal to the material passions of man' and that without the whip of poverty there is an insufficient incentive to the effort required to maintain a civilisation like our own as a going concern. That is why journals like *The Economist* can urge the desirability, in England, of allowing the number of unemployed workers to grow up to some such figure as one million and a half. That is why there is the persistent claim that our taxes are too high;

[1] *Le Droit au Travail au Luxembourg et à l'Assemblée Nationale.* (Paris, 1849). Vol. II. p. 71. These two volumes constitute the sixth volume of the collected works of Emile de Girardin.

we are, it is said, discouraging the initiative of the able by taking from them so much of their earnings that they are deterred from an effort they are no longer inclined to regard as worth while. At the same time, it is urged, we are spending too much on matters like the social services, or food subsidies, and the like, too much on housing, while our taxation of corporate profits for such purposes as these discourages the re-equipment of industry. We have, we are told, replaced a society based on a requirement that the individual citizen should exercise his own responsible initiative by one in which the 'welfare state' imposes upon him at the will of an ever-increasing horde of officials, habits which suppress in him the habit of adventure which makes a civilisation great. So far, indeed, has this gone that the Royal Commission on Population noted in its *Report* 'the remarkable approach to agreement (among a group of specialist witnesses) on the two essential points (1) that a considerable element in intelligence is inherited, and (2) that the more intelligent have smaller families on the average than others.' If this were true, the Commission concluded: 'all advances towards equality of opportunity might only have the effect of making matters worse in the long run, since a growing proportion of the intelligent members of society would move up into the social group whose fertility is too low for replacement.' While the Commission is careful not to affirm, with the specialists whose evidence it received, that the national intelligence is being lowered because the social groups with the highest incomes, on the whole better educated and more intelligent, have smaller families than the groups with lower incomes, they remark that 'this evidence, tentative and inconclusive though it is, but backed by an impressive weight of expert authority, raises very serious issues.'[1]

Here, once again is the inference, stated, of course, with far greater caution by the Commission than by its witnesses, that income is a function of intelligence, and that the implication of this is the contingent danger of extending the area of equal opportunity. Translated into terms of government action that would leave the society with three choices. It might choose to decide that its government abstain from action for social wel-

[1] Report of the Royal Commission on Population. Cmd. 7695. (London, 1949) Chap. 5, esp. pp. 153, 156.

fare; or it might decide not to attempt to expand equal opportunity for all social groups; or it might decide to give the main weight of its effort to the encouragement of the higher income groups, on the ground that these comprise the most intelligent portion of the community. Any one of these choices would then throw the weight of state-power on the side of those citizens with more property than others on the ground that the intellectual level of the nation would be raised if they could be encouraged to increase the size of their families. Poverty, here, is not the consequence of sin, but of inferior intelligence; though it may well be that the inferior intelligence which results in poverty is itself the twentieth century phrasing of what an earlier and less secularised era was content quite simply to regard as sin.

At the back of the hostility to a planned society is the conviction that the less the state intervenes in any of the categories of social or economic life, the larger is the area of freedom which remains to the individual citizen. In fact, this is simply not true for the immense mass of mankind. Since it is in general true that larger possessions mean larger power, the greater the concentration of wealth in any community, the greater the privileges those who control this wealth are likely to seek for themselves; and the outcome for those who do not share in this control is more likely to seem like tyranny than freedom. How easy it is for the absence of public law to leave the field open to private coercion was dramatically shown by the Senate Committee on Civil Liberties in its *Report* of 1936. What those who dislike planning forget is that business is a system of power, and that the degree of freedom in economic life that any citizen enjoys depends, where the state does not intervene, upon the volume of power at his disposal. Economic life, moreover, cannot be effectively separated from political or social life. If it is decided by a private corporation to shut down the great shipyards of Jarrow, for example, all its citizens are impotent unless the government steps in. And unless there is vested in the government the authority to subordinate the interest of a private company to the larger public interests of the whole community it affects by its policies, the company will obviously be able, as it was able in Jarrow, to dominate the life of the town. On the experience of economic history in the last century and a half, it seems obvious to conclude that the framework of policy shall not be left to be defined by a small body of private interests constantly liable, no doubt in genuine sincerity, to confuse with the freedom of the whole community the privileges they enjoy as a result of their grip on economic power.

It must be realised, moreover, that the supposedly unplanned nature of capitalist society which enabled it to offer 'freedom' to all its citizens on equal terms is a sheer illusion; what it does is to transfer the right to impose legal imperatives to the realm of economic relationships. These imperatives are static in character, empty concepts into which capitalism pours a changing content in terms of its relations of production and the ways in which it distributes the commodities which result from their operation. The framework of policy in a capitalist system is set by giving power to the owner of a factory or to the proprietor of an estate to use them as they think best. Freedom of contract, the law governing succession, the right to close a factory or to leave land unused, the power to form a private partnership into a public company, all these are categories of law which are filled by decisions made by the owners of property; these provide the law with its dynamic and thus clothe it with the social functions it performs. Thus to the owners of property, the capitalist society of the early nineteenth century appeared a 'free society' because they were virtually free to make contracts for its use by other persons, or for employing other persons to assist in its use, without a mass of legal imperatives which set limits to the contracts they could make. They argued that the worker who had nothing but his labour-power to sell was also free because, as a matter of legal form, he could accept or reject a proffered contract for the use of his labour-power at his own discretion; no owner could compel him to work on conditions which the worker found unacceptable. It is, of course, obvious that the 'freedom' of the owner of property, and the 'freedom' of the worker whom he employs operate on wholly different levels in the absence of equality of bargaining-power between the two; and it is no less obvious that, to the worker, the greater the equality of bargaining power he possesses the more genuine seems his freedom to sell his labour-power, or to refuse to sell it.

The history of law in the last eighty years has been, very

largely, the history of an importation into freedom of contract of limitations and conditions which are less and less the result of agreements of the parties to the contract, and more and more the result of the intervention of society which uses the authority of the state-power to deprive the owner of property of the economic sovereignty his possession of which seemed 'natural' to Dunoyer or to Thiers. It then becomes easy to see that the owner of property feels less free when his power to dispose of his own becomes limited by a will in the shaping of which his share may be, as he thinks, pitifully small. This is what Mr. Justice Holmes termed 'the paradox of form and substance in the development of law'. The form may look the same; the substance has undergone wholesale transformation for the most part because considerations of public policy are decided increasingly by legislation approved by the state-power and decreasingly by conditions imposed by the owner of property. The Factory Acts, the limitations recently imposed in the interest of the family upon freedom of testamentary disposition, the Rent Restriction Acts, with the complementary Furnished Houses (Rent Control) Acts of 1946 and 1949, the immense changes in company law, are all of them illustrations of the fact that a large part of what was once private law has now become unintelligible except in terms of public law. The judge may say, like Lord Atkin, that 'the right to choose for himself whom he would serve . . . constituted the main difference between a servant and a serf'.[1] That is, in form, legally unexceptionable; the freedom to choose one's master is, in law, the difference between a serf and a servant. What the law disregarded was whether the economic conditions in which it operated gave reality to that freedom. The great change is that public law has set those economic conditions in a wholly new perspective. So, too, while the Courts still try to interpret housing legislation as though it was dealing with a freely willed contract between landlord and tenant, the truth, of course, is that the legislature has intervened over a wide area of this relationship to prevent the excessive exploitation of the tenant by the landlord when we have entered an era where the shortage of housing accommodation might make such exploitation a very grave danger to the stability of society.

[1] *Nokes* v. *Doncaster Amalgamated Collieries, Ltd.* (1940) A.C. 1014.

CHAPTER V

NYONE who considers the general pattern of our society at the present time cannot, I think, mistake the confusion in the results to which it leads. In the last four hundred years, man has been torn from the hierarchical society of the middle ages, with its relatively fixed groups within the hierarchy, its stable faith, and its slow pace of change, to the individualist society of bourgeois capitalism, which made security a function of success, and success in large part the outcome of skill in the acquisition of money. Production for the world-market replaces domestic economy. When, in those four hundred years, we have spoken of an enlarged freedom, of a wider individuality, of a greater control over nature, of a refusal to look upon man as the prisoner of an original sin from which he could never escape, we have omitted, as a general rule, to add that these benefits of bourgeois capitalism were overwhelmingly confined to a relatively small aristocracy of wealth. It is, of course, true that they shared their wealth, and the power that went with it, with remnants of the old ruling class, and with the politicians and the major officials of the new régime. But it is not an exaggeration to say that, in order to be sure that their wealth and power could not be invaded by the masses, they had to create for their society criteria of conduct which excluded the masses from any serious chance of enjoying freedom in any positive sense of the term. Having established the market economy, they declared that the career was open to the talented; but that only meant, in the immense majority of cases, that freedom was open to the man who had the gifts necessary to win his way to success in a fiercely competitive struggle imposed by the morally neutral rules of supply and demand in the open market.

That capitalism, in the first era of its development, had remarkable achievements to its credit, there is no reason to deny; it enabled man to obtain a fuller mastery of his physical environment in three hundred years than in all the previous centuries of human history. But that mastery grew more full

81

only at the cost of increasing technological complexity; and this involved the need for an even greater accumulation of capital, not only to repair or replace the worn-out machine, but also to develop its possibilities as the source of increased production. The profits of the capitalist gave him security in the degree to which he ploughed them back into development. If he used all his profits for consumption, he risked his chance of survival against a competitor willing to refrain from excessive spending in order to win a bigger place in the market. There thus was evolved an environment in which the worker without capital was dependent on the employer who, in his turn, had to judge of the workers' usefulness to him in terms of what the workers could do for him in his fight to maintain his position in the market. That is why their position always drove the worker to form, if he could, a trade union in which he could join with other workers, similarly placed, to safeguard himself from the exploitation of his helplessness, when he stood alone. And, parallel to the evolution of trade unions, the capitalist sought to ensure the safety of his own position in a market economy by devices like limited liability and the various forms of trusts and cartels with all their devices for dominating the market. As the nineteenth century drew to its close, what became ever more obvious was the diminishing initiative of the individual citizen, the control of his spontaneity, his sense that, however courageously he might fight for his freedom, he was in the hands of an immense impersonal power against whom he was bound to wage a battle in which his defeat was only a matter of time. He was no longer master of himself. There towered above him the great giant forces, war, depression, the corporation like Standard Oil or Unilever, like General Motors or Imperial Chemicals, which left him with a sense that he was alone and powerless, perhaps futile as well, in a world so complex and so bewildering that the key to its understanding had been lost to him beyond the chance of discovery.

It is not very surprising that, in a civilisation where the dimensions of significant activity seem more and more beyond his power to attain, the individual should seek every means of escape from the personal responsibility to act. In his economic life, he can search out the routine in which to habituate himself to an automatic performance of some function in living through which he can persuade himself that his very dependence is fulfilment. Or he may regard the economic activity by which he lives as an inevitable payment for relations of fulfilment outside his working hours. He may have a hobby; he may play games; he may link the satisfaction of his personality to the life of another person or organisation in whose success he finds his own. It may be a girl he loves, a 'movie' star, his distant adoration of whom brings colour and romance into his life; it may be working for a church or a political party, or becoming an enthusiast for some baseball team or cricket club. It is clear that, in the great society, one of the ways of escaping from the torture of an unattained freedom is by a subordination so complete that the selfhood and uniqueness of individual personality are lost. It is obvious that, after the British monarchy began to recover its prestige in the later 'seventies of the nineteenth century, many thousands of people found a happiness in their devotion to, and pride in, Queen Victoria and the Royal family, from which they derived a fund of emotion making them one with a world in which previously they had felt themselves to be alien. All over our civilisation there are, as Dostoievsky knew, people whose supreme need is 'to surrender as quickly as possible the gift of freedom . . with which they, unfortunate creatures, were born'. For them surrender is security; and they think they are free because they have abdicated from the social obligation to achieve individuality. These are the people whose sense of impotence, or loneliness, or frustration, at the root of all of which lies fear, who make possible the maintenance of authority by men like Hitler or Mussolini.

It is here, I venture to think, that there lies the true meaning of that first famous sentence with which Rousseau began his *Social Contract* : 'Man is born free, and now everywhere he is in chains'. Man, that is to say, is born for freedom; it is his nature to expand, to initiate, to find ways of expressing by spontaneous activity, the thing that is himself. Then he is, in very truth, free, and, being free, is capable of a happiness that is sane and not neurotic. But our civilisation has pushed him to a point where his search for the freedom that fulfils his nature is at war with the social and economic conditions by which he is compelled to subordination, to lose hold of individuality, to be made to feel dependent, isolated, fearful, and thus to require some false mask under which to conceal the destruction of his integrity. One of these masks is subjection to the false ideals which insist to him that the more he sacrifices of himself the more fully he will be free. It may be an ideal which represents itself as patriotism, as devotion to a church, as love of parents, as service to a political party. It is an important index to the character of our time that each false ideal becomes more and more revealed as a chain which binds those whom it professes to set free. All of them intensify our critical position because all of them compel attack wherever they are examined in terms of their power to liberate and not in terms of their power to undermine freedom. The false ideal is always the irrational ideal, asking for a faith that reason may not examine, clothing itself in an authority that lives by coercion, fearful that anyone may escape its power, and thus always ready to attack or to destroy. It is rare not to find it the outcome of a tradition in decay, a privilege that is obsolete, a claim that is empty at the first dissection by hands which have either learned its sterility by experience, or approached it on their own terms without admitting the assumptions by which, previously, it exacted submission.

What our era has somehow to find ways of understanding is the fact that we have arrived at the point where man can be genuinely free because, adequately organised, his control over the forces of production is near the point where he can throw off his chains. To be genuinely free is to cast away the barriers that have stood in the way of the social and economic order which releases individuality in each of us, and does not maintain itself by the repression of that individuality. The *malaise* of our civilisation lies in the contradiction between the pressure to liberate this individuality and the refusal of so many powerful interests to recognise the validity of this pressure and make way for its release. That is why there is increasing resentment of democracy, increasing attack upon civil liberties, increasing insistence by the traditionalists and their advocates that a planned society seeking, by the rational ordering of its resources, to prevent unemployment and hunger and war, must result in slavery. Those who have been accustomed to command, find the refusal to submit intolerable. They demand submission, ignorance, the preservation of the steep hierarchy which permitted them to impose authority and call it co-operation, to make parliamentary democracy, in all its forms, as much a method of slowing down, as of quickening, the advance of society to freedom. To affirm this is not to deny that, in its early phase of growth, capitalism aided in that advance. Where the unit of enterprise was small, and the room for individual initiative great, there can be no doubt that the chance open to men to test their capacity, to find themselves, to discover the fullness of personality, gave the sanction of high prestige to the values attendant upon its immense success. No one can fail, for example, to see that in the period of American history roughly spanned by Emerson's life. The expansion of opportunity seemed so immense that the doctrine of a self-reliance which asked only to be left alone by the government semed almost as rational to those who failed as it was to those who were successful. It exacted, indeed, a far heavier price than men like Emerson were ready to admit; that is evident from the early history of socialism in the United States; and in the maturity of American capitalism, it is evident enough that most people are employed on terms that leave them no room to exercise any initiative during their hours of work. The sanctions of disciplined routine, indeed, are too often methods intended to drive the workers into habits of frightened acquiescence and to injure, not seldom to destroy, their sense of dignity as human beings.

The social organisation of the future must, if it is to serve freedom, plan its economy in such a way that the members of a community share in the shaping of the effort to produce in a way that evokes from them both the sense that what they are doing is worth doing, and that they can bring to their task an activity of reason that prevents the widespread conviction that they have been emptied of what makes life an adventure in responsibility. Few people resent authority and discipline which have a rational foundation they can understand; and, in the present phase of our economic life, over wide areas, no such rational foundation is possible. Partly, that is because owner-ship and management have become so remote and impersonal that the impact of their power dehumanises those over whom it is exercised. Partly, it is because the habits of capitalism in

decay have become a breeding ground for that type of successful man whom John Ruskin described so vividly in the hey-day
of the system. 'In a community regulated by laws of supply and
demand,' he wrote, 'but protected from open violence, the
persons who become rich are, generally speaking, industrious,
resolute, proud, covetous, prompt, methodical, sensible,
unimaginative, insensitive and ignorant. The persons who
remain poor are the entirely foolish, the entirely wise, the idle,
the reckless, the humble, the dull, the thoughtful, the imaginative, the sensitive, the well-informed, the improvident, the
irregularly and impulsively wicked, the clumsy knave, the
wicked thief, the entirely merciful, just, and godly person.' It
may well be that the government of industry in its contemporary phase, calls forth from those who direct it that energy
of mind and eager devotion to the task in hand which one can
observe in the scientist or the artist; they are free because they
find fulfilment in their task. But the price of their fulfilment,
as innumerable investigators have testified, is the reduction of
the workers to a soulless drudgery in which it is rare to find
that their problems find a consideration equal to that given the
problems raised by the need of the corporation to respond
successfully to the challenge of the market. That is one of the
major reasons for the steady dissolution of the marriage
between capitalism and democracy.

For the condition of that marriage was an implied agreement to develop democratic principles in the political sphere,
while leaving relatively undisturbed authoritarian forces in the
economic. The agreement became ever more impossible of fulfilment with each year after the twentieth century began. The
negative state became, increasingly, the positive state; its rulers
had to satisfy the demands of the electorate in any society
based on universal suffrage by ever greater concessions of
welfare. Even so, those concessions did not produce a society
in equilibrium; whatever was conceded usually seemed to its
recipients too little and too late. The striking disparity, moreover, between the remarkable productive power in an advanced
industrial society, and the grave failure to solve its problems
of distribution brought out its inner and inherent contradictions
with ever greater force. The power to make profit began
increasingly to depend on finding new markets, on organising

scarcity, or on government intervention to prevent complete breakdowns in a country like Germany, where defeat in war was followed by psychological humiliation and by the destruction in the inflation of 1923 of the prestige and self-confidence of the middle class, in whom hope died out, especially in the younger generation, because none of the old values they had been taught to respect had any meaning. They joined the Brownshirts with zeal because Nazism seemed the one chance of restoring their self-esteem and their conviction that they ought not to be deprived of the superiority over the workers which they regarded as an integral part of their right to self-esteem. In the Germany of Kaiser Wilhelm, everything seemed orderly, secure, and solid. In the Germany of the Weimar Republic everything seemed upside down; no one knew what the morrow might bring forth, and the combination of inflation and depression gave them a sense that all the foundations were insecure. They accepted Hitler in the belief that he would be able to restore their self-esteem by removing the causes of their anxiety and resentment. It was only after he came to power that they began to realise how complete was his partnership with monopoly-capital, with the Prussian junkers, and the General Staff. It was then too late to save the political democracy which the Weimar Republic had sought to build. The power of monopoly-capitalism was expressed through a lawless despotism in which the gangster, the soldier, and the business man united in a common effort to win the loyalty of the masses by offering to them a new prestige and a new well-being to be obtained from the domination of the world.

The lesson of German experience is unique only in the horror of its intensity. Where the strain was less, both the horror and the intensity were less also. But where the strain was clear, it always expressed itself in an attack upon the foundations of capitalist democracy. That was true in the United States under the New Deal; it was true in France where it found expression in the swift breakdown of the Third Republic, and the attempt, after the capitulation of 1940, to impose the fascist categories of Vichy upon a people attached with passion to freedom. It was true, also, of Italy under Mussolini; and, if there are complicating international elements in both cases, it was still the inner secret of the victory of Nazism in Austria,

87

and of Franco in Spain. In Great Britain, the basis of capitalist democracy, though challenged from a number of angles, remained on the whole secure; but even there, it must be remembered that, from 1931 until the breakdown of the Munich Agreement in the spring of 1939, the MacDonald-Baldwin-Chamberlain policy of 'appeasement' meant nothing so much as an attempt to win the goodwill of Hitlerite Germany by surrendering to Hitler. It surrendered Austria first and then the main democracy of Eastern Europe by permitting him to ruin the remarkable achievement of the Czechoslovak Republic of Masaryk and of Benes, in the hope that, with the immense diplomatic gains he had won, he would turn his forces against Soviet Russia. The Western nations, which did not doubt that he would win, were willing to let him plant the German flag on Moscow and Leningrad, in case his primary aim changed and he turned his attack upon the West of Europe.

Hitler was defeated in the early spring of 1945, by the patient resistance of the British people, by the proud resistance of Russia, and the decision of the American Government to make itself the architect of munition supplies for the grand coalition against Hitler in which it played so prominent a part. After its initial and almost disastrous defeat at Pearl Harbour in December 1941, the United States showed a power of military and naval potential which probably, even proportionately, has never been equalled in the history of the world; in that mobilisation, the assembly of the atomic bomb was certainly one of the most remarkable achievements. The use of two of them only was able to secure the unconditional surrender of the Japanese Government in August 1945. But the immense technological advance of the United States no more solved the problem of economic democracy than did the wholesale socialisation of the means of production in Russia. Both leave the mass of workers instruments to be manipulated for ends in the definition of which they do not in any decisive way share. Both of them elevate the few at the price of leaving the many disciplined and insignificant because the routine they are told to follow evokes from them nothing of that initiative and

88

spontaneity without whose evocation the quality of freedom in society is inevitably depressed.

If this be true, we need to get rid of an economic system in which ownership, by definition, becomes a method of exploiting men and women, with the power of the state mobilised to protect that exploitation. We do not achieve this objective merely by transferring ownership from private to public hands, and then seeking to plan the processes of production. The problem is the much more complicated one of planning the whole economy of the society in such a way that each worker is able, at the level of his effort, to co-operate in defining the end and the means of that part of the plan in which he is involved as producer, while as consumer and as citizen he can participate in judging the operation of the plan as he experiences its results upon himself. That clearly involves decentralised machinery of consultation both on the side of production and on the side of consumption. It is not enough merely to change the forms of ownership in a society; it is necessary to democratise them too. Men whose nature calls for creative activity will only feel free when they are given the opportunity to go forward from the present system which makes them so largely automata, empty, without self-respect, citizens of a friendless world, to a system which, believing in man, works out in concert with him the conditions in which his full individuality has room for genuine expression. It is, of course, an immense task and it may well take generations before its problem is solved. But, unless it is solved, and unless, during the period when the effort to solve it is being made, men can see that it is being tackled with energy and in good faith, we shall watch the present crisis in values grow deeper and more serious, partly because the area of frustration will be more wide, and partly because, given the number of people whose elementary wants must be satisfied, our technological methods may require that those who act by reason of their frustration must be ruthlessly suppressed. Were that to occur we should move into a new age of slavery, however cunningly the fact might be concealed. For slavery, after all, is still what Aristotle called it —a system in which most people are animate tools, subordinate to ends they are not permitted to examine, and with no choice between submission and rebellion. In a slave system, all men are insignificant save those who have the power to rule; and, in the main, the sanctions of their power are both cruel and irrational. Nor does it make any difference that this annihilation of the longing for freedom may make possible material security for the slaves. The annihilation of freedom denatures mankind. It is the triumph of barbarism over civilisation, even when the superstructure of its organisation presents an appearance of splendour. The foundations of a social order are always broken when the condition of being respected is the surrender of self-respect. That was why Joseph de Maistre could say with truth of the system he approved that the executioner is the corner-stone of society.

CHAPTER VI

I WROTE *Faith, Reason and Civilisation* in 1943, when it was already clear that the war of 1939 was not itself the cause of the world-crisis, but an expression of it, the intensity of which only made the world-crisis still more profound. I argued then that Russian communism was an attempt to re-state values in terms of a new social order, the emergence of which it was legitimate to expect; and I suggested that it summarised an effort to prepare for that new social order by providing men with a new fighting faith which would enable them to co-operate with those who were compelling its emergence. I compared it, in this respect, with Christianity in the first epoch of its history. The early Christians developed a system of values which protected those who accepted them from the unhappy and pessimistic view that civilisation was breaking up before their eyes. It was, I suggested, unimportant that it came from the experience of lowly men in a nation of relatively small political power; unimportant even, that it based the validity of its claim upon a mythology no longer acceptable since it could not stand the test of historical criticism, and became, very rapidly, a church built upon a magic foundation, the secret of which could be recognised only by those who accepted its mythology as true. Magic always fails in the long run because its practitioners promise people the fulfilment of their desires; and the original promise of Christianity to its votaries that they would be saved for a heaven of eternal bliss after the brief interval before the end of the world has all the characteristics of magic about it. As the small groups of devout believers grew in numbers, and became the powerful religious organisation to which Constantine lent the full power of imperial recognition, the function of Christianity, at least as it was expounded by its orthodox leaders, changed also. The Christian Church became an organisation the main purpose of which was to promise salvation to those who accepted the social order of the Empire as one which manifested the will of God; it beatified the *status quo* by finding in it the expression of a Providential

91

pattern, and thus persuading men of their duty to obey rather than to rebel against the implications of that pattern. There were, of course, from the outset, men who protested passionately against this view. Many of them could not accept as valid an orthodoxy which, by beatifying the *status quo*, left the problem of evil unsolved, or noted that the behaviour of leaders in the Church, or of persons renowned for their piety, was in secular life, undistinguishable from that of a world the Kingdoms of which were, as Saint Augustine had said, *magna latrocinia*.

The Church, broadly speaking, was able to defeat, or to drive underground, all the rebels against the doctrines it regarded as unorthodox until the Reformation. It was then met by the challenge of Protestantism which, relatively swiftly, emphasised the importance of accepting a direct relation between man and God instead of insisting that such a relation, to be real, must pass through the channel provided by the Church as mediator. The Reformation coincided with the economic revolution in Europe which undermined the foundations of feudal society and, by providing the conditions under which the middle class rose to power, enables the Churches, new and old, to adapt themselves to the acceptance of the new values which sought to protect, first, the validity, and, next, the stability of bourgeois capitalism. What was broadly implied in the values emphasised by the new Churches was that, given faith in God, the goodness of a Christian consisted in fulfilling the duties of his secular life. From this it was easy to deduce the inadequacy of a creed at the very centre of which lay the ideal of retirement from the world for prayer and contemplation. Assisted by the immense secular changes involved in geographical discovery, scientific and technological development, and the impact of the new perspective given to all thinking by the re-emergence into men's lives of the speculation of Greece and Rome, aided above all, perhaps, by the realisation that the result of diligent economic enterprise offered a marvellous road to self-fulfilment, the standards of moral conduct underwent a remarkable change, and, if always at a distance, and with a minority expressing with different degrees of vehemence their dissent from this outlook, the Churches found ways of blessing the new standards in the name of religious truth. The business men did not separate the qualities required for economic success from the faith that made possible their access to the Kingdom of God; on the contrary, they found, with the co-operation of the Churches, that the road to wealth was identical with the road to the Kingdom. Activity replaced contemplation as an ideal; systematic accumulation of wealth became the fulfilment of one's calling; success in business became the proof of grace; and poverty became the proof of sin. From the ruthless attack on almsgiving, and the equally ruthless promotion of enclosures, it was easy to move to a position where even a man like Bishop Berkeley could propose that the sturdy beggar be taught the habits of industry by undergoing a term of enslavement, and Sir William Petty could warn the nation that wages above subsistence level did nothing but promote idleness and debauchery. The famous remark of Arthur Young in 1771 that 'everyone but an idiot knows that the lower classes must be kept poor, or they will never be industrious', can be read either as the epitaph engraved by the Enlightenment on the tomb of the mediaeval ethic, or as the signal for the recognition that the separation of economics from ethics had been finally achieved. It is possible to document decade by decade from the Reform the truth of that sweeping denunciation in the *Communist Manifesto* where Marx and Engels describe how 'the bourgeoisie, wherever it got the upper hand, put an end to all feudal, patriarchal, idyllic relations, pitilessly tore asunder the motley feudal ties that bound man to his "natural superiors", and left remaining no other bond between man and man than naked self-interest and callous cash-payment.'

The separation of ethics from economics gave birth to the individualist society of which Great Britain provided the outstanding example between the Napoleonic wars and the Revolution of 1848. Do not let us for one moment imagine that the harsh words of Marx and Engels paint an exaggerated picture. It was no embittered socialist revolutionary, but that fervent Evangelical Christian, Lord Shaftesbury, who could write, in 1842, that 'over a large surface of the industrial community man has been regarded as an animal, and that not an animal of the highest order; his loftiest faculties, when not prostrate, are perverted, and his lowest exclusively devoted to the manufacture of wealth'. When, in 1847, the British Government enquired into the state of education in Wales, the commissioner who visited Monmouth reported that he 'regarded their degraded conditions as entirely the fault of their employers, who give them far less tendance and cure than they bestow upon their cattle, and who, with few exceptions, use and regard them as so much brute force, instrumental to wealth, but as nowhere involving claims to human sympathy.' The indictment that can be drawn up against the new rich of the post-Napoleonic years is, on any ethical grounds, an overwhelming one. It was only slowly repaired by social legislation like the Factory Acts, by the growth of trade unions, and, in part, by the development of a competent and incorruptible civil service. The individualist society of the eighteen-thirties and eighteen-forties was beginning to be recognisable as moving about 1880 towards what it has become customary to term the 'welfare state'. Yet it remains immensely significant that, in the great years of British prosperity, when its economic supremacy was unchallenged, there were no forces powerful enough to tackle either the misery of the unemployed or the slums, which were a by-word of shame all over the world. It is, indeed, far from an exaggeration to say that what Disraeli called the 'condition of England' question only became a permanent and living issue in British politics at the end of the First World War in 1918.

By that time, the Bolshevik Government had seized power in Russia, and all our thinking became set in a new perspective. When I wrote six years and more ago, it looked as though one of the beneficent results of the War would be the discovery of terms upon which there could be accommodation between the horizons a triumphant communist society had opened, and the traditions of bourgeois democracy. Had those terms been achieved, world-recovery might have been more swift, and we might have been moving towards that effective peace upon the urgency of which all except the extreme reactionaries are agreed.

In place of the accommodation, we have had the 'cold war'. I do not think anything is gained by the attempt to measure the degree of responsibility for its inception which all the great Powers have incurred; it is as foolish to blame Russian Communism and its devotees in other countries, for the cleavage

94

from which we suffer as it is to insist that America and Great Britain are seeking by different ways to arrest, and, ultimately, to destroy, the communist idea in the interest of the privileged classes which are fighting to retain their traditional authority. We must approach the problem of this cleavage dynamically, and not statically, in its full historical background, and not as though we had a standardised ethic, that of Christianity, for example, by which to establish which side is right and which side is wrong. There is, of course, the same kind of danger on the Russian side; not least among the leaders of its dependent parties in other countries. They, too, have developed a standardised ethic which enables them to assume that they are the guardians of a rigid orthodoxy from which they will permit no deviation. It is difficult, moreover, not to feel that central to their outlook is a disposition to resent all criticism with a sensitivity so excessive that they are unable to examine their own experience with any detachment. They enforce conformity with a ruthlessness that reminds us of Diocletian seeking to root out the Christians, or of the Inquisition seeking to destroy the Albigensian heresy. If the work of the Un-American Activities Committee is loathsome, so, also, is the way in which Lysenko was permitted by the Soviet authorities to drive Vavilov to his death, and to compel the eminent scientist, Orbeli, to a recantation as foolish and as humiliating as that enforced upon Galileo three centuries ago. The 'cold war' was born of fear; and it has intensified fear as it has developed. Men who have to take decisions in the atmosphere where fear prevails are rarely capable of scrutinising their own activities with either disinterestedness or imagination.

We shall not see the significance of all this unless we set it in some sort of comparative perspective. Anyone who watches the slow rise of Christian culture from the early days of the Empire to the aftermath of its recognition by Constantine can hardly fail to see the significance of the analogy to our own condition. The Empire was based on the barbarous exploitation of slaves and *coloni* who were organised by a *conductor*, often himself a slave, on behalf of the absentee owners of the latifundia; in the towns was the urban proletariat which, despite the bread and circuses by which its rulers sought to purchase its loyalty, was full of a deep-seated resentment which no bribery could stifle. How deep that resentment was we can see in some of the writings under the Empire, as well as the real hatred of the stifling mental climate produced by the combination of absolutism and plutocracy. Out of the agony and suffering there were born not merely a belief in an original golden age where, as Seneca said, 'there was no sharp sting of want to rob a man of his sleep', but also the growth of a conviction that, somehow, the gods were preparing a happier destiny for mankind. Oppression gives birth to a new faith in the coming of a millennium. Philosophy becomes transformed into a religious hope. The poor slave, like Epictetus, begins, almost secretly, to have a new faith in the dignity of man, a sense that there are ways in which neither humble origin nor wretched poverty can degrade him, a confidence, enormously intensified by the wide revival of the mystery-religions, that salvation awaits him in the world beyond.

I cannot attempt to trace here the coincidence of this outlook with the evolution of Jewish Messianism, as shown, for example, in the Book of Daniel which dates, significantly enough, from the reign of Antiochus Epiphanes. Nor can I discuss the fascinating problems of the relation between the apocalytic visions of Daniel and Ezra, with their vision of a world-kingdom in which there is no longer private property, and the Essenes, on the one hand, and the growth of the Christian communities of the early Empire, on the other. What is unmistakable in all of them is that they express, in different ways, and over a wide geographical area, a sense of protest against the injustice of this world, and, in particular, of protest against an economic order which condemns the vast majority to poverty and oppression. The Christian community, in its early days, has an obvious resemblance to, even kinship with, the socio-religious organisations that were found in all parts of the Roman Empire. What makes it more striking is that it combines its emphasis upon mutual aid with an ethic which has behind it a profoundly religious sanction. Obedience to its claims becomes the condition of salvation and it claims an allegiance which exacts from its votaries behaviour different from that of the Roman citizen who does not accept the Christian faith. It develops into an *imperium in imperio*, with a conviction of its own self-sufficiency and, indeed, of its own

96

certain triumph, which easily becomes regarded, as the famous correspondence between Pliny and Trajan makes clear, as a challenge to the supreme authority of the empire. It is also a challenge on the economic plane; that is evident from writers like Clement of Alexandria and Saint Basil, like Chrysostom and Saint Augustine; with all of them, to have more than one needs without recognising that the surplus is the rightful possession of the poor is, in Augustine's phrase, criminal usurpation. It is so on the military plane also; the good member of the Christian community renounces the profession of arms. At the outset, he is even eager to be separate from the Empire on the plane of law; the Christian settles his disputes with a fellow-Christian in a communal court rather than take him before a secular court. It is an attempt to build an autonomous world in which the citizens find salvation through rules of faith which ensure the equality of men. It is thus a challenge to the Empire. The Christian denies its authority as supreme, repudiates its gods, even denounces them, and lives by values which are the direct antithesis of those behind which there is the sanction of the imperial power. In the light of these contrasts, it is easy to understand why the Roman Government began persecuting those whose whole outlook was a denial of its own. The persecution is perfectly logical. But what is most important in its evolution is that not all its barbarities can prevent the growth of the Christian faith or the development of it into a great international organisation whose leading figures are men of immense influence.

It is, of course, a long and hard struggle before the little communities of Christians of whom we read in apostolic times become transformed into the great Church which Constantine adopted as his own. On its way, the new faith has to compete with many rival faiths, and, like all successful ecclesiastical organisations, it absorbs ideas from them, and adapts its own principles to the need for victory over them. But there is more than this. As it begins to accept the devotion of men and women whose economic and social status is wholly different from that of those early beginnings, the new faith begins to reshape its doctrines to their habits. Its theological metaphysic assumes a larger proportion in its life than its original economic principles. Salvation becomes increasingly a matter of orthodoxy, and not of behaviour. The idea of stewardship becomes a technique for passing beyond its original asceticism. It can, indeed, slowly provide the economic criteria of the mediaeval world, with its conception of the just price, its prohibition of usury, and its emphasis on the obligation to give alms. But as the Christian community passes into the Christian Church, recognised, powerful, wealthy, it is transformed from a community of equals into an impressive hierarchy, where the great clerical figures are hardly less the devoted agents of the Empire than the great soldiers of the army or the great functionaries of the court. And after 321, when Constantine conferred upon the Church the status of corporate personality, it achieved therewith the right to receive bequests, and to hold landed property. Within a century, it had become one of the richest proprietors in Europe, and it naturally sought to impose upon the municipal law of every community which it penetrated the spirit and purpose of its own Canon Law. But to achieve this end, it was bound to enter into close relations with all who shared in the government of any community; its spiritual power becomes so interwoven with its economic and political power that it cannot effectively distinguish between them. From a spiritual fraternity it achieves the position of a great temporal power, international in character, claiming a divine authority for its principles and purposes, and using its secular authority to reinforce its spiritual supremacy, as it used its spiritual supremacy to strengthen its secular authority. With the collapse of the Roman Empire it became the central institution in European civilisation until the time of Luther, claiming an ever greater authority, able, with the collusion of secular states, to destroy or to drive underground the challenge of any heresy, and able to prevent the claim of the individual Christian either to spiritual or moral fulfilment except through the power of its mediation. Only after the Reformation did the individual autonomy of the individual Protestant begin to be possible; and the answer of the Church to that challenge was the increasing centralisation of its claim at Rome until, at the Vatican Council of 1870, the dogma of infallibility was recognised as residing in the Pope's person, whenever he spoke *ex cathedra* to Christendom.

Anyone who considers this development can hardly avoid

98

the recognition of its extraordinary resemblance to the history of Communism. This, too, begins with small groups of men holding passionately to a common faith, believing that their faith colours every aspect of their lives, hostile to all who do not share their principles, and convinced that the era of emancipation is very near at hand. They struck for power when they sought, in 1848, to lead the masses to the overthrow of the systems which denied them a share in their benefits. Thenceforward, all over Europe and America, their members are hunted down and persecuted by the government of almost every national community. Nevertheless, they grow in numbers, and their persecution only extends their ability to secure an increasing popular support. It is tempting, even, to argue that the breakdown of the First International, in 1872, was to the Communism of Marx and Engels very much what the Reformation was to the Roman Catholic Church; for, after 1872, the doctrines of Marx and Engels are, for most of their followers, a formal corpus of ideas which rapidly lose their revolutionary content even though that corpus continues to be the envelope in which the new ideas are contained. That was made abundantly clear in the history of the Second International from 1889 to 1914. The organisation which was intended to be the general staff of the Revolution was transformed into a Congress of Ambassadors, many of whom, on behalf of the Socialist parties they represented, professed Marxism as their faith, even though, like the German Social Democrats, they had, in fact, become social reformers to whom the recitation of Marxian principles was no more than the performance of an historic ritual; other members, the representatives for example of the different sections of the Labour movement in Great Britain, were, like the Fabian Society, and the Independent Labour Party, hardly influenced by Marxism at all, while the representatives of the Social Democratic Federation merely believed in the Marxist Revolution as some far-off event towards which, under the leadership of H. M. Hyndman, the whole creation was ultimately bound to move.

As the dissolution of the First International marked one great era in Socialist history, so the breakdown of the Second on the eve of the War of 1914 marked the beginning of a second far greater in significance. For the central fact in the War of 1914 was the success of revolution in Russia in its third year, and the central fact in that revolution was that between February and October 1917, the power to direct it fell into the hands of Lenin and the Bolsheviks who alone grasped the possibilities it implied. There is an interesting resemblance between the visionary hopes of the earliest Christians and those of Lenin and his colleagues. Just as the former expected an imminent Second Cöming, so the latter expected a European Revolution to follow their seizure of power. When, in each case, the hopes were unfulfilled they set out to build, respectively, a church and a state. Each was afflicted by the need to grapple with persecution and with heresy; and each must have seemed to themselves to have survived by something like a miracle. Moreover, both the early Church and Soviet Russia placed great reliance upon the efforts of missionaries in their cause who were ready, on its behalf, to suffer imprisonment, and even death, if thereby they could deepen its hold and spread its influence. The Christian Church and the Soviet State both saw the slow onset of assured stability, though both had to face lean years of agony in which each was bound to suspect that its enemies were organising its overthrow. Nor is it an exaggeration to argue that, in their different ways, each applied to the analysis of its problem a body of sacred scriptures the interpretation of which was entrusted to a relatively small number of adepts who were in large part regarded as the guardians of orthodoxy. It is, too, difficult not to say that Lenin was virtually canonised after his death, and that Trotsky became the great heretic, as Stalin became the Gregory VII of Bolshevism. Thenceforward, Church and State alike are threatened, attacked, deeply involved in the catastrophe of war. Each of them, also, had to preserve itself from the contagion of an external world which, while professing goodwill, was, in fact, deeply anxious for its destruction. Each used as the method of self-preservation a censorship, the right of excommunication, and a powerful Inquisition, served by a network of secret police, to impose all penalties, including that of death, upon those who were persistent in their heresies and dangerous by reason of the interest and sympathy they aroused.

No one can say of Christian culture that there was a single moment when it had triumphed over the pagan culture it replaced. But no one, either, can doubt that, by the era of Justinian, the triumph was beyond dispute. What is clear in the building of that triumph is how large a part was played by the tenacity with which orthodoxy was imposed, the ability to regenerate hope, and the certainty that present sacrifice meant ultimate salvation. Nor can one omit the power of its self-assurance, the vision before men's eyes of impressive material improvement, and the conviction that its doctrines were unassailable by all the alternative winds that blow. To these must be added the fact that attack from outside engendered an internal unity which no external criticism was powerful enough to threaten; even the Reformation was followed by a Counter-Reformation which left the spinal column of the Church as fighting, and certainly as determined, as those who sought to challenge its assumptions. Christian literature between, say, the age of Constantine and of Justinian was never wholly safe from the danger of pagan revival; but it was, at least, even more sure that it could count upon the growing victory of the principles for which it stood. There is a great truth in Maitland's famous aphorism that the Church of England was Protestant before the Reformation and Catholic after it.

The development of the Christian Church was extremely like the development of the Bolshevik party. Like that Church, the party regarded criticism as unwelcome, and insisted that its heresies could not find room within the catalogue of its categories. It, too, offered its votaries the offer of a certain hope of victory in the end. It was optimistic, victorious; able to convey the assurance that despite occasional victories against it, not even the forces of hell could prevent its triumph. It had immediate material triumphs to its credit. It held to its victories with a triumph with which no opponent could hope to compete. It had evil enemies to hate, devils which always tempted the victors from their enthusiasm for its triumph. It had a power of adaptation to new circumstances which enabled it to seem the same to its votaries even while its critics knew that it had changed. To be on its side seemed to the overwhelming bulk of these to be an inevitability they could not doubt; when they chose to support it, they were choosing a future they saw emerging before their eyes. It, too, had its heroes and its martyrs, and the enemies who knocked at its gates were challenged with a ferocity that made them seem as though they were devils from hell. Much of what it foretold of pain and tragedy in other countries had come to pass; and by always opening new avenues of opportunities to its own adherents, it seemed, not unjustly, to be expanding the opportunities it offered to them. Russian Communism was optimistic, convinced of the ultimate outcome, proud of the fear it caused among its enemies, and the obvious divisions it created among its half-hearted friends. It abhorred neutrality. It urged that it must, as a philosophy of life, be all or nothing; it could brook no rival upon the theatre it occupied. It was able to point proudly to the need of its services by its previous enemies after 1941, and to adopt to its aid a transformed account of the past history which added to its strength that mystic folk-lore which was almost the lost record of its slow rise of ascendancy. Even when it was beaten back by the enemy its leaders were able to insist that, on a wider view, it was moving forward; the capture of Berlin was its insistence upon a new German Canossa, as the half-broken Church had compelled Henry IV to kneel in the snow before the papal feet. When challenged, the whole world saluted it at Stalingrad, and thereby recognised the miracle of the morale of which it disposed. Before the conferences at Teheran and Yalta, it might have had to consider the prospect of some accommodation with its enemies, even with the enemies who were its allies; after those conferences, it stood for the one faith whose ultimate principles were inflexible and beyond the power of opponents to change. It had the immense satisfaction of ensuring that, by the late summer of 1945, its determination to push its principles forward could only be broken by a renewal of conflict; and it was convinced that, despite high-sounding phrases, impacts and declarations, it was in the highest degree unlikely that its surviving enemies would take the risk of conflict. In so far as they made a display of organising opposition, it could take comfort in the knowledge that nothing was more likely to strengthen its structure than its power to announce to its own people that its enemies were willing to sacrifice the destruction of civilisation rather than admit the truths of the great doctrine which, on the basis of the discoveries of Marx and Engels, its own great leaders, Lenin and Stalin, had been able to discover.

Whether Bolshevism, as Stalin stated it, was the central idea the world required was far less important than the fact that it left those who accepted it with the conviction that it was the one true doctrine; and, even more, that there was no competing doctrine which possessed even a portion of its appeal. Liberalism, in its historic sense, was dying before men's eyes. Conservatism promised little more than a revival of all the evil conditions which led to the War of 1939, with an occasional prospect of some minor reform, here and there, where circumstances permitted. Democratic socialism had, in its view, a deeper and more dangerous appeal. But it was possible for the Soviet leaders to say of it that, as soon as its right-wing enemies showed signs of active opposition to the reforms it urged, the leaders of democratic socialism drew back, and laid their emphasis upon the consolidation of the past rather than upon the movement of the future. Social Democrats, they would argue, pretended to ignore the very class-struggle by which they had climbed to power. They ignored the fact that, in taking the offensive, it was urgent to win new successes every day; and they gravely underestimated the real fact that while they had possession of political power in appearance only, the essential power, which was economic, remained overwhelmingly in the hands of their opponents By preserving, therefore, the classic machinery of formal democracy, whether Parliamentary or Congressional, they were leaving in their opponents' hands the real instruments with which the victory of the working class could be forged in the class-struggle. When they had done all they could, the authority that mattered was still beyond their control. They had struck the shield of the bourgeois knight, but they had wholly failed to strike his lance from his hand or to demand his admission of defeat. They respected, in fact, the dictatorship of the capitalist, even when they announced, with futile solemnity, that they had emerged the victors of the tournament.

'Tournament,' said the Bolsheviks, was indeed an appropriate word. For the fact was that in none of the countries where democratic socialism prevailed, in Great Britain or in

Scandinavia, in Australia or in New Zealand, had it touched more than the outworks of the capitalist fortress, or achieved more than large-scale, in some cases even spectacular, social reforms of a kind that were always within the compass of a bourgeois democracy based upon universal suffrage. Since the example of Great Britain was by far the most outstanding in its influence, it is worth examining the most closely. All the nationalised industries meant a transfer of ownership; but though large policies were subject to Parliamentary control in the hands of the government, the day to day control remained in the hands of the central and regional boards, the members of which came from much the same social strata, and had much the same outlook, as their predecessors when the industries were in private hands. It was true, and it was important, that a minority of trade unionists were put on to these boards. But it is difficult to infer from the evidence we have of how the nationalised industries are operating that the men who governed them had a more democratic relation to the ordinary workers than was the case under private ownership. It may well be that in the next decade they will discover the road to such a relation, and, thereby, evoke a deeper loyalty and a more profound initiative than private ownership was able to do. There is great need of both; and it is, thus far, obvious that no way of answering the need has yet been found.

There has been an important advance in agriculture, in which, for the first time in British history, the agricultural worker has been given a square deal, and it has become possible to deprive an inefficient farmer of his land, under suitable safeguards. But it is not less important to realise that this advance has not involved any serious change in the relations of production in agriculture. The nationalisation of the health service, the immense improvement in the scale and area of social insurance, the increased recognition that education, especially the higher forms of education, can no longer be neglected, are all of them big and impressive gains. But, in education particularly, it must be remembered that there still remain two systems of education in Great Britain, one for the rich and one for the poor, and that it is to the bright boy or girl from the working classes that a wider horizon has been opened rather than for the children generally of the working class. A brave effort has been

104

made to tackle the housing problem of much greater proportions than any previously attempted; but there is nothing yet
which permits us to say that a still predominantly capitalist
society can solve the housing problem, even when the state-
power is in the hands of a democratic socialist party. And it is,
clearly, of immense importance that, in a period of economic
difficulty the government has continued both the rationing of
food, and subsidies through taxation to reduce its cost, so
that the diet of the people generally is, if monotonous, nevertheless adequate, and the national health, not least of younger
children, has maintained a remarkably high standard.

But, on the economic side, three grave problems remain and
cast dark shadows over the future. The first is the ability of
Great Britain to maintain its competitive position in the international market, independently of financial aid from the
United States; there is, as yet, no permanent hope of exporting
enough to foreign markets, especially in hard-currency
countries like America, to pay for the imports by which the
nation maintains its standard of life. A socialist government is
necessarily committed to the maintenance of full employment
as well as the revision of the foundations of the national
economy. This involves high taxation, which bears with special
hardness upon the middle classes, and, amongst them, upon
those who live by what they earn and have no inherited capital
upon which to fall back. Given the traditional background of
the manufacturer and the trader, this involves the discourage-
ment of capital accumulation either for re-equipment of existing plant, or for new investment, and, therefore a discourage-
ment of the policy of low dividends; while, in addition, full
employment necessarily makes labour costs a cause of high
prices which, in their turn, reduce external competitive power.
And since the British economy is honeycombed with price
rings of every shape and size, the ability to lower prices, as
well as willingness to do so, is discouraged by the fact that
firms which are half-efficient, or incapable of efficiency at all,
survive by the support of the price ring; this enables the really
efficient firms to make very large profits without any communication of their efficiency to the firms which are mainly
parasitic upon price-fixing machinery. The Labour Government has sought to remedy this position by the establishment

of a Monopolies Commission which has been given the power to investigate practices of this kind, and to make recommendations to the President of the Board of Trade to put an end to them. This, and its proposal, if it continues in power, to enter into direct competition with industries where monopolistic practices have gone too far, will, it is hoped, cure what is an unhealthy economic condition. But, on the evidence, these are pillls to cure earthquakes; for even half a century's experience of the Sherman Act, and a generation's experience of the Federal Trade Commission in the United States, does not suggest that any government can, by such weapons, even hope seriously to reverse the trend towards monopolistic practices back to the intensely competitive conditions of the first half of the nineteenth century and, of course, even if it were successful, it would not thereby have taken a step on the road to socialism.

The third great problem is whether, in any foreseeable future the gap between the nations of Europe and the United States in productive power will not be so great as to create something like a permanent dollar shortage, with all its consequences. And we must not mistake the scale of these consequences. It means an inability to purchase food, raw materials, and machinery, because the demand for European commodities is not large enough to pay for these and thus maintain, let alone increase, the standard of life. And as new markets develop in South East Europe and Asia, and in Africa also, the American claim to penetrate these markets will be ever more emphasised for the simple reason that American manufacturers will face mass-unemployment if their plant is idle or be forced to make an immense re-adjustment in the purchasing power of their own citizens; these are the alternatives to a continuing Marshall aid to which there is no definite limit in time, unless European purchasing power is not merely restored, but raised proportionately to the increased productive potential in the United States. Asia, of course, is in a still more difficult position; and we are just becoming aware of how much is likely to be involved in the awakening self-consciousness of Africa. Looking at all this, it is not surprising that President Truman, in his 'fourth point' should have stressed the importance of an American policy which should set out deliberately, by large-scale grants-in-aid, to assist the backward areas in equipping

106

themselves to raise their standard of living both by developing their material resources on the one hand, and by modernising their methods of production on the other. What, indeed, is surprising is not that he should have made the suggestion, but that there should have been critics opposed to its implementation. Civilisations are only made secure when taxation makes life tolerable by a national transfer of wealth from the rich to the poor. In the long run, history has usually shown that what can be done by reason and consent in peace is otherwise done by anger and coercion in war.

Round these three great questions the future of the world may fairly be said to depend. What has happened is that between 1914 and 1945 the pattern of the world which was made by the sixteenth century has been broken in pieces. The centre of power is no longer in Europe. Part of it has become dependent upon the United States and part of it has become dependent upon Russia. In both parts of Europe, moreover, especially in its Eastern part, the supremacy of the middle class has been broken. It cannot maintain its privileges in the face of the deliberate demand of the working class to share fully in the amenities which were not only the outcome of middle-class rule but in large part and, again especially in Eastern Europe, confined to a middle class and an aristocracy which were a very small fraction of the population. And, alongside these two immense changes—the end of European supremacy and of middle class domination—there is that awakening of Asia which I venture to regard as the outstanding event in the twentieth century, bigger even, in its long-range consequences, than the Russian Revolution. India and China, Japan and Indonesia, overwhelmingly peasant populations which, in all their poverty, constitute something like three-quarters of the inhabitants of the world, have begun to realise that the application of modern science to their problems would not only enormously better their material conditions, but also, thereby, enormously raise the spiritual values by which they live, giving to them the chance of that life of grace and dignity which, at its best, Western civilisation has offered to its middle classes and to its aristocracies.

No one is likely seriously to suppose that the rise of Asia will be accomplished through middle-class leadership either from

107

within or from without. Certainly not from within, partly because the middle class is much too small to maintain domination over the vast peasant masses, and partly because—as the contemporary history of China has made evident—the middle class has revealed itself as an exploiting class, corrupt, oppressive, and incapable of magnanimity. It is, indeed, important to note that in Russia the middle class was only able to maintain an uneasy hold of power from February 1917, to October 1917, when it was swept ruthlessly on one side despite the efforts of middle-class governments in Europe to assist it against its enemies. It was therefore natural that, with the destruction of the Russian aristocracy and the Russian middle class, the values to which they attached importance should be destroyed also. Since the Russian party which led the Revolution was aware that if it accepted the peasant ideal of peasant ownership of private farms there was no serious chance of applying modern science to the development of Russia, it embarked upon its immense experiment of large-scale industrialisation and the replacement of private by collective farming. The leaders of the Russian Revolution were seeking to by-pass one hundred and fifty years in the history of Europe and America by imposing upon the mainly backward and illiterate peasantry with whom they had to work new values they had never known by a discipline that was bound to be both stern and drastic. They had, moreover, to implement their decisions in a world overwhelmingly unfriendly to the values they sought to impose. They had to do so in the continuous shadow of the war which broke upon them in 1941. Now they have to pick up the threads of the pattern they were seeking to weave under the shadow of another and even more catastrophic conflict which the 'cold war' casts over their lives.

That is the reason why I believe that the American decision to make the successful waging of the 'cold war' the pivot of their foreign policy is so disastrous a mistake. It is built upon an erroneous diagnosis of the world-situation, and it proposes to apply remedies to what it regards as the disease which are, in fact, irrelevant to its nature. For American foreign policy, the expression of what is to-day an immensely wealthy and powerful middle-class civilisation, is seeking to impose the values of that civilisation not only upon a Europe where those values are losing their hold, but upon a Middle East, a Russia and an Asia, where they are either already dead or have never existed. To do so the American Government must ally itself with those forces in Asia and Europe which share its own outlook, and assist them to make a stand against the new values which it regards as a challenge to its own. To do so it has not only to 'contain' Russia and its satellites. It has also to discourage the emergence even of democratic socialism in Western Europe—hence the pressure upon it by American business men to make further aid to Great Britain conditional upon the abandonment by the Labour Government of any further measures of nationalisation—and to welcome the advent to power of groups eager to retain the authority of a dying economic order associated with a system of values with an ever smaller ability to maintain its hold upon the people.

But this is not all. The American Government cannot apply this policy in Asia because it is itself aware that the overwhelming mass of the population is hostile to it both on economic and psychological grounds. To do so it would have to divide every Asiatic people and arm, as in China, the corrupt and reactionary forces which can only express themselves as fascist. This indeed is increasingly true in Europe and the Middle East. The Truman doctrine, as soon as it is seriously applied, means the endowment with American strength of all the interests which seek to prevent the working class from winning its place in the sun. That is why American aid is given to what is, in essence, a middle-class government in France, a middle-class and near fascist government in Italy, and an obviously fascist government in Greece. The aid, indeed, is extended to the Labour Government in Great Britain, and to governments, as in Scandinavia, which are mildly socialist, or, as in Holland and Belgium, to coalition governments in which socialist parties have had a minor share without, however, being able to secure any acceptance of socialist measures. The American aid to Great Britain, despite the real element of magnanimity it contains, has nevertheless something paradoxical about it. For the inherent sympathies of the American Government are not with the Labour Party now in power, but with the Conservative Party which seeks to regain power and to arrest the forward movement of all the tendencies to socialism the Labour Party represents. That is why the policy of the Conservative Party has been so consistently dualistic since 1945. For, on the one hand, it must not allow the British working class to think that a Conservative victory would mean the loss of the strategic gains that class has made since 1945, while, on the other, it must convince the United States that the British advance to socialism will stop if there is a Conservative victory in the next few years. Mr. Churchill and his followers therefore promise the British workers freedom and democracy, which the workers are asked to believe will include both the welfare and the opportunity they did not win under the rule of the middle class, while assuring the United States that, by freedom and democracy they mean, in essence, the American 'way of life'. That is why, even while they are out of power, their whole appeal is based upon the insistence that the difficulties of the British position are not due to the decay of capitalist civilisation in Europe, a decay which began slowly to reveal itself after the panic of 1873, but to the experiments in social welfare and socialism which began in 1945, in the unfavourable conditions of a country not only physically devastated by war, but economically in great danger because, in two world-struggles, it had lost the overseas investments which enabled it to maintain its economy in equilibrium.

This view, is not, I think, impaired by the fact that the Labour Government in Great Britain is hostile to the idea of violent revolution in the Russian manner of 1917 and to the stern dictatorship which has grown out of its success. The historical traditions in Great Britain are rooted in a constitutionalism which goes back for over two hundred and fifty years. They enabled the Labour Party to take office, after its victory of 1945, in a perspective of almost universal acceptance. They conditioned it, indeed, to the obligation to act within limits the overpassing of which might outrage the emotions and opinions of those whom it replaced. The traditions bound the Labour Party to attempt, as a government, to make a revolution by consent, to win the support of the large and powerful middle class, and not to drive it to that desperation where a social group will fight rather than accept the measures of its opponents. Granted that view, the Labour Government of 1945 was bound to look to the United States for aid in its attempt at revolution by consent; and, granted the polarity of American and Russian ideals, its foreign policy was generally bound to developments which, thus far, have culminated in the North Atlantic Security Pact, and the effort of the American Government to protect it in doing so by aid towards its rearmament in case the 'cold war' became a 'shooting war'. What is most important in the Atlantic Pact is what Great Britain as its major European signatory would do, not with a Labour Government in power, but with a Conservative Government in power. For there would then be a coincidence of governmental ideologies in both London and Washington. There would be equal concern to protect the principles broadly termed the 'American way of life'. There would be a great insistence on the political and economic integration of the West European Powers. It would be necessary, in order to achieve that integration to buy all the possible support that could be won by securing that the potential strength of Western Germany at least is associated with that integration. In partnership with the United States, the new pattern of union could not avoid two things. It could not avoid becoming the apparatus for defending middle-class supremacy in America and maintaining it against the challenge of socialism in Western Europe; and it could not avoid becoming the patron of the opposition to Russia and its allies in Eastern Europe, and of the old order both in the Middle East and in Asia. Dependent as it would long be upon continuing aid from America, it would necessarily evolve into the active instrument of counter-revolution. It then becomes difficult not to argue that the next stage is a third world war.

In all these developments, there is a grave tendency to take for granted the long-term viability of the American economy which thus enables the Government of the United States permanently to safeguard the standards of life among its dependent allies in Western Europe. That is a very large assumption. Immense as are its natural resources and unsurpassed though the level of its technological skill may be, the present American relations of production offer no prospect of a permanently expanding economy. The Great Depression of 1929 and the 'little depression' of 1937 remind us that neither the 'rugged individualism' of President Hoover, nor the 'New Deal' of

President Roosevelt, had discovered the key to full employment. There is an important sense in which the programme of Marshall Aid, and the military implications of the Truman Doctrine, can both be regarded as a safeguard against a slump. It is sixty years since the frontier was reached; the period when a man could escape to free land from the weary search for an urban job has, therefore, long since passed away; and it was, above all, the grim experience of organised labour which compelled Congress to place grave restrictions upon the right of immigration in 1921 and 1924—restrictions which have not seriously been relaxed even in the face of the wholesale misery of the vast horde of displaced persons made helpless and homeless by the War of 1939. No nation has contributed more than the American to heal the wounds left by that war; but nothing it has done has, as far, even suggested grounds for believing that its economy will continue to possess some power of continuous expansion denied to capitalist economies elsewhere.

Rather the contrary is the case. The great American dream, as Emerson depicted it, and as Walt Whitman saw it, began slowly to fade after the Civil War. The small farmer began to lose his independence to a capitalist agriculture which made the land simply another element in the normal economy of the market. The overwhelming growth of large-scale manufacture destroyed so much of the free enterprise and individualism that were the Jeffersonian ideals as to make their use as battle-cries little more than recourse to incantation. We can trace the decline of toleration in America, the growth of a fear of discontent, suspicion of subversive ideas, limitation upon the freedom of teaching. No one can study with any closeness the fears of Communism, even more the activities that are brought under the vast rubric of Communism, the growth of the secret police, the way in which the Government of President Truman is driven to spend millions of dollars in assuring itself that its officials are safe and sound, the persistent endowment year after year by Congress of its incredible 'Un-American Activities Committee'—I take a few examples only—without seeing that the right to speak freely and to act upon that freedom, which Jefferson wrote of as the very heart of Americanism, has been transformed relentlessly into the very antithesis of Americanism. And, allied to this, there is a growth of doubt about

112

the validity of democratic institutions which hides like a lush undergrowth beneath a loud eulogy of them. It is not only that Americans before the war gave help to Mussolini and Hitler; there is the fact that after the war Americans support ugly and evil régimes in Greece, Turkey, China and Spain. In the United States itself even, there is a cult of inequality, a growing faith in the *élite*, which does not hesitate to associate success with biological worth. Even so normally sensible an economist as the late F. W. Taussig could write that 'innate superiority is the secret of the greater productivity of the business and professional classes . . . [They have] a higher ratio of biologically superior individuals . . . The degree of achievement has [not] been conditioned to any considerable extent by the environmental factors.[1] To this doubt about the validity of democratic institutions there must be given the perspective set by the continuing hostility to Negroes in the South, and the growth, which I do not think would be seriously denied, of anti-semitic feeling, a condition which actually accompanies a decline in the conviction that democracy is the best form of government.

It is important also to note the shrinkage in the opportunity for promotion. Here we have the evidence of Professor Taussig, and his collaborator, C. S. Joslyn, neither of whom can be accused of hostility to the ethos of bourgeois capitalism in its American expression. 'Contrary to an American tradition of long standing,' they write,[2] 'the typical figure among present-day business leaders in the United States is neither the son of a farmer, nor the son of a wage-worker . . . The proportion of farmers' sons among successful business men is tending to decrease, and that of business men's sons [specifically, the sons of major executives] is tending to increase. The slack created by the decreasing proportion of farmers' sons is being taken up not at all by the sons of manual workers. The representation of sons of major executives is on the increase. If this tendency continues for many decades, the well-to-do classes will be contributing the major share of business leaders, and the middle classes but a minor share. This tendency—as yet in its first

[1] F. W. Taussig and Carl Joslyn, *American Business Leaders* (N.Y. 1932). pp. 243, 251.

[2] F. W. Taussig and Carl Joslyn, *American Business Leaders* (N.Y. 1932) p. 234 f.

stages only—to narrow the sources of business leadership, and to relate that confinement to a growing habit of nepotism, is, of course, an important witness that there is a decline in the power to expand, and that there is a decrease in the class-mobility which was one of the important differences between capitalist democracy in America and Europe respectively.' What is disturbing in this picture is that despite its immense wealth, its technological superiority, its massive productive power, the rulers of America are afraid. They are afraid in the same sense as Pagan Rome feared Christian Rome, as the land-owners of the sixteenth century feared the rising middle class. The order of things has got out of focus for them. They feel as though they cannot see clearly ahead, and they are afraid of the obscurity. They repeat with passion the old formulae, and instead of hearing over most of the world the echo of their words, they catch fragments of new formulae which they find uncomfortable, challenging, disturbing. They are not at ease with themselves. They are unable to affirm the conviction that Franklin Roosevelt strove to persuade them to accept, that 'they have nothing to fear but fear itself'. They have an unhappy sense that a new idea is abroad in the world to the implications of which they cannot accommodate themselves. They are afraid to discuss the idea lest by argument in the market-places of the world they find that it is more persuasive than the old. They point to their faith in education, their confidence in science, their desire to solve their problems, internal and external, by the light of reason. Yet, with all their protests, they are still afraid, and they communicate their fears to others. They have an inner sense that bourgeois democracy has reached a grave turning point in its development. They suspect that, if it is to keep its bourgeois character, it cannot remain democratic; yet they suspect also that if it remains democratic, it cannot keep its bourgeois character. If that bourgeois character were once to be lost, they recognise that the tide of a new social order would sweep over them, and that they, too, would be like those dreary exiles who are so interesting for the few months in which they almost convince ruling America that the new idea is already losing its hold, and become so heavy a burden when, the stimulus of their freshness over, they persist in repeating the stale prophecies that never come true.

Professor Gilbert Murray has discussed, with his usual penetration and insight, what he has called the 'failure of nerve' which characterises the twilight of Hellenistic civilisation. Something like that 'failure of nerve' again oppresses capitalist civilisation. There is unending uncertainty about our ability to be sure about the things we thought were certain. There is a persistent anxiety everywhere which makes us wonder whether the appearance of things is in fact reality. In the famous phrase of W. B. Yeats, the centre does not seem to hold. And it is all complicated by the fact that Americans are not patient people, that they want things done quickly, that delays irritate them, that they find it hard to argue with people who do not agree to start from the premises most Americans have come to deem not only permanent, but obvious. They are not a steady people, who can take disappointment and frustration as part of the day's work. They find it very difficult to understand other national communities which have never had the impressive margins of wealth and security they have possessed for over half their history. They do not know what it costs another nation to shake itself free from the repressive burden of a semi-feudal despotism, still less to move, almost at a stride, from a mediaeval primitivism to all the massive complexities of modern technology. Least of all can they understand the profound discipline the movement requires, the pain and harshness involved in the conquest of immaturity. That is why, with all their tremendous power, they have a lack of serenity, of self-confidence, of that responsibility in the use of power which gives men the wisdom of patience. They feel that the world ought now to see its centre in Washington, that, so to say, the 'American century' ought to begin. They are angry that other nations seek to examine the meaning of that century in which America sets the pace and character of the world. They have given so much to aid in the conquest of Fascism. They have been so outstandingly generous in seeking to heal the tremendous wounds that Fascism inflicted upon civilisation. They find the refusal of Russia to accept the assumptions upon which they propose to reshape the pattern of ordered living exasperating and threatening. Russia has thus become the symbol of all that blocks the way to peace, and, with peace, security and prosperity. It is for Americans a symbol the more

115

dangerous and more evil not only because it is arrogant and unyielding, but because there is something in the blueprint of the future that Russia offers which is clearly more attractive to some of the nations than the American blueprint; and it is more attractive even though America is anxious for the friendship of those nations and ready, with its inherent generosity, to aid them in recovery and their search for a higher standard of life. Russia thus becomes the symbol of all that America denies. It becomes the source of hate and fear, the more so because Americans are justly aware that the Russian victory over Fascism was in no small part of their making. The return for their aid seems to them insolent enmity, dangerous efforts towards the disintegration of the American way of life and a morbid refusal to make any serious response to repeated offers of co-operation.

Hence, in the American mind, the picture of expansionist Russia, of its Communism as nothing but Fascism in a different uniform, of its enmity to all the freedoms for which the Second World War was fought and won. As the government in Washington scrutinises the record of Russia from Potsdam, perhaps from Yalta, onwards it sees it as a challenge which the Kremlin is prepared to thrust by force down the throat of civilisation. Stalin becomes for Americans the successor of Hitler, of Mussolini, of General Tojo, only on a more gigantic scale. He is the enemy of freedom and democracy, the tyrant who seeks to impose his cruel and relentless ideology upon the world, he brooks no opposition to his will; all his satellites are driven to servile imitation of the pattern he has imposed upon Russian civilisation. Impatient America, not less convinced that its destiny is the salvation of mankind, begins out of hate and fear to organise the nations over which Russia has not yet extended its influence into a combination with the will and the power to defeat what it has already come to accept as a monstrous conspiracy against the way of civilised life.

CHAPTER VII

A L L these tensions are reflected, even though indirectly, in the crisis of our culture which weighs so heavily upon our time. Mr. T. S. Eliot has very wisely said[1] that 'culture is not merely the sum of several activities, but a *way of life*'. He pleads[2] for 'a form of society in which an aristocracy should have a peculiar and essential function, as peculiar and essential as the function of any other part of society. What is important is a structure of society in which there shall be from "top" to "bottom" a continuous gradation of cultural levels; it is important to remember that we should not consider the upper levels as possessing *more* culture than the lower, but as representing a more conscious culture and a greater specialisation of culture. I incline to believe that no true democracy can maintain itself unless it contains these different levels of culture. The levels of culture may also be seen as levels of power, to the extent that a smaller group at a higher level will have equal power with a larger group at a lower level; for it may be argued that complete equality means universal irresponsibility; and in such a society as I envisage, each individual would inherit greater or less responsibility towards the commonwealth, according to the position in society which he inherited —each class would have somewhat different responsibilities. A democracy in which everybody had an equal responsibility in everything would be oppressive for the conscientious and licentious for the rest.' To these intensely significant sentences Mr. Eliot adds the emphases, first, that 'the primary vehicle for the transmission of culture is the family', and, second, that 'if we agree that in a more highly civilised society there must be different levels of culture, then it follows that to ensure the transmission of the culture of these different levels, there must be groups of families persisting, from generation to generation, each in the same way of life'.

[1] *Notes Towards the Definition of Culture* (London, 1948) p. 41. The italics are Mr. Eliot's.

[2] *Op. cit.* p. 48.

Mr. Eliot rejects a classless society, but he is equally opposed to a 'society of strict and impenetrable social barriers'. There should be constant mobility between classes, and though they remain distinct, they should all have a community of culture with each other which will give them something in common, more fundamental than the community which each class has with its counterpart in another society. There must, of course, be social unity, but it must be compatible with the 'useful diversities'. In a society like England, culture is inconceivable without an acceptance of the Christian faith; and though 'Christendom should be one', yet, within its unity 'there should be an endless conflict between ideas—for it is only by the struggle against constantly appearing false ideas that the truth is enlarged and clarified, and in the conflict with heresy that orthodoxy is developed to meet the needs of the time'. We should expect, Mr. Eliot tells us, not only 'regional' forms of Christianity—the Anglican Church, for example—but also forms of it suitable—as in the different dissenting sects—to the social strata in which it is finding expression; otherwise there is a loss of the genius which 'useful diversities' contribute. But diversity does not mean anarchy; 'there must also be a force holding these classes and these areas together' for a national culture, while it must be healthy in its parts, must itself be part of a larger culture, ideally, indeed, a world-culture, in which a common faith binds nations together.[1]

Mr. Eliot approaches the relation between culture and politics from the same direction. Save in small areas, he assumes that, crisis apart, politics on the national level would be the business of a governing *élite*. 'In a healthily *stratified* society,' he writes,[2] 'public affairs would be a responsibility not equally borne; a greater responsibility would be inherited by those who inherited special advantages, and in whom self-interest and interest for the sake of their families ("a stake in the country") should cohere with public spirit. The governing élite, of the nation as a whole, would consist of those whose responsibility was inherited with their affluence and position, and whose forces were constantly increased, and often led, by rising individuals of exceptional talent.' Mr. Eliot, of course,

[1] *Op. cit.* chap. iv. esp. p. 82.
[2] *Op. cit.* chap. v. p. 84. Italics Mr. Eliot's.

is not contemplating a political ruling group shut off from ruling groups in other spheres of social life. 'A society is in danger of disintegration,' he urges,[1] 'when there is a lack of contact between people of different areas of activity—between the political, the scientific, the artistic, the philosophical and the religious minds. This separation cannot be repaired merely by public organisation . . . Men who meet only for definite serious purposes, and on official occasions, do not wholly meet.' It is thus desirable to have a society 'in which persons of every superior activity can meet without merely talking shop, or being at pains to talk each other's shop'. It is in this way that a man will learn the things outside his métier which, otherwise, he would be too occupied to learn. Otherwise, he confronts the danger that he will miss the significant ideas in discussion about him. By this easy social intermingling of élites the politician merely knows 'the ideas which flatter a current tendency or an emotional attitude' among a large public incapable of appreciating profundity. In those circumstances, Mr. Eliot warns us[2] the politician will not, 'as a rule inhale any fragrance they [the current ideas] may have had when they were fresh; he only noses them when they have already begun to stink'.

Born of this outlook, Mr. Eliot is deeply critical of most contemporary aims in educational discussion, above all of the aim of equality of opportunity, which he calls 'jacobinism in education'. 'It is an ideal,' he writes,[3] 'which can only be fully realised when the institution of the family is no longer respected, and when parental control and responsibility passes to the state. Any system which puts it into effect must see that no advantages of family fortune, no advantages due to the foresight, the self-sacrifice or the ambition of parents are allowed to obtain for any child or young person an education superior to that to which the system finds him to be entitled. The popularity of the belief is perhaps an indication that the depression of the family is accepted, and that the disintegration of classes is far advanced.' Indeed, he goes further, and argues that the enthusiasm for more education irrelevantly to the function a person must perform in society is a proof of

[1] Ibid.
[2] Ibid. p. 87.
[3] Op. cit. p. 103.

119

'cultural breakdown', and that the aim of making everyone share in 'the appreciation of the fruits of the more conscious part of culture is to adulterate and cheapen what you give. For it is an essential condition of the preservation of the quality of the culture of the minority that it should continue to be a minority culture'.[1] Mr. Eliot, indeed, is convinced that the more ardent the zeal for universal education the more certain it is that the standards of true culture will be degraded.

It is natural enough, in the light of this approach, that Mr. Eliot should condemn, with what may perhaps be termed a disdainful vigour, what he calls the Russian 'subordination of culture to political theory'. He looks upon the Russian attitude to racial equality as mere appearance. He suspects that the grant of autonomy to the smaller republics and the satellite states is mere illusion, an attempt merely to flatter their vanity; and he infers this from the fact that such republics have, on occasion, been reduced in status to the position of 'a kind of province or crown colony'. Since, he argues, culture is subordinate to political theory, the greater the success of Russian 'imperialism', the greater is likely to be the sense of superiority of the Great Russians as the main authors of that theory. He does not deny that the 'harmless' part of local culture—'harmless', of course, from the standpoint of political theory—will be preserved, and even fostered; local arts and customs,·language and literature, for instance. But he prophesies that, under the existing Russian system, we shall 'find the increasing assertion of one dominant Muscovite culture, with subordinate races surviving, not as peoples each with its own cultural pattern, but as inferior castes'. Not only is this the case; Mr. Eliot also foresees that the Russians are bound to attack alien cultures which are highly developed with a special determination to destroy them 'by elimination of those elements in the subject population in which that culture is most conscious'.[2]

I have summarised at some length and, I hope, fairly, Mr. Eliot's attitude because it is at once one of the most clear and far-reaching attacks upon the emerging tendencies of our age. If we call this, as I think we are entitled to call it, a revolutionary period, Mr. Eliot is seeking to enunciate what is hardly

[1] *Ibid.* pp. 106-7.
[2] *Op. cit.* pp. 92-3.

less than the outline of a counter-revolutionary philosophy. He argues that our present values are in a condition of disintegration. But his desire is not to discover how to move forward from this condition to a new integration, but how to restore values which were already in advanced decay at least half a century ago. The influences which have gone to shape his outlook are pretty clear. Some of it derives from Plato, and, more generally, from that Greek view of life which excluded the workers by hand from a part in the higher expression of civilisation. Some of it comes from an admiration of the still fairly tight hierarchy of seventeenth century society, where each class had its place, its own habits and customs and outlook, and social mobility in an upward direction was, if always possible, nevertheless difficult, even infrequent. Some of it, above all the stress on the immense importance in the West of active ecclesiastical life, and of the desirability of rule by an hereditary aristocracy free from material cares and so suffused with public spirit that the interest of the whole society becomes identical with its own, seem to come directly from Edmund Burke; Mr. Eliot might have taken as his own the famous sentence in the *Reflections* that 'Englishmen know, and what is better, we feel inwardly that religion is the basis of civil society and the source of all good and all comfort'. Nor, I suspect, would Mr. Eliot be unsympathetic to Burke's hatred of political metaphysics: 'One sure symptom of an ill-conducted state,' Burke wrote, again in the *Reflections*, 'is the propensity of the people to resort to theories.' Burke's ideal of an aristocracy delegated to do its work on behalf of the mainly incompetent masses, an aristocracy which combined the hereditary influence of birth with the power of great wealth, a system of government in which, while office should be open to all, it should be out of the reach of most, has an obvious kinship with Mr. Eliot's own purpose. And he, like Burke, would agree that 'the characteristic essence of property . . . is to be unequal', and that where that inequality is perpetuated by inheritance we have built into the foundations 'that which tends most to the perpetuation of society itself'. Even Burke's contempt for the 'swinish multitude' is shared, if with far more sophistication, and a skilful indirectness, by Mr. Eliot. The higher culture is open only to the élites; it is degraded when an attempt is made to share it

121

with the masses. And there is a similar insistence upon those unconscious social influences which reason cannot penetrate, so strongly emphasised in Burke's famous aphorism, 'we ought to venerate where we are unable presently to comprehend'.

The higher culture is for the few, and the élites in a society must mingle closely with one another; that is how the politician is rescued from the ever-present danger that he may mistake the voice of the people for the voice of God. As Mr. Eliot paints, rather faintly, the outline of his doctrine it is difficult not to think that he dreams of a revival of those delicious days at Great Tew when, before the intrusion of the agonies of the Civil War, Falkland could entertain in its enchanting garden not only the lawyer-politician like Edward Hyde, the aristo-cratic philosopher like Herbert of Cherbury, but poets of the intellectuals like Crashaw and Cowley, and grave theologians like Chillingworth and the 'ever memorable' John Hales who, at port, almost a generation before, had, with such grace, bade good-night to Calvin and his doctrines. It is the slow disap-pearance of a society where an élite of this character may combine the power to govern with the capacity to live on the heights in all the realms of thought that disturbs Mr. Eliot. For him the centre has lost its hold because liberty, which is the art, for him, of an aristocracy, has been set in the context of equality, by the influence of which it is bound to be debased. The highest is always for the few; the many may have their joys and rights and dreams, but they must be content to possess them on a lower level lest their inability to appreciate what is profound or original or sublime should destroy these qualities by their popularisation. Civilised living means hierarchy and inequality, or it ceases to be civilised living. In nothing, per-haps, is this proclaimed so defiantly by Mr. Eliot as when he assigns sectarian forms of Christian organisation to the lower strata of society, leaving the Church-form, with its vital duty of guarding the central themes of orthodoxy upon which the preservation of the Christian tradition depends, to that hereditary aristocracy to which he entrusts the high function of governing the whole society. The common man can rise no higher than some minor nonconformity in religion, and the issues of the parish-pump in politics. The great questions beyond he degrades when he enters into their decision.

122

There are at least three major barriers which an approach like that of Mr. Eliot is unable to overcome. The first is the failure of Mr. Eliot to realise that politics is the art of the possible. Into the matrix of the economic life of the middle twentieth century he seeks to restore the pattern of the institution of an age which was already beginning to fade when the American and French Revolutions made their immense impact upon social organisation. He fails to see that the vast changes in the forces of production have brought with them changes not less vast in the relations of production, and that these changes are themselves caught in a vast dynamic which no man or groups of men can do more than temporarily arrest in its sweep onwards. He deals with the epoch of his affection with a wistful regard that shuts out from his survey all that it contained of yearning unappeased, of hopes unrequited, of grave wrongs and oppressions unredressed. He yields himself so fully to the graceful ease of Great Tew and the meditative communion of Little Gidding that he fails to see them in their proper setting as two luxurious oases in a society bitterly rent by deep dissension on fundamental matters, which was about to express itself in bitter civil war. He is so wrapped up in the beauties of John Donne and Lancelot Andrewes that he hears nothing of those angry murmurings that were presently to declare themselves in the harsh clarity of Cromwell, the strident claims of John Lilburne, and that call to a complete social reorganisation which, at its best, made the prose of Gerard Winstanley hardly yield in eloquence to the beauty of Traherne or in piercing insight to the penetration of Thomas Hobbes. Mr. Eliot, to adapt the phrase of Tom Paine, so admires the plumage that he has hardly time for interest in the bird and its life.

The truth is that, on his historical side, Mr. Eliot perceives none of the causal relations between the culture of a society and the material environment of which it is the expression. In an economy such as ours, an aristocracy of wealth and leisure, separated through its isolation from the hard effort to earn its daily bread, does not retain a wide or profound sense of public spirit; it concentrates upon its privileges, and not upon its duties, and exhausts the major part of its energies in angrily protecting them from invasion. It therefore seeks, not seldom with grim ferocity, to deny to those outside its frontiers not merely the means of crossing them, but, still worse, the very amenities in which the masses are to find the hopes of that lower culture to which Mr. Eliot assigns them. He has only to observe the lack of integrity in most of those whose part in an inherited aristocratic tradition is supposed to breed public spirit, the zest with which, like flies on carrion, they fatten themselves upon the public funds, their lack of sensitiveness to any pain but their own, to realise that his political élite, at any rate, has no more resemblance to the portrait he paints of them than Burke's fantastic idealisation of the Whig oligarchy of the eighteenth century.

Nor is the historical argument upon which Mr. Eliot leans made better—I do not think he would wish to claim it is—when the victory of the middle class replaces the privileges of birth by the privileges of wealth. No one can read of the discipline exacted by the new political élite as they drove their way to power without a sense that, even if there is an immense gain in man's control of nature, the price paid for that gain is an intense suffering in the masses and an amazing indifference to that suffering on the part of their new masters. In one sense, the whole is summarised in the death, both of hope and exhilaration, in the great experience of 1848-9. In another, it is recorded in the passionate struggle against corruption in government, both central and local, and the effort to secure education, a decent standard of health, relief from long hours of toil, safeguards against unemployment, the means, as in public libraries and parks and museums of art and science, to create the very possibility of that culture from which Mr. Eliot restricts all outside the boundaries of his élites. It is surely no accident that there were few creative minds in the nineteenth century, in Europe or America, who had direct experience of the price paid by the masses for the higher culture made possible for the different élites who did not passionately protest against the immensity of that price. Heine and Marx and Engels among the Germans, Louis Blanc, George Sand, Proudhon among the French, Herzen and Tolstoy and Chernichevski among the Russians, Carlyle and Mill and Matthew Arnold among the British, Emerson, Whitman and Melville among the Americans are all aware, even when they

124

have confidence in the doctrine of progress, that the values of a bourgeois civilisation involve contradictions that are fatal to its ultimate survival. I speak only of men who saw that civilisation at the height of its power; and it is important to note that their protest became, in the voice of the great pessimist and reactionary Dostoievsky, the anguished cry of what can only be termed utter despair.

The second major barrier in the way of Mr. Eliot's thesis is his insistence that, since all cultures are bound up with the acceptance of a religious faith, the culture of Europe is dependent upon the continued acceptance of Christianity. Here it is far from easy to be certain precisely what Mr. Eliot has in mind. If by Christianity he means the system of ethical values formulated in its sacred texts, it is, of course, historically obvious that these values are not specifically Christian, and that, were they to be applied in all their amplitude, they would involve a new society utterly incompatible with the ideal society Mr. Eliot himself recommends. If, rather, he means by Christianity the acceptance, within some broadly defined limits, of a body of theological dogmas which derive their authority from the postulated authenticity of certain events in time, one is bound to reply that the rational examination of the evidence upon which authenticity is claimed becomes ever more damaging to acceptance the more honestly and closely that evidence is examined by the normal canons of historical verification. In the endless quest for the historical Jesus through whose power the central dogmas of all Christian Churches claim their authority there are now no foundations left acceptable to reason. Mr. Eliot is, of course, wholly right in insisting that European culture cannot be separated from the history of the Christian Church; but he could equally insist with truth that it cannot be separated from the history of Greece and Rome in epochs separated by long centuries from the birth even of Christianity. Nor would it be easy for him to affirm that what is best in the moral behaviour of men is the outcome of their belief in the Christianity urged or imposed upon them by the different forms in which it has been expressed as church or sect; only too often, indeed, and too continuously, churches and sects alike have been the enemies rather than the advocates of the moral values for which Christianity has stood; and it has

125

often been the great infidels, like, supremely, Spinoza, who have embodied those values best in their time. And, in this context, finally, it is clear that if Mr. Eliot makes Christianity a matter not of rational evidence, but of non-rational faith, his claims on its behalf have merely a private validity which has no public significance save where those who accept it out of some inner and incommunicable experience are prepared to impose that experience upon others to whom the vision has not been vouchsafed. At that point, it may be argued, the Christian believer becomes a persecutor; and, by the very act of persecution, he then creates the conditions under which a Christian culture is either the means of breeding sycophants or hypocrites if it is successful, or is defeated by its opponents, and then ceases to influence the society in the way Mr. Eliot has in mind.

The third major barrier he fails to surmount is the sociological barrier. Mr. Eliot sees no direct relation between the relations of culture and its content on the one hand and the totality of social relationships on the other. It is fantastic utopianism to imagine that, at this stage of economic evolution, it is possible to rebuild the structure of a society divided into classes in which the supreme political functions of the state-power are mainly confided to an hereditary aristocracy of birth and wealth. The alternative before us is between a planned society in which, if its citizens have different functions, it is nevertheless agreed that they are entitled to equal consideration, and a society controlled by a dictatorship, whether of some Caesar or of some self-perpetuating oligarchy. There are, no doubt, small sectors still in the Western democracies in which the family has remained a basic unit in the formation of a culture; but, in a general way, it is broadly true to say that for the overwhelming majority of any national community the family has ceased to perform any such function for well over one hundred years. Nor can Mr. Eliot seriously maintain the possibility of keeping the institutional pattern of a society stable as long as the dynamic inherent in its relations of production is as swift and as massive as it has necessarily become with that discovery of the 'invention of inventions' which not only makes for unceasing and large-scale technological change, but makes absurd the refusal on the part of any ruling élite to adapt its political institutions to the pace and implications of that change. I do not know whether Mr. Eliot believes that he has made provision for this adaptation by agreeing that, while his hierarchical society is in general desirable, and while its citizens should as a rule stay in the situation they have inherited, there may nevertheless be a movement from base to apex where there is extraordinary capacity to justify it. If that is so, the answer, of course is that only in a maximum of opportunity for such movement, of refusal, therefore, to maintain a generally hereditary hierarchy of any kind, are we likely to discover the volume of capacity a society requires fully to develop the forces of production at its disposal.

There is a relatively simple illustration of this immediately to hand. The Barlow Report has carefully examined the manpower position in Great Britain in the light of its bearing upon our technological future and emphasised the gap between demand and supply. There is no evidence to suggest that the gap has been caused by the lack of enough inherited ability in our population to make supply possible; on the contrary, the evidence is abundant the other way. The causes of the gap seem to lie first and foremost in the unwillingness of the governing élite until only our own day to tax that part of the community which could bear the burden of securing an adequate educational system able to provide the necessary trained personnel for agriculture and industry. A second cause was the birth among that governing élite of a profound complacency about its future born of its long years of hardly challenged supremacy in the field of international trade. A third cause was, quite bluntly, a fear in that ruling élite that, if it were to open wide the gates of educational opportunity to the masses, its own authority would presently be jeopardised. There are, of course, many subsidiary reasons for the gap. When Mr. Eliot speaks of the demand for equality of opportunity in education as a proof that there is no longer respect for the institution of the family and that the State has taken over the responsibility of parents, with the result, in his view, that 'the disintegration of classes is far advanced', he does not mean any more by this formidable phrase than that we have reached a situation in which the kind of society he desires is no longer possible. When he warns us that 'any social system which puts it into effect

127

must see that no advantages of family fortune, no advantages due to the foresight, the self-sacrifice, or the ambition of parents are allowed to obtain for any child or young person an education superior to that to which the system finds him to be entitled', he is really asking us to accept as valid his own ideal society, and thus to agree with him that refusal to accept this ideal means disintegration which, in his view, has 'induced the expansion of envy' because it underrates a desire to be trained above one's station. He rejects this as an example of that 'half education' which he believes to be a special disease of the modern world. 'In earlier ages,' Mr. Eliot writes,[1] 'the majority could not be said to have been "half-educated" or less: people had the education necessary for the functions they were called upon to perform. It would be incorrect to refer to a member of a primitive society, or to a skilled agricultural labourer in any age, as half-educated, or quarter-educated or educated to any smaller fraction.'

It here becomes obvious that what Mr. Eliot has in view is a system in which the child or young person is to be functionally educated, to be trained, that is, to the use of the skills necessary for the vocation he is to follow in life. For most, subject to exceptional capacity, that vocation will be determined by birth or the 'advantages of family fortune', with the chance of special opportunities where the parents display 'foresight, self-sacrifice, or ambition' for their children. What Mr. Eliot forgets is that, in the large majority of cases, we have far too little knowledge of the vocation for which the child is really fitted, and that, for most of them, there is no real choice when the final educational decision was, until only the other day, taken when the child was under twelve years of age. We approach an age which is likely, one hopes, to approach the matter with wholly different criteria of value. It becomes ever less possible to believe that an insight into the heritage of our civilisation, its art, its literature, its music, its science, its history, can be confined to a few without the grave danger that

[1] *Op. cit.* p. 105. It will be noticed that by slipping in the adjective 'skilled' in the last sentence, Mr. Eliot is really refusing to face the real issue which is precisely to define the area and volume of skill an agricultural labourer must be given by education in order properly to be called 'skilled'.

the many are deprived of the sight of those things which evoke what is most dignified in human nature. To train a man to be a 'skilled agricultural labourer' does not mean that we waste our energies and our substance if we teach him also to appreciate the beauties of Shakespeare or Dickens, to recognise why Goya was a greater artist than W. P. Frith, to realise that the music of Bach and Beethoven can bring things into his life more precious than he will find in the music of Sousa or George Gershwin, to explain to him at least in large outline, what science is, and how it has developed, and to give him some sense of the movement of world-history, not least of the place of his own country in that movement. None of these things ought to be the private possession of an élite; they are all of them part of the process of making man at home in the universe, of giving him perspective, of helping him to grasp how those forces work which determine his own destiny. When Mr. Eliot talks of our 'half-educated' people, of our education as an 'abstraction', it is not unfair to retort that the curiously functional view of education he takes is in truth, especially in an age of machine technology, a method of making all outside his élites little more than dependents upon the machines they serve, and thus to intensify in most of them that subjection to the poorer appetites—the *panem et circenses* of our own day—which has done so much towards the very end Mr. Eliot himself denounces most strongly, the disintegration of our way of life, by leaving the masses to be the ignorant prey of that raucous leadership which has most to lose when beauty and knowledge are made available to them.

It is important, moreover, to recognise that, despite Mr. Eliot's bitter distaste for all that is crude and ugly in our civilisation, the very essence of his political philosophy, indeed, by implication, of his religious philosophy as well, is his lack of reverence for the life that, outside the relatively few with special gifts, it is now, and will be for any future we can realistically imagine, the fate of most men and women to live. He has not grasped the meaning of that vast experience summarised so superbly by William Morris in his famous sentence that 'no man is good enough to be another man's master'. That is why we are learning so swiftly that freedom is rarely adequate unless it is set and operates in the context of equality; we have no other means of assuring equal consideration for all human beings. Once the ultimate power to make decisions is associated with a small élite, either of birth or of wealth—and that is what in actual fact Mr. Eliot's hierarchical society means — that small élite will come to exercise irresponsible power. It will define the good of the community as its own good, and it will become corrupted by the effort to force that identity upon those over whom, as an élite, it exercises authority. It will abridge the stature, as it will impede the development, of all who are not admitted within the ramparts it builds for its own protection against claims which seem to diminish its own privileges. Such a system as Mr. Eliot envisages as his ideal offers the great body of citizens in the society he describes no sort of compensation for their slavery.

Here, after all, we are not discussing an abstract problem, outside of space and time, but one about which we have considerable knowledge in the period between the Civil Wars in England in the seventeenth century, and the supreme statement of the outcome and the aspiration of their victors in Adam Smith's *Wealth of Nations,* or, more harshly and more briefly, in the *Thoughts on Scarcity* of Edmund Burke, written, significantly enough, in the years when the French Revolution had brought not merely European society to one of the great cross-roads of history. In a century and a half the social attitude to the poor and to the unemployed turned from one in which they were recognised to have a claim upon the resources of the community to one in which their position was overwhelmingly regarded as due to some perversity which caused them to prefer charity and laziness to thrift and work. Hence, with but rare exceptions, the literature is mainly a mass of pamphlets directed to the discovery of how they can be forcibly disciplined to effort. 'The reason why so many pretend to want work,' wrote Daniel Defoe,[1] 'is that they can live so well with the pretence of wanting work, they would be mad to leave it and work in earnest.' By the time that the idea of the workhouse has crossed the sea from Holland, the workers have begun to be thought of as a class the members of which were either employed or idle; in the latter case they were a burden upon

[1] Defoe, *Giving Alms No Charity* (Works, ed. 1713) Vol. 2, p. 430.

the nation and must be coerced into industrious habits; there is little evidence of any idea that they had, like their masters, any right to improve their chances in life. One writer in the *Gentleman's Magazine* speaks of the poor in 1731 as 'rogues too lazy to work, squandering one's charity in drink'[1]. Dean Tucker, in 1751, asked 'whether the manufacturing poor in any country are so debauched and immoral as in England? Is there not therefore greater danger that the English should corrupt the foreigners than be corrupted by them?'[2] An anonymous writer, in 1767, criticises indignantly the foolish weakness which forbids the imposition of hard labour upon children; and he condemns with vigour any effort to teach them to read and write since it makes them less ready for heavy toil which, he insists, is what persons without property need and are unfitted for if they have access to learning.[3] The incredible Richard Wakefield cannot see why proposals to keep children at work 'for at least twelve hours a day' are not regarded by the parents as 'agreeable and entertaining'.[4] Arthur Young, as is well known, was always emphatic on the moral value of low wages, not only to the national economic effort, but to the character of the workers themselves.[5] He was only repeating the earlier views of Petty[6] and Houghton[7] a century before. Writers like Jonas Hanway and Joseph Townsend were always insisting that the higher the cost of living, the better the work to be got out of labour; and David Hume, in his *Political Discourses* (1762) speaks of a 'considerable manufacturer' who held when bread and other provisions were scarce and at high prices, his workmen did better than in times of plenty.

The men who wrote so strongly in this way were not especially harsh or incapable of a kindly feeling for the poor. They were convinced that the volume of production must be raised, and that, since this was the cause of prosperity, what-

[1] Vol. I, p. 114.

[2] Josiah Tucker, *Important Queries* (1751) p. 40.

[3] Anon. *The Management of the Poor* (1767).

[4] *A Letter to the Landowners* (1602), p. 43.

[5] E. G. *Eastern Tour* (1771), Vol. IV, p. 361; *Northern Tour* (1770) Vol. I p. 192, 197.

[6] *Political Arithmetic in Hull*, Works of Sir W. Petty.

[7] Houghton, *Collection of Letters* (1681), p. 177.

ever encouraged the worker to slowness in effort, or to take a holiday, or to secure high wages, was bound to lower individual output because of the natural tendency of the worker to indolence. They therefore, with rare exceptions, were accustomed to insist not only that low wages were a benefit to the nation, but even that they prevented the deterioration of the worker's character. As early as 1669, Thomas Manly[1] had laid emphasis upon the need 'to subdue our wages,' and if Sir Josiah Child said that he was opposed to the reduction of wages, in the same pamphlet he argued that 'dear years' helped the workers themselves.[2] English workers, wrote Dean Tucker,[3] 'are as bad as can be described . . . (they) become more vicious, more indigent and idle in proportion to the advance of wages and the cheapness of provisions'. He did not doubt that unemployment was due to immorality. Temple, writing in 1770, insisted that 'the labouring people should never think themselves independent of their superiors, for if a proper subordination is not kept up, riots and confusion will take the place of sobriety and good order'.[4] Perhaps it was partly fear of the French Revolution that induced Thomas Ruggles to argue that 'the art of writing is not necessary to a performance of the duties of the poor . . . There must be in society hewers of wood and drawers of water; If all are good penmen where are those who will contentedly live through a life of toil?'[5] And to all this must be added the evidence adduced by Mr. and Mrs. Sidney Webb to show that the central purpose of Wilberforce's fantastic 'Committee for the Reformation of Manners among the Lower Orders' was to suppress, with the widespread aid of the Justices of the Peace, any source of innocent pleasure or recreation which might tempt the workers to neglect their primary obligation of unending toil.[6] Even Henry Fielding could attack 'too frequent diversions among the lower kind of people' and justify his view by saying 'I confine myself to the

[1] Thomas Manly, *Usurie at Six Per Cent* (1669), p. 22.
[2] Cf. the preface to his *New Discourse on Trade* (1693) with his statement on p. 18.
[3] Josiah Tucker, *Brief Essay* (1750), p. 46.
[4] William Temple, *An Essay on Trade and Commerce* (1770), p. 56.
[5] Thomas Ruggles, *History of the Poor* (1793), Vol. II, p. 180.
[6] S. & B. Webb, *English Local Government; The County* (1906) pp. 406, 536 f.

lower order of the people . . . to the upper part of mankind, time is an enemy . . . Their chief labour is to kill it'.[1]

It is in the context of the attitude these quotations illustrate that Mr. Eliot's approach should be examined. These writers, and very many others like them, were not especially harsh men. Some of them, like Petty and Child and Arthur Young were outstanding figures among their contemporaries, and ardent in their zeal for the public good. They had no desire to do injustice to the workers or their children. They had a profound faith in the need for hard work as the basis upon which the national prosperity was founded. What had happened was that, with but little awareness on their own part, they had completed the separation of the economic world from the religious, and, in doing so had destroyed the popular feeling which, as Professor Tawney has so well said, 'had lent a half-mystical glamour, both to poverty and to the compassion by which poverty was relieved, for poor men were God's friends'.[2] From being God's friends, the poor had been transformed within the space of one hundred and fifty years into the enemies of society, unless they accepted the obligation to toil unceasingly for low wages; and charity had become transformed from a Christian duty into connivance at evasion by men and women, and even children, prone by nature to idleness and rescued from its attendant evils not by almsgiving but by the imposition of a severe discipline which compelled them to fulfil the duty to labour.

Here, obviously enough, the new social philosophy is an attempt by men to find reasons to justify intellectual and social changes, above all, changes in the productive relations between masters and men, which have resulted from profound changes in the material environment. The rise of a new class has demanded the creation and acceptance of new values in order to put authority behind the change, and to enable those who are rising to a ruling position to justify to themselves the relations they find themselves compelled to impose. They had not thought out those relations before they were all, masters and men, rich and poor, involved in them. Theory is the child of practice; it is not its cause. It is not until the practice becomes

[1] Henry Fielding, *Enquiry* (1751), p. 6.
[2] *Religion and the Rise of Capitalism* (Pelican edition, 1944) p. 239.

a conscious aim that the arguments brought forward in its service begin to cohere into an integrated system; and it is then that the system itself becomes a body of principles which the ruling class uses that, so far as may be, a cosmos may be built from a'chaos. The cosmos is never complete. There are always men to protest against its postulates or its conclusions. We can see that in the famous debates of the Army Council at the close of the Civil War when Ireton's cold defence of the rights of property makes Colonel Rainsborough so angrily exclaim that, if Ireton is right, the common people have won an empty victory over the Crown, since they have merely exchanged one tyrant for another. We can see the protest again, after Adam Smith had given the 'simple system of natural liberty' its supreme expression alike in the judgments passed upon it by Charles Hall and Robert Owen, in the opening of the new century, in the work of Hodgskin, William Thompson and Bray in England, and of Sismondi in France. Their protests are an attempt to provide safeguards against the horrors of Juggernaut; but it is not until the system has begun plainly to exhibit it inherent contradictions, that their protests begin to make a direct impact on its destiny.

It is not, I suggest, an exaggerated comparison to look upon Mr. Eliot's approach, despite its aloofness and fastidiousness, as not dissimilar from that which such different men as Cobbett and Charles Dickens approached the new capitalism in the great hour of its triumph. Mr. Eliot, perhaps, is most distressed by the cheapness and the vulgarity of a ruling élite which he despises; Cobbett and Dickens worked themselves up into a passion of fury at its brutalising cruelty. But, just as Cobbett and Dickens had no remedy to propose but the return to an earlier pattern in which the ruling élite was either, like the Cheeryble brothers, steeped in the milk of human kindness, or, like Mr. Scrooge, converted to it, so, also, Mr. Eliot seeks refuge from a society he deems hateful and hopeless by retreat to an age in which he finds some, at least, of his ideals in operation. But he offers us no clue as to how we can find our way back. Either he assumes that we can, by some interior magic, will our way back there, or, as in his *Idea of a Christian Society,* he seeks to maintain some small group of the faithful who will keep alive a cherished tradition until such time as the community recognises that there is no other way to its salvation. Yet, historically, there is no foundation for either of its assumptions. Our will to change operates always within spheres the boundaries of which not one or even two generations can hope to alter; and the little group which attempts to act as the guardian of a tradition beyond which the community has moved finds itself in a backwater of history. It has the often joyous escapism of a dream; but it has abandoned the pursuit of reality that it may find fulfilment in a dream that is, inevitably, an empty one. It is impossible, as Trotsky said, to play with history; and Mr. Eliot's utopia is an incantation rather than a remedy for our problems.

One other comment upon his argument it is necessary to make. At the back of it all, as he shows, perhaps, most clearly in his comments upon Soviet Russia, there is in Mr. Eliot a profound disbelief in the quality of the ordinary man. He belongs to that esoteric group of thinkers in our time who, hating its disorder and violence and scepticism, find no release save in the rejection of seeking to pilot their craft down the mainstream where Everyman journeys, and, in their despair, seek some back-eddy of the stream where the boat may lie quietly at anchor. 'The centre', to quote Yeats once more, 'does not hold' for them. So the poet writes for poets, the novelist for other novelists, the philosopher for other philosophers, admitting to their private worlds those critics who can luxuriate in the refinement of their different specialisations. They are afraid of the deep anger and the hearty delight, they dread the speed of the world's dynamic, the opening of new windows through which the general public may gaze into the rooms, to change the metaphor, into which they have locked themselves and their group of friends and acolytes. They weave complex patterns of thought and sensibility to make certain that their rooms will remain closed and secure. They do not want things to happen for fear that they happen wrongly. They speak in a dialect of remote and technical symbolism by which they seek to assure themselves that what they have to say will not be heard by the world outside. They watch life; they do not live it; they are so sensitive to the immense dangers of the actual and the concrete that they devote their talents, often immense talents, to the minute examination of some detail on the peri-

135

phery of events. They want no word of theirs to echo in the heart of Everyman, as Dickens did or Tolstoy or even, in his intense personal way, Carlyle. So the plea even of so eminent an intellectual as Virginia Woolf for 'a room of one's own, exquisite in its decoration, dignified in its spaciousness', sometimes seems as though it were rather a plea for a tomb of one's own, where action is separated from thought, and death has come to mean life. They seek to arrest the dynamic of civilisation at the moment when it challenges them to search in all the dangers it unfolds in order to find, as the fifteenth and early nineteenth centuries were able to find, the clue to a new vitality and a wider hope. They have surrendered to despair. They refuse to discover the means of renewing the spirit of man.

CHAPTER VIII

THE immense influence that Mr. Eliot has exercised, especially among the younger intellectuals of Europe and America, is not merely a measure of the persuasive power of his gift for precision of statement. It is a measure, also, of the degree to which those whom he has influenced are fearful of the future, and anxious to find refuge in a known and safeguarded privacy from the dangers that are always involved in a changing civilisation. It is probable that Mr. Eliot's influence was at its height in the period between 1919 and the advent of Hitler to power in 1933. Then it seemed possible, at least before the Great Depression of 1929, that economic recovery might give birth to a new political equilibrium, and that there would be no narrowing of the boundaries within which the intellectual might choose. Indeed, it could be urged, as by Julien Benda, that a decision to choose on the intellectual's part was a betrayal of his central function. It was no part of his function to attempt to solve problems. He was to be indifferent to results; he was to be satisfied with self-expression as the motive of his effort, the values he should seek to communicate were to transcend all those which have their roots in material passions, especially those which involve the political ordering of society. M. Benda castigated in particular those who, like Sorel and Péguy, like Kipling and Charles Maurras, had urged the validity of violence as a means of achieving the ends they deemed desirable. His outlook indeed was not without kinship to that of Mr. Eliot. He asked the intellectual to desert the deed for thought. He insisted that what was the most important concern of the thinker was to discover and to propagate transcendental truths the acceptance of which would once more produce a stable society in which the intellectual could pursue his task in peace and freedom.

M. Benda, like Mr. Eliot, was too late; Hitler was already upon the scene. And from 1933 until the outbreak of war in 1939, there was an increasing area in which the intellectual learned by direct and often tragic experience that he had small hope of either peace or freedom unless he chose to fight for it, and that, even if he sought to remain above the battle, the contending armies still denied to him any chance of peace or freedom. The famous protest against action which Villiers de l'Isle Adam had expressed in his 'as for living, our servants will do that for us', had little meaning for the intellectual who could find no servants. It is of those who thus sought to turn their back upon the ugly and the evil, and felt that in their emotion of disdain for the world in which ugliness and evil were daily omnipresent they were living for beauty when they retreated into their ivory tower, that Mr. Shaw has so wisely said that 'they did not wish to realise Utopia for the common people; they wished to realise their favourite fictions and poems in their own lives'.

They learned after the outbreak of the Second World War, perhaps after Munich even, that they could not 'play with history'. They were engulfed by the torrent of the conflict with a speed that swept away the foundations of all the ivory towers, and when Hitler was broken in 1945 there was security for none of them either in Heartbreak House or Horseback Hall. It was then that the intellectuals sought so eagerly to discover whether there was not, perhaps, a temporary refuge in existentialism, which vied with logical positivism for the favour of those who found the confrontation of reality too harsh an exercise to be endurable. The formulae, indeed, were not new. Schopenhauer had given them partial expression before the crisis of 1848; and that immense adventure had given birth to Kierkegaard who sought, by the renovation of a Christian faith, to destroy that confidence in reason which enabled the critics to attack the foundations of society; for it is no accident that he bade men choose between Christianity and philosophy, that he disliked the idea that the masses should rule, and that he was strongly opposed to political change. Nor is it accident either that the next great figure in the development of existentialism should be that of Nietzsche—the contemporary, be it noted, of Bismarck's Germany—who transformed the pessimism of Schopenhauer with its despairing acceptance of life into an ardent optimism which is expressed in a passionate will to power. By making power into good, he identifies life with the assertion of strength, and when he sees the world passing to

138

the hands of timid, unwarlike, mediocre people seeking, the vast majority of them, for a peaceful democracy, he cries out that its urge to make universal the doctrine of Christian love is a depressing gospel of slavery, and that the world can only be cleansed from its pitiful disease of cultivating impotence by the strong man so passionate in the iron will to power that the world becomes simply an idea in his mind made and remade in his image. His passion thus takes him beyond reality and above truth. He can turn his back upon them because by his inner vision, with its Faustian zeal for an all-inclusive experience, he can become, as he wills, the master of the world.

I cannot, of course, even attempt here to trace the detailed history of the complex existentialist philosophy which in all the rich diversity of its phases corresponds so interestingly with the different stages of bourgeois evolution from the great crisis of 1848 to our own time. Its outstanding figures, Lagarde, Sorel, Ortega y Gasset, Jaspers, Heidegger, with all their often important nuances of difference, have important elements in common. They dislike democracy; they distrust reason; they deny the validity of progress; they give their energy to fortifying the importance of subjective idealism in the construction of a theory of knowledge. They may be Christian or agnostic or atheist; what is characteristic of them all is the fact that they have a troubled sense of impending doom, that they seek to understand the world by intuition rather than by the diagnosis of experience, that they make the mind which perceives the creator of the material world about them. They are, almost by compulsion, myth-makers, men who stress the impotence of reason, hostile to the dialectical analysis of those contradictions lest that attain a synthesis which is able to unite them. In the sociological field, as with Scheler and Dilthey, Mannheim and Kelsen, the world they depict is supremely an intangible subjective world, often imaginatively grasped by intuition in some special aspect but rarely seen in its totality as materially out there for all to inspect as something outside themselves. They have not only atomised the social sciences, often giving to each a formal methodology of its own, but they have even argued that the picture of reality they make is bound to be partial and subjective, a *mystique* as it were, since each social science takes the findings of the others on a trust which, because not self-experienced, is irrational. To take an extreme example, it then becomes possible for an eminent jurist like Hans Kelsen to insist that the science of law is bound to regard the origins of legislation as 'a great mystery' which it cannot penetrate. This is perhaps even more true of the abstractions rigorously endorsed by the modern economist to whom the subjectivism of individual choice makes the character of the market, and who is able thereby to refuse consideration to the interpenetration of economics with law and politics, with history and anthropology. It is not surprising, in circumstances like these, that a sensation is created when an economist of Keynes's supreme distinction insists on pressing forward questions which admit of an answer by the recognition of a dialectical process in life itself. There were those who came forward angrily to urge the tactlessness of putting forward proposals the nature of which admit the unity of thought and deed; if his method, they saw, became general, the economists would descend into the market-place and deal there, not with refined abstraction, but with crude reality in which all the contradictions were as imperative as the 'pure essence' with which otherwise they could be happily concerned.

It is illuminating to watch the increasing interest in existentialism, both in Europe and in America, since just before the war; and it is not less interesting to observe the dramatic vigour with which this philosophic attitude has, most notably in France, sought to extend its influence by striking a revolutionary pose at a time when the abyss between academic philosophy and public attention is so wide as itself to be a social problem of increasing importance. We have now Christian existentialism and atheist existentialism. We have not only existentialist treatises but existentialist plays and existentialist novels. It has aroused the kind of fashionable excitement which, before the First World War, was aroused in the Faubourg St. Honoré by the famous lectures of Henri Bergson at the College de France. I do not think that anyone can read the work of Sartre, or Simone de Beauvoir, or Gabriel Marcel in France—I take examples only—of Jaspers and Heidegger in Germany, or of those who have given such devoted effort to translating and commenting upon the works of Kierkegaard without the conviction of their earnestness and their sincerity.

140

They are as anxious to rescue our world from annihilation, to rebuild its foundation upon a new basis, as Marx and Engels were at the time of the *Communist Manifesto,* or as Lenin was when he set out to destroy the attempt of Bogdanov and his followers to ally the philosophy of Marxism to the neo-Kantian principles which would, as they thought, give it new freshness and wider appeal.

With the metaphysics of existentialism, of course, I cannot here concern myself, though it is worth remarking that they reflect pretty directly the special character of our time; I must limit myself to the social and political implications it involves. Here, as I think, its significance is of great importance. Its exponents deny that we can hope to attain any real knowledge of the objective relation between the human being and life. Man being his own human reality, to claim a knowledge of man would at the very outset mean the abandonment of existentialist principles. The world is an irrational and unmeaning world in which all we know is that each of us makes his own complete universe, that each of us is, so to say, self-caused, and is free to make the content of that universe what we will. That freedom in Sartre, for example, is so vast that he denies any relation between the choice I may make at any given moment and the whole of my past; I begin again, as it were, at each act of choosing free from, because above, all limitations of causation. On this basis it is evident that freedom is at once irrational and arbitrary in the sense that it is born of motives inside my self which, as they receive external expression, attain the status of universality, for, as Sartre himself tells us: 'I cannot put forward liberty as my aim, without also taking liberty as the aim of all others.'[1] If it be said that this seems curiously close to Kant's categorical imperative, Sartre, seemingly, would reply that 'it is useless for us to respect another person's liberty . . . since every attitude we take in relation to him violates the very liberty we are pretending to respect'.[2] But if this is not solepsism, it is nihilism, and it would then follow that there can be neither continuity nor legitimate expectation of social relation. To avoid this dilemma, Sartre explains that all social activity is built up out of individual acts, and that, whatever

[1] *L'Existentialisme est un Humanisme.* (Paris, 1946) pp. 25-6.
[2] *L'Etre et le Néant.* (Paris, 1946) p. 480.

influence the external environment may exercise, each person has a certain area of freedom left to him which no environment can determine. None of us can have social relations; we have relations only with other individuals, isolated and self-contained like ourselves. My liberty, therefore, is unlimited because it is bounded only by my own choice; and my responsibility, therefore, must be unlimited also since it is the outcome of a liberty similar in nature.[1]

There is, no doubt, a certain logic in this view. If the individual person is alone real, and cannot be made to act with others save as he wills to do so, we have arrived at a completely irrational world whose ultimate character is, since anything may happen, necessarily nihilistic. It could not in this aspect provide any basis for coherent action; on the contrary it would become a weapon of the extreme individualists whose outlook it rejects, in the same way as the outlook of Nietzsche became an instrument of Prussian militarism which he passionately despised. Granted the basis of German existentialism, at least, this is not surprising; for it is not easy to forget how Heidegger, as Rector of the University of Freiburg, led his students in organised formations to vote for Hitler's proposals that a plebiscite should confirm his decision in favour of Germany leaving the League of Nations. But Sartre is anxious to escape the situation in which his philosophy leaves the individual isolated and self-contained in an irrational universe, a nihilist swept in any direction by forces which impel him, like Nietzsche, to the creative fulfilment of action. Sartre seeks also that creative fulfilment, but his anxiety is to secure an activism of the Left and not of the Right. That is why, as he has said: 'I cannot make my own freedom an end without seeking also the freedom of all others'. That is why, also, he insists that we are bound to choose the good, and that we cannot choose good for ourselves without choosing the good of all other persons. 'Each man,' he writes,[2] 'must ask himself: 'am I really a person whose right to act is of such a kind that all humanity is ruled by my acts?' He stresses the anguish of decision, but he emphasises that this anguish leads, not to

[1] *Ibid.* p. 640.
[2] *L'Existentialisme est un Humanisme* (1946), p. 31.

quietism, but to action. 'Man,' he says again,[1] 'without help and without support is compelled at each moment of time to invent man,' and to be responsible for him.

What is interesting in the ethic Sartre here formulates is that he seeks to keep it on a purely existentialist basis by insisting that we must all make our own decision from an internal drive to action about which no one can advise us except ourselves. He is thus able to conclude that a general ethic built upon the basis of social experience in time is impossible. But he is then involved in the difficulties with which he does not deal, of explaining why there results from within a choice of freedom wholly internalised an external freedom, and why my choice of good should result in the good of others as well as my own. He tells us that he is compelled to reject Marxism because it destroys subjectivism and thus deprives man of his freedom. But this is, of course, to identify Marxism with fatalism, a position which was vigorously rejected both by Marx and Engels. And it assumes, contrary to all experience, that a particular moment when a decision is made—by a worker, for example, to go out on strike—is internal and subjective and is independent of similar decisions taken by his fellow-workers. It enables Sartre to save his meaningless universe, but he is able to save it only at the expense of common sense. That is why he can argue that Marxism, as far as it builds upon objective material reality, is the philosophy of the oppressors. For, in making man free by acting with other men to destroy the relations of oppression, Marx, for Sartre, is annihilating his power to make the act the outcome of a consciousness which itself creates the act. He makes practice the antithesis of reflection, and from this he concludes that the contemplation of the world as it is implies a conservative outlook. What he has omitted to emphasise is that the Marxian view emphasises the need to know an objective world for the very purpose of changing it. It does not, as Sartre does, make revolutionary class-consciousness something outside an objective material situation from the relations of which it gains both its existence and its drive to change. It denies that knowledge of objective reality is the necessary pre-condition of its transformation since the knowledge which is internal to the free mind itself

[1] *L'Existentialisme est un Humanisme* (1946) p. 38.

creates the objective situation. So, too, concrete historical reality originates nothing; change is made by the free will in the individual's consciousness. 'No social overturn and no moral conversion,' writes Mme. Simone de Beauvoir, 'can suppress what has no existence in the human heart.' Yet this leaves obviously unresolved the source from which the human heart derives its impulse to evocative change.

The French school of existentialism has a curiously dual view of revolution. Mme. de Beauvoir, for example, while convinced that all violence is wicked, nevertheless agrees that political action makes violence inevitable. But while she is prepared to forgive a man guilty of offences, even of crimes, if his purpose is self-affirmation against society, she finds it unforgivable if any man should employ violence to degrade another man. But this leaves wholly unresolved the question of the morality of violence; all we are told is that the problem is an 'agonising' one when it arises out of some cause which benefits man, and that we must repudiate 'the myth of the future', the background, that is to say, of historical understanding, in favour of 'the living future' which emerges when the individual is driven from within himself to some concrete idea. She has no doubt that violence is evil if it is, for example, the lynching of a negro by a Southern mob. But it is different when one considers violence in Russia where its use is part of an effort to improve the conditions of an enormous mass of human beings. Was it right, for example, to shoot Bukharin in order to save Stalingrad? Her answer broadly is that, if the Russian victory over the Germans could not have been won without the Moscow trials, then it was right to execute Bukharin. But she seems to be anxious to avoid a criterion which, though excessively abstract, is nevertheless utilitarian in its essence. She then argues that one knows from an inner intuition of conscience what is right by knowing whether it will add to freedom or no. That must, of course, be decided without reference to an objective and material world. As an existentialist, therefore, Mme. de Beauvoir tells us that 'the reconciliation of ethics with politics consists of the reconciliation of man with himself'. This is surely no more than a verbal rhetoric which indirectly means that, in terms of her philosophy, there are contradictions which she confronts, but is unable to solve.

What is above all interesting in this approach to the problem of action is the nostalgia which Mme. de Beauvoir exhibits towards the France of the Resistance period, above all because it was not then necessary to choose positive solutions. 'The Resistance,' she writes,[1] 'did not tend towards any positive efficacy. It was negation, revolt, martyrdom; and it was in this negative movement that liberty was positively and absolutely confirmed.' Upon this there are two things to be said. There is little difficulty in understanding the nostalgia for days when all members of the Resistance movement had the simple and concrete purpose of fighting an evil enemy in occupation of France; it bred a comradeship in which the only qualities required were the courage to face danger and the skill to concert plans of maximum hostility to the Nazis. No doubt these were, both of them, qualities which tested character in an exceptionally high degree. But they were, so to speak, qualities of the soldiers in the line, not the qualities either of the Resistance leader who plans the campaign, still less of the statesman who knows how to use the victory and the victors for high constructive ends. 'Only the revolt itself is pure', Mme. de Beauvoir writes. She not only fears its end; she even fears that its victory may result in the degeneration of the pure principles with which it started. So she opposes the transformation of the negative revolt into a positive revolution. That may, she warns us, 'create a church where one buys salvation by joining a party as one buys it elsewhere by baptism and the purchase of indulgences.'[2]

Quite obviously there emerges here the nihilism and the paralysis of collective action which are typical of the French existentialists. They loathe the decadent France which sold itself to the Nazis in a pitiful surrender. But their loathing is paralleled by the horror of what a revolution may mean if it cuts down to the roots of that decay. It would compel the intellectual to act instead of leaving him alone, contemplating with loathing the spread of decay, content, like Sartre, to bemoan a situation in which 'it is absurd that we are born and absurd that we shall die'. It thus emphasises the irrationalism of the world and the resultant folly of believing that revolutionary

[1] *Temps Modernes*, Vol. XVII, p. 856.
[2] *Ibid.* p. 857.

action can rid that world of its fundamental contradictions. We have thus no choice but to decide between evils and that choice becomes a matter of personal discretion instead of political responsibility. It is worth while, in passing, to note that this is the clue to the evolution of Koestler's ideas, for Koestler has passed from communism through humanism to a nihilism which is nothing so much as an effort to escape from both. He denounces both of them because he finds in each a dual ethic, one high and noble, one low and base, and he insists that it is the low and base ethic which permeates the practitioners of the ideals, for, in his view as in that of the existentialists when they seek to transform the world to the shape of their ideal, they are compelled by the actions to which they must resort to commit the very crimes in protest against which their ideal took its shape. So Koestler, too, ends in a rootless nihilism which leaves him a dissatisfied wanderer who has enjoyed the comradeship of battle but repudiates the victory to which it has led.[1]

So that the French existentialists end by the insistence that there is neither direction nor pattern in history. Chance, as it were, cancels out any effort to see in social relations any road either to rationality or to justice. We remain baffled by a mysterious process in which there is no clear relation between cause and effect, no apparent proportionality between means and ends. We can only, as it were, know when the curtain goes down what the play was about; we can never be sure, at any given moment, what its end will be. We have possibilities at which we can guess, but the data given us are always too small, the intrusions of the unexpected always too numerous, for us to make predictions assured enough to justify our choice of a definitive road down which we march with confidence that we shall reach a chosen goal. 'To-morrow,' Sartre has said,[2] 'when I am dead, men may choose to establish fascist society . . . if they do, fascism will be the truth of mankind, even though it be to our detriment; in reality, things will become what men choose to make them.' There is thus no progress; there is only

[1] This seems to me the general outcome of *Darkness at Noon, The Yogi and the Commissar,* and *Thieves in the Night.* It is illuminating to remember that, in the last of these books, Koestler's main sympathies are with the terrorists in Palestine; once Israel had been established, he became a bitter critic both of their habits and their purposes.

[2] *L'Existentialisme est un Humanisme* (1946) p. 63 f.

change. 'Man,' he says again,[1] 'is always the same in face of a situation which is always changing, and his choice will always be a choice made in some given situation.'

Yet it is obvious that the political and social developments in the post-war world have not been without their influence on Sartre and his colleagues.[2] He has thrown overboard any faith in the methods of capitalist production. He sees in the continuance of bourgeois democracy not only 'the diseased crisis of monopoly capitalism', but an opening 'to the temptations of state capitalism'. He calls for a new point of view. He seeks, by the foundation of the 'Rassemblement Démocratique Révolutionnaire' to give a new directive to social and political effort which will renew self-confidence, and enable men to pass 'from the old intellectual habit and social prejudices' to a new creativeness.[3] Sartre is hostile to the movement of General de Gaulle because he sees in it merely another expression of the reactionary influences which have corrupted France. He is hostile also to the Socialist Party since, in his view, it has shrunk to the position of a minor sect unable to influence more than a fragment of the working class or the small bourgeoisie. He will not work with the Communists on the ground that the major accomplishment of Russia and the states allied with it is to replace the proletariat which it abolishes by a vast serf class exploited by the state-power and deprived of any hope of achieving political and social maturity. He has contempt for M.R.P., which he regards as 'not only paralysed by its mediocrity . . . not only a part of the Right Centre, but, above all, a confessional party'. While the class war is real, and while most of the demands made by the trade unions which, like the miners, are driven to strike, should be granted because they are just, he notes the danger that they may evoke repression which involves the creation of the totalitarian state. He would, for the present, retain the bourgeois republic, because, though it is in a state of decay, it is not yet so diseased as to destroy freedom of discussion and of organisation. It would be a grave error of tactics, therefore, to overthrow it at this time. To all this must

[1] *Ibid.* p. 79.

[2] Cf. Sartre, Rousset-Rosenthal, *Entretiens sur la Politique* (Paris, 1949), *passim.*

[3] *Ibid.* pp. 208-9. Here it is Rousset who speaks, but, clearly, with the full agreement of Sartre.

be added that he sees no reason to suppose that social forces are moving towards war, and that he thinks it urgent to heal the split in the French trade union movement.

How, then, does M. Sartre propose to overcome the disease which he thinks is killing France? His answer is a curious and complex one. The 'Rassemblement' is not to be a party, though members of political parties. Marxist and non-Marxist alike, are to belong to it. It is to have a committee of direction; the impulse of ideas is to come from below, communicated to it by the large number of groups and sections. Some of these will be bourgeois, the intellectuals, for example; some will be working class. All of them from their separate experiences will contribute doctrines born of their 'situation', and that will lead to a vast ideological current which will sweep each man, in his given place in society, whether it be a class or a political group, to a unity in which each will win his emancipation. That will be the outcome of the class-struggle, the daily reality of which sets in motion those forces which will end the antithesis between individual and society and seek to integrate the free individual in a society to be conceived as the union of the free activities of individuals. It will be a democracy which liquidates the structure of a capitalist society without the need of violent revolution. It must not be regarded as a renovation of the *Cartel des Gauches* in the sense which fitted the union of 1935. If it contains political parties, their whole nature will have changed, since they will have no authoritarian character as a result of which, as in the Communist Party, the masses merely obey the orders of their leaders. Not least, it will be built on a recognition that the régime of Stalinist Russia is not to be confused with socialism, since it is clear from Soviet experience that the abolition of classes is not equivalent to socialism. There is now through technological change a new dynamic in the class-structure of Europe, and this provides the basis for a new grouping of the mass-forces to permit the expression of the new social reality.

No one can seriously mistake the limitations of this existentialist position. A dying bourgeois republic, a party system which breeds in an ever-increasing proportion of the population a distaste of and apathy towards politics, an economic structure which is rotten to the core and gives daily nourishment to the class-war, workers who strike for demands no government ought to refuse, and are then put down by the armed forces it can command, natives in the colonies who ought to be free to determine their own destiny, with the right, if they wish, to separate from the mother country, leadership so centralised that there is no effective consultation of the masses, and no profound reality in the diverse groups they form—all this is one side of the account; on the other, all that Sartre can call up in its defence is that the decaying bourgeois republic has not the strength to prohibit freedom of speech and association. His magic formula is to create in some mysterious way a profound and ardent sense of democracy backed by so widespread a support from the masses that reaction is to give way before its élan, and urgent discussion from below will permit the executive committee of the 'Rassemblement' to build, without conflict, a new and genuine democracy in which at long last the French people move from the realm of necessity to the realm of freedom.

It is not necessary to deny the depth of hostility to reaction, especially to Fascist reaction, which is common to the leaders of French existentialism. But it is also evident that, when they reject the impact of an objective material reality and the relations of production which arise from it as the basis of social philosophies for which men live and die in favour of an incoherent grouping of men who have little else in common but the desire to see a France in decay transformed into a France in regeneration, they are, in fact, guilty of that 'revolutionary romanticism' of which they have been accused by their Gaulliste critics. They are really utopia-mongering in the sense of insisting that the continuous discussion of high ideals will, of itself, create the situation in which the ideals impose themselves. A philosophy of historical evolution which is independent of any material foundation is no more than an academic exercise; a theory of social change which assumes that serious analysis can begin by taking an individual in isolation, and examining the different states of mind which move him to action, does not lead to action; it leads to a fatigued scholasticism which sooner or later becomes interested in its own intellectual refinements, and ceases to consider action as in any serious way important. It supports an abstract socialism;

149

it does not set out to build a socialist society. It seeks refuge from reality in revolutionary phrases, but it does not seek to translate the phrase into the deed. It fears the consequences of action and, therefore, seeks an escape from it in insisting that since history is irrational in itself, men must discover the path to rationality by a comprehensive exchange of ideas in which, so long as their differences are made known to one another and exhaustively analysed so that their content is clearly known, social amelioration will come of itself. Given this outlook, it is not really strange that Mme. de Beauvoir should exclaim that she and her colleagues 'ont peur devant la liberté'. They resemble unmistakably the Russian revolutionaries of the mid-nineteenth century. They see all that is evil in the existing régime; its ugliness compels in them a sense of sin which in its turn drives them to endless discussions of how what is evil may be transformed into good. They have even some hope of success because, despite its evil, the social order still leaves them some room for free discussion. What they refuse to see is that while they talk, other men act; and that they play with history who are satisfied to argue when the time has come to choose between the old world and the new. Twice in the twentieth century opportunity has knocked at the door of the French people; it would be tragedy indeed if existentialist philosophy gave birth to the quietism of that formalist approach to freedom which recognises the value of a concrete liberation only after the enemies it faces have captured the power without which it cannot be brought to life.

CHAPTER IX

I HAVE already quoted the remarkable phrase by which Professor Gilbert Murray distinguishes what he calls the 'difference of tone' that is felt by any reader who 'turns from the great writers of classical Athens to those of the Christian era'; there is, he says, 'a failure of nerve'.[1] He speaks of the later Hellenistic age as 'a period based on the consciousness of manifold failure, and consequently touched both with morbidity, and with that spiritual exaltation which is so often the companion of morbidity. It not only had behind it the failure of the Olympian theology, and of the free city-state now crushed by semi-barbarous military monarchies; it lived through the gradual realisations of two other failures— the failure of human government, even when backed by the power of Rome or the wealth of Egypt to achieve a good life for man; and lastly the failure of the great propaganda of Hellenism, in which the long-drawn effort of Greece to educate a corrupt and barbaric world only seemed to lead to the corruption or barbarisation of the very ideals which it sought to spread'.[2] Despite all the immense differences which separate the mid-twentieth century from the last phase of Hellenism, and despite also the immense difference in the results of this failure of nerve, the characteristics Professor Murray describes as characteristic of Hellenism as it was dying, bear a striking resemblance to those of our own day.

We, too, have a 'consciousness of manifold failure'. Our theology, like that of Hellas, is breaking down before our eyes. The system of representative democracy which, certainly until 1918, was the ideal held up for an almost universal emulation, is ever more confined to an area small enough to let its self-confidence be threatened, if not by semi-barbarous monarchies, at least by semi-barbarous communities where government by consent has not yet been able to triumph over

[1] *Five Stages of Greek Religion* (Thinkers' Library edition, London, 1946) p. 123.
[2] *Ibid.* pp. 3-4.

government by coercion. It is certainly doubtful whether we are now more able to achieve a good life for man by our methods of rule than was the case between, say, the defeat of Napoleon and the outbreak of the First World War in 1914. And despite the scale of the effort made to carry propaganda for representative democracy over Germany and Italy, South Eastern Europe and Russia, and the Middle and Far East, there is much to be said for the view that the classic picture of representative democracy has been more changed by those whom it sought to alter than it has been able to change either their ends or the means by which they attain them. All of us have a deep sense that what we mean by the life of civilisation is threatened by grave perils which we lack either the power or the courage to overcome; and to-day a far larger number of people are either sceptical about, or indifferent to, what we have traditionally called civilised life than at any period within the memory of a living man or woman. Fear of a complete breakdown is never long absent from the thought of any observer in the West who is honest enough to admit that what was generally accepted, say from Hume and Adam Smith to the Peace of Versailles in 1919, as the permanent aims of our civilisation, are now under microscopic examination by the very peoples whom we hoped to persuade to its acceptance.

I want to examine their standing in the two great communities which for the rest of this century are most likely to set the perspective of the international scene—Soviet Russia and the United States. I take these not merely because their power is so immensely greater at present than that of any other peoples, but because their very polarity throws a special light upon the problem I have raised. If I examine Russia first, I do so only because the revolution of 1917 committed it to a profounder experiment than any which the United States has thus far undertaken, and because, so far, most large-scale changes elsewhere, and not least in America, have themselves been undertaken in partial emulation of what the Russians have done in the generation since Lenin. It is the more important to be clear about the purposes of Russia since, at the present time, the main theme of world policy is in large part built around the attitude which Lord Palmerston made almost the central theme of his diplomacy. 'The policy and practice of the Russian government,' he said, 'have always been to push forward its encroachments as fast and as far as the apathy or want of firmness of other governments would allow it to go, but always to stop and retire when it met with decided resistance, and then to wait for the next favourable opportunity to make another spring on its intended victim.' It is interesting to note that, despite the entire change in the nature of the Russian régime since 1917 Palmerston's outlook is still that adopted towards Russia in the 'cold war'. There are, however, added to it, first, emphasis on the view that, properly regarded, Russia is an Asiatic power the Westernisation of which, begun by Peter the Great, is now being brought to a stage of further completion by Stalin; and, second, that the impotence of the Russian intellectuals combined with their sense of the immensity of Russia, produced a passionate Messianism which, in varied forms from Tolstoyan primitivism to Leninist Marxism, gave to its votaries the obligation to rebuild the whole world in the image of the supreme dream by which they were haunted. It is this apocalyptic character which gives to the revelation of each school of Russian thought its fierce intolerance, its assumption that if it cannot win all, it will lose everything. It is an essential part of the moral and intellectual climate of the Russian intellectuals, that, with all their realisation of Russian backwardness, with all their admiration for the achievement of Western Europe, they felt in Russia an inexhaustible primeval force, not yet sophisticated, as yet untried, which, when at last yoked to what was worthy in the outer world, would give to Russia the power to lead in a universal regeneration of man.

To anyone who bears in mind the fantastic, though capricious, repression of ideas in nineteenth century Russia, above all in the area of political thought, there ought to be no surprise at the intensity of the energy released in 1917, or at the fantastic vigour with which, in almost all forms of life, ideas were argued upon with fanatical vigour, so that in their loneliness, above all in the loneliness of exile, every detail of a theory of liberation became fundamental, almost a decisive criterion by which to judge orthodoxy and heresy. It was an unending debate, which went on for almost a hundred years—from the Decembrist conspiracy of 1825, to the enforced abdication of the Tsar in February 1917. It was a debate in large part accom-

153

panied by a conspiracy, in which, whether the participants were in London or Geneva, Zurich or Vienna, Prague or Siberia, they knew that they might well be gambling for their heads. They could not talk without the sense that everywhere the police were watching them, that, sometimes, as with Azev, Father Gapon, and the member of the Bolshevik Central Committee, Malinovski, the agents of the police actually helped to shape their policy, and assisted them to destroy the basis of Tsarism, even while assisting the Tsar's Ministers to discover and to punish those who sought to lay the axe at the roots of Tsarism. Any one who looks at the different segments of the revolutionary movement, in these long and fatiguing years, and compares their fierce intensity, outside Russia as well as inside it, with the slow, almost dreadful monotony of the masses, or with the dull and half-meaningless intrigues of the Russian Court, can hardly fail to understand why almost every group of revolutionists was bound to build its doctrine in an extremist form. The extremism was, for the most part, the sublimation of frustration, the half-conscious suspicion—until the significant, if abortive, revolution of 1905—that they were condemned to something like a perpetual exile in which there were only brief intervals of hope, and in which the occasional act of terrorist revenge brought with it widespread and ruthless punishment from a government able as late as the period of Stolypin to make even the unbreakable optimism of Lenin change into doubt whether he would ever live to see the revolution.

Any revolutionary movement which established authority compels to work in the darkness is driven to the fanaticism which erects minor differences into major principles. That was so in the early history of Christianity; those who shaped its official form found it far easier to absorb ideas from the pagan cults it replaced than to accept the realism of Marcion, the attempt of the Montanists to return to a simpler primitivism, or that Pelagian heresy of which the logical result would have been to make the doctrine of the Atonement unnecessary. How barely the early Church survived its early struggles with its 'heretics', until it was able to evoke in its support the direct, though not always reliable, authority of the Empire is a history which bears a deeply interesting resemblance to the internal

154

dissensions of the revolutionary parties in Russia until the reaching of a dividing line which was hardly attained until the closing phases of the Civil War. No one can read the passionate controversies between the different groups in the Russian Social Democratic Party between 1903 and 1917 without seeing that in politics as in religion, where what is in issue is less power than the taut strength of orthodoxy it is far easier to bear unbelief than to tolerate heresy. The character of Bolshevism as orthodoxy in the period before Lenin's conquest of power is maintained with increasing force after it for two reasons. The first is that, given the deep antagonism of its opponents both inside and outside Russia, it would have lost the defensive strength given to it by the rigid unity it imposed had it been easily accessible to variation. The second is that, with Lenin's victory, his interpretation of Marxism acquired a prestige to which no alternative could claim a rivalry simply because he was able to give Marx a kingdom over which to preside, when his other disciples in Germany, or France, or Italy, or Great Britain, were still discussing its implications abstractly without being able to take the concrete steps to power, or, when they did take it, as with Kurt Eisner in Bavaria, or Bela Kun in Hungary, they could maintain it only for a brief moment. With half the world expressing its hostility to the Russia of the October Revolution, with even its own leaders convinced that they but held a temporary line until the inevitable and overdue European Revolution came to its rescue, it is not really surprising that Bolshevik survival seemed something like a miracle, and that Moscow came to be, like Mecca, a holy city to which, year after year, innumerable pilgrims would resort for an inspiration which seemed to renew and to deepen their faith that October, as it has been reached, was a junction and not a terminus.

What I am concerned here to note is that the extremism of the Russian revolutionists is, like that of any kindred movement that lives for so long a half-underground life, bound to develop intolerance and a faith in the compelling power of rigorous orthodoxy, for tolerance is always the outcome of the social security of a ruling class aware that no amount of discussion can seriously disturb its authority, and that, even if it is able to make its dream of power come true, the intolerance

155

and the insistence upon orthodoxy will remain so long as it has reason to suspect that its power is either unstable or incomplete. There is nothing novel in all this. Kerensky himself, whom Lenin broke in pieces, affirmed it strongly. 'Let no one say that Lenin is an expression,' he wrote, 'of some kind of allegedly Asiatic "elemental Russian forces". I was born under the same sky. I breathed the same air. I heard the same peasant songs, and played in the same school playground. I saw the same limitless horizons from the same high bank of the Volga.' All that Kerensky can suggest is that the relentless determination with which Lenin 'deliberately and cruelly' mutilated Russia was the outcome of a long exile from his native land which had caused him 'to lose all natural feeling for it'. It is not, indeed, an explanation which carries weight with any who have read the massive sequence of pamphlets and letters in which, behind every move in plot or tactic for the control of his party, we can read the depth of Lenin's *Sehnsucht* for his native land. The ruthless intolerance with which Lenin treated all his opponents was the outcome of his conviction that those only can bring about the vast changes he had in view who live for nothing but the power to make those changes. 'There is not another man,' Axelrod was to tell a member of the Bureau of the Second Socialist International, 'who for twenty-four hours of the day is taken up with the revolution, who has no other thoughts but thoughts of revolution, and who in his sleep dreams of nothing but revolution.' The man who felt this way, who moreover trained others by twenty years of revolutionary agitation to think, as he thought, if with less intensity, was not going to loose his grip on power once he had seized it. If revolutionary terror was needed to maintain his hold, he felt no more doubt of his right to exercise it than Thiers had, when to suppress the Commune he exercised amid the applause of most of Conservative Europe counter-revolutionary terror to consolidate the authority of the bourgeoisie. The Church had acted in the same way when it sought to break its heretics in pieces.

Nor, as I think, is there any validity in the claim that Russia among the rest of the nations has formulated some special claim to a Messianic nature which makes the right of its people to expand exceptional in character. The same sense of unique-

156

ness has been felt by every great nation—by Great Britain, by Spain, by France, by Italy, by Germany, by the United States. America's 'manifest destiny', indeed, is proclaimed with vigour as early as the time of Thomas Jefferson. Here, he said, is a unique country, free from the vices of the old world, displaying special virtues, created to provide effete Europe with an example upon which, if it purge itself of its evil habits, it may one day hope to build its future. He did not hesitate to justify even the Terror in the French Revolution. 'The liberty of the whole earth,' he wrote, 'was depending on the issue of the contest, and was ever such a price won with so little innocent blood . . . Rather than that it should have failed, I would have seen half the earth desolated.' He told his fellow citizens, on March 4, 1809, that "the station we occupy among the nations of the earth is honourable but awful. Trusted with the destinies of the solitary republic of the world, the only monument of human rights, and the sole depository of the sacred fire of freedom and self-government, from hence it is to be lighted up in other regions of the earth, if other regions of the earth shall ever become susceptible of its benign influence . . . And to what sacrifice of interest or convenience ought not these considerations to animate us? To what compromises of opinion and inclination, to maintain harmony and union among ourselves, and to preserve from all danger this hallowed ark of human hope and happiness'. Neither Lenin nor Stalin would have written otherwise of Russia's place among the nations.

It is not otherwise with Germany. 'We want to become a world people,' wrote the eminent historian, Friedrich Meinecke, 'let us remind ourselves that the belief in our mission as a world-people has arisen from our originally purely spiritual impulse to absorb the world.'[1] 'The frontier of Western civilisation,' wrote Oswald Spengler,[2] 'was always placed at the point where German colonisation had come to a standstill.' The attitude to other nations is set in similar terms. 'Everything,' said Spengler,[3] 'that Marx said about "capitalist society" applies to the English, and not to a human universal economic instinct.' 'Is the United States,' he asked,[4] 'a power with a

[1] *Die Deutsche Erhebung vom 1914.* (Berlin, 1914) p. 37.
[2] *Jahre der Entscheidung* (Munich, 1933) p. 25.
[3] *Ibid.* p. 50.
[4] *Ibid.* p. 67.

future? . . . All we know is that so far there is neither a real nation nor a real state. Actually, what it amounts to is a boundless field and a population of trappers, drifting from town to town in the dollar-hunt, unscrupulous and dissolute, for the law is only for those who are not cunning or powerful enough to ignore it.' 'The Latin race,' wrote von Moltke, in 1870,[1] 'is a worn-out race. It is condemned to extermination and disappearance probably in its entirety, or at least in the character of a constituted whole.' 'How can we teach the German worker,' asked Hitler,[2] 'that Bolshevism is an infamous crime against humanity?' I do not need to prolong the hideous catalogue. Its point is the simple one that there exists an immense volume of literature which claims for each major nation the title to dominate civilisation and justifies, in the name of its greatness, the right to use methods to validate that title even when it condemns their employment by other nations with which at the particular moment it is not on friendly terms.

Obviously, the central problem which Russia presents to the world is not that of its strength; nor is it the possession of a different ideology from that of the Atlantic Powers. For the time being, at any rate, the United States is stronger than Russia, and its ideology existed peacefully alongside that of all the capitalist powers from 1918 to 1939 without any general sense that the issues between them would have to be settled by conflict. Until 1917, indeed, Lenin had no doubt that, after a brief period of proletarian dictatorship, the revolution in Russia would assume a democratic form; a socialist, he wrote in 1914, ceases to be a socialist if 'he decides to pronounce the questions of political freedom and democracy as of no consequence to him'. It is clear from all that he wrote after 1905 and before 1917 that he was gravely preoccupied with the problem of how, in a country where the proletariat was a tiny minority, a provisional government could be prevented from becoming a minority dictatorship. It was in answer to the view of Trotsky that the provisional government created by a revolution would be socialist with a socialist majority, that he answered angrily 'That cannot be ! It cannot be because a revolutionary govern-

[1] *Gesammelte Schriften* (Berlin, 1881) p. 97.
[2] *Mein Kampf* (London, 1939) p. 538.

ment can endure for a time, only if it rests on the enormous majority of the people.' It was in answer to Trotsky's view that he threw out the slogan 'for the democratic dictatorship of the proletariat and the peasantry'. In 1914, once more, he emphasised that 'a socialist revolution is out of the question unless the masses become class-conscious, organised, trained and educated by open class struggle against the entire bourgeoisie. Whoever wants to approach socialism by any other path than that of political democracy will inevitably arrive at absurd and reactionary conclusions, both economic and political'. Certainly, after 1917, the policy for which the Bolsheviks stood was fairly described by Trotsky in his attack on Lenin's famous stand at the Social Democratic Congress of 1903: 'the organisation of the Party takes the place of the Party itself; the Central Committee takes the place of the organisation; and, finally, the dictator takes the place of the Central Committee'. What Trotsky vehemently asserted in the aftermath of that Congress, Rosa Luxemburg asserted with brilliant insight in 1918. But when Trotsky was in the first years of his exile, he repudiated the earlier and startling prophecy he had made. 'I did not fully realise,' he wrote, in his *Autobiography,* 'what an intense and imperious centralism the revolutionary party would need to lead millions in a war against the old order.' He was then accepting the principle Lenin described so starkly in his pamphlet *One step forward, two steps backward.* There Lenin had written : 'The organising principle of revolutionary social democracy strives to go from the top downwards, and defends the enlargement of the rights and plenary powers of the central body against the parts.' That was the view of the Bolshevik Central Committee after its brief coalition with the Left Social Revolutionaries was over. They made the Party the Government of Russia, and kept the sovereignty of the state in its hands. But even before Lenin died the sovereignty of the Party had passed to its Central Committee; and within five years of his death, the Central Committee had virtually surrendered its independent power of decision to one only of its members whom, it might well be, it could advise, but whose decisions it had no real choice but to accept.

What begins with Marxist analysis has been transformed by world events in what has now been for over thirty years

159

nothing so much as a permanent Committee of Public Safety on the Jacobin model. As early as 1918, Rosa Luxemburg had foreseen this danger. She did not fail to praise the remarkable achievement of Lenin and Trotsky; what disturbed her was the fear that what had succeeded in the special conditions of a defeated and disintegrating Russia might be transformed into a universal formula which Communists would try to force upon all the socialist parties in the rest of Europe. 'By the vigour of their attitude to revolution,' she wrote in 1918 in *Die Russische Revolution,* 'their exemplary force of action, and their unshakeably faithful attachment to international socialism, they have truly done everything it was possible to do in such diabolically difficult conditions. But now the danger begins. For they are now at the point where they make a virtue of necessity. They are turning the tactics they were driven to adopt by the terrible conditions which they faced into a full-blown theory. They have commended its acceptance as a model of socialist tactics to the international proletariat. This involves them in putting forward their own personalities where they are really irrelevant. They thus hide their real and incontestable historic merit under the mass of faults which necessity imposed upon them. In doing so, they render a bad service to the cause of that international socialism in whose name they fought and struggled. For this is a claim to add new truths to the general body of socialist ideas when, in reality, these new truths are simply old errors committed in Russia under the pressure of necessity, and, at bottom, as the consequence of the bankruptcy of international socialism in the world war.'

This was not only Rosa Luxemburg's view. Even more interesting is the fact that, in one of his most famous pamphlets, *The Infantile Disease of Left-Wing Communism,* Lenin carried her doctrine to its logical conclusion. For there Lenin sought to make it clear that it was folly on the part of excited Left-Wing Communist minorities to adopt the strategy possible in the Russian situation, and to throw overboard the central Marxist principle that a socialist society can only be born when a mature and informed working class is able to take over the state-power where capitalist authority is collapsing. There is nothing in Marx to suggest the desirability of a totalitarian dictatorship which accretes to itself all power, and regards all

160

criticism of itself as proof of treachery. It is obvious enough that each step taken by Lenin after 1917 was a response to what he thought the needs of the Russian situation, and that, wherever the Russian pattern was imposed either by him or by his successors on the ground of its universal validity, it did harm and not good. That was clearly seen by Rosa Luxemburg in the autumn of 1918. She did not doubt that, in the consolidation of its power, a socialist party making a revolution might well have to safeguard itself against the danger of counter-revolution. But, like Lenin himself before 1914, she regarded that as a temporary measure. When the Bolshevik party began to argue that only by their own methods, which should be given the status of universal authority, could a socialist revolution succeed, she pointed out with vigour what would follow the permanent translation of freedom and democracy into their opposites. 'The suppression of political life throughout the country,' she wrote,[1] 'must gradually cause the vitality of the Soviets themselves to decline. Without general elections, freedom of the press, freedom of assembly, and freedom of speech, life in every public institution slows down and becomes a caricature of itself, and bureaucracy rises as the only deciding factor. Public life generally dies, and a few score party leaders with inexhaustible energy and limitless idealism direct and rule; amongst them, the leadership is, in reality, in the hands of a dozen men of first-class brains, and from time to time an élite of the working class is called together in conference, to applaud the speeches of their leaders, and to vote unanimously for the resolutions they put forward.'

This has, in fact, been an accurate prophecy of the qualities of Communist life as its parties organise it not only in Russia, but in most parts of the world. The 'iron discipline' of the 'monolithic' party has resulted in splits and purges, in an omnipresent secret police with exceptional powers, in mass-trials and wholesale executions, in the equation of opposition with treason, in the dismissal of foreign leaders from their posts when they did not accept the directive approved by Moscow, the denunciation, at one moment, of men and women who, as it were the day before, had been enthusiastically praised, and in the ruthless separation of Soviet Russia from

[1] *Die Russische Revolution*, p. 113.

the possible poison of contact with the socialists of other countries. Nor is it possible to forget the contrast between the direct and simple relation of Lenin with the masses and the deification of Stalin in his own lifetime. And to all this there must be added not only the denial of that right to national self-determination, upon which Lenin himself laid so much emphasis, but the treatment of the nations allied to Russia which are regarded as such junior partners in the alliance that any independent thinking on their part is, as in the Yugoslavia of Tito, dealt with as a crime so grave as to merit a call to the organised overthrow of the régime by way of punishment.

These are grievous qualities all of which not only diminish the influence of Russia abroad, but stand in the way of developing the maturity of its own people at home. Only too often, they turn Marxism into 'putschism', or, as in the programme of 1949, published by the Communist Party of Great Britain, lead to the making of quite delusive promises which its leaders themselves know perfectly well they would have no chance of fulfilling even if they came to power. Those who direct Communist parties are led not only to a carelessness about truth, but even to its suppression when this seems best to serve the temporary interests of the Party as these are defined for that moment by its Executive Committee. We have books suppressed which were once regarded as of classic quality, like John Reed's *Ten Days that Shook the World,* or that *Short History of Russia* by M. N. Pokrovsky which Lenin praised so highly. Not only are the notes to Lenin's *Works* altered from one edition to another to suit the immediate exigencies of party conflict, but even the recollections of old party members are compulsorily altered by their authors when they are not deemed sufficiently serviceable to Generalissimo Stalin's reputation.[1]

In some ways, perhaps, nothing is more significant in this process of adaptation than the way in which new histories of

[1] The worst instance of this is Enukidze, for so long so close a friend of Stalin that his recollections of the Generalissimo in the Caucasus were part of an official volume published in honour of Stalin's birthday in 1930. Enukidze has now been executed as an 'enemy of the people', though his supposed falsifications are confirmed by both Krassin and Krupskaya.

the Russian Communist Party appear in which the events are given new emphasis, and even new patterns, with old evidence suppressed, and new evidence adduced, to support the outlook in official favour at the time of their publication.[1] It is doubtful to-day whether the younger generation of Communists, both inside and outside of Russia, are aware either of the part played by Trotsky in 1905 and again in 1917, or how far greater, after the October Revolution, his importance was than that of Stalin until the first illness of Lenin enabled Stalin to use the machinery of the party organisation for encompassing his rival's ruin. Grave as were the defects of Trotsky, he served the Russian Revolution superbly; and there is no possible justification for the effort, made by every hireling upon whom Stalin could count, to represent a Communist of Trotsky's stature as a social fascist intent upon the betrayal of his country merely to serve his own ambition.

It would be folly to deny that all this is not only a deformation of Marxism, but also a deep stain on the character of the men responsible for it. On the side of international organisation, Lenin denied the very thing that Marx set out to accomplish. 'The International was founded,' the latter wrote,[2] 'in order to replace the socialist or semi-socialist sects by a real organisation of the working class for struggle . . . and the history of the International was a continual struggle by the General Council against the sects and amateur experiments which attempted to assert themselves within the International itself against the genuine movement of the working class.' Marx and Engels always believed that since, in every country, the working class was at a different stage of maturity, it was natural that their practical activities would find very diverse theoretical expression.[3] So Engels warned the German socialists in America not to try 'in the face of a mighty and glorious movement, not of their own creation, to make of their imported and not always understood theory the kind of dogma which they put forward as the only road to salvation. Our theory is

[1] This can be seen by comparing the various party histories of Zinoviev, Yaroslavsky, Popov, and that edited, and in part written, by Stalin himself.
[2] Letter to Bolte, Nov. 23, 1871.
[3] Cf. Franz Mehring, *Life of Karl Marx* (London, 1936) p. 143.

163

not a dogma, but the exposition of an evolutionary process which involves successive phases.'[1] And a year later he reaffirmed his conviction. 'Had we from 1864 to 1873,' he wrote, 'insisted on working together only with those who openly adopted our platform where should we be to-day?'[2] His answer was that those who stand aloof from 'the great national movement' will 'dwindle down into a dogmatic sect, and will be brushed aside as people who do not understand their own principles'.[3] That is assuredly a very different climate from that in which the famous 'Twenty-One Demands' were sent to the Independent Labour Party of Great Britain as the conditions of its affiliation to the Third International.

Yet none of this harsh narrowness, regretful though it be, can be held to justify the attempt to present Soviet Russia as simply Nazi Germany in another and more dangerous form. When we examine the leaders of the Bolshevik Party what at once emerges in them is that 'limitless idealism' of which Rosa Luxemburg spoke. They have not sought personal wealth. If they have fought passionately for power, even for personal power, they have never failed to keep in view the idea of a great Russian civilisation leading in the great task of emancipating the workers of the world. I do not believe that they have lost the sense of mission which that idea has evoked from them and their followers all over the world. I am sure, indeed, that the history of Bolshevism, both in its origins and development, has distorted the perspective of its exponents. We shall never understand it unless we think of it beginning almost as a secret society within a party which was itself a conspiracy whose members were, if they stayed in Russia, always gambling for their heads, or, if they lived mostly in exile abroad, like Lenin, were deeply affected by the febrile psychology of the *émigré* who is never quite certain whom it is safe to trust. If the Bolsheviks were able to seize power by a brilliantly planned and superbly executed coup, none of them thought that they would be able to maintain their power unless a European

[1] *Selected Correspondence of Marx and Engels* (London, 1934) p. 315 f.
[2] *Ibid.* p. 455.
[3] *Briefe und Auszüge aus Briefen* (Stuttgart, 1921), Letter of February 9th, 1887.

Revolution came to their aid. The leaders, especially Lenin, counted greatly on that wider revolution mainly on the ground that, otherwise, the price of an attempt to build a socialist society in a backward country dominated by peasants would be overwhelming. Not only did the European Revolution not come, but, for over two years, the Soviet government had to cope with civil war within, and external invasion from without, with little aid, and even less sympathy from European socialists; the German Party, indeed, which had taken over the government in defeat actually collaborated with the General Staff to destroy the elements of a genuinely revolutionary effort led by Liebknecht and Rosa Luxemburg, whose murder it can fairly be said to have observed with some detachment. At this stage, it is not really surprising that a deep estrangement should have developed between the Bolshevik government straining every nerve to keep alive in a starving country devastated by war and Social Democratic parties which, for the most part, rendered it no effective aid. Nor, indeed, is it any more surprising that it should have welcomed those socialist elements in European countries which broke away from their comrades in a furious insistence that refusal to co-operate with the new Russia was to play the traitor to Marxist principles.

In this first phase of the split thus caused in the ranks of the Socialist Movement of Europe, it is difficult not to sympathise with the Russian indignation. The Bolsheviks were fighting for survival; elsewhere, the main scene was one in which other socialist parties broadly accepted the restoration of capitalist authority as inevitable, and made no profound effort to hinder it from doing all in its power to prevent the Bolsheviks surviving. Even *de facto* recognition of the new government was slow in coming; commercial relations were only restored after complex and painful efforts in which the representatives of the new Russia were more often than not treated with calculated discourtesy. It is not an exaggeration to say that it was not until Hitler seized power in Germany that the possible importance of Russia began to be weighed; and the contrast between the welcome given to Mussolini and the enthusiasm for his supposed achievements, and the obvious hope of Bolshevik failure at each stage of its development is, in retrospect, overwhelming. Even when it became obvious that the whole interest of

165

Russia lay in peace, its government rarely received the consideration that was its due. After the outbreak of the Spanish Civil War, appeasement of Hitler was the main item on the programmes of most European powers. Not only did the British Government, for example, accept the destruction of Czechoslovakia as part of Hitler's price for peace; even after March 15, 1939, Mr. Chamberlain, without consultation with Russia, took the risk of guaranteeing semi-fascist countries like Poland, Greece, and Rumania against aggression, while, at the same time, he made faint signs of a half-hearted desire to find terms upon which Russia would give aid in making possible the fulfilment of his guarantee. Yet it was common knowledge, at least from May, 1939, onwards, that while his second-class delegation to Moscow was leisurely negotiating there in an atmosphere made futile by Mr. Chamberlain's acceptance of the Polish refusal to receive any aid from Russia which involved the presence of Russian troops upon its soil, he was also having conversations with German ministers which are largely unintelligible except as preparations for a still larger appeasement. Had he succeeded, Hitler would have been free to turn east and sweep through Poland into a full-scale attack upon Russia in the knowledge that he could count upon the neutrality of the Western powers and the probable aid of Japan. If the Russo-German Pact of August, 1939, was the necessary release of Hitler from the military danger of a war upon two fronts, it is vital to remember that Stalin merely achieved swiftly and successfully that relief from attack at the expense of the Western Powers which Mr. Chamberlain was seeking slowly, and unsuccessfully, to achieve for the Western Powers at the expense of Soviet Russia.

It is not, therefore, excessive to say that there was no period from 1917 until 1939 when Russia was free from crisis in almost every part of which foreign hostility was involved. Its government was regarded throughout those years as the embodiment of evil, and there was no socialist party in Europe which strove with any serious continuity to develop a friendly relation with it. No doubt it is true to say that in those years some of its blunders were immense; but it is also true to say that, as a rule, their immensity was the outcome, first, of the drive for industrialisation, and, second, of the necessity to over-

166

come the individualism of the peasants, both of which were essential to its preparations against attack from outside. It is difficult to forgive that internal fight for power which drove Trotsky into exile, and resulted in the execution of so many of the leading Bolsheviks after trials which, even half a generation later, remain as mysterious as when they were being held. It is not less difficult to forgive the deliberate strategy of seeking, with some success, to break the unity of the working class in practically every European country, so that socialist and trade union leaders became far more estranged from Communists in their own countries, than they were from the forces of capitalism. It is impossible, for instance, to doubt that the mutual hostility of Social Democrats and Communists was a factor of genuine importance in the rise of Hitler to power.

The scale of the terror, the deliberate conditioning of the mind by a censorship which extends, for political reasons, even to the highest realms of the arts and sciences, that 'disease of orthodoxy', as the Webbs termed it, which remains, after thirty-two years, an outstanding feature of the régime, the reckless and all-pervasive habits of the secret police, the large-scale use of forced labour, arrest without warrant, and both imprisonment and execution without trial, all of these are, on any showing, indefensible. The so-called 'iron curtain', lamentable though it is, admits of an easier understanding. It operates, almost wholly, against foreigners who are not Communists, and is at least partly the outcome of the belief that foreign diplomats and journalists are all engaged in conspiracy to defame or to destroy the Soviet Union; to be judged in proper perspective, it must be remembered that a Communist, not on an official mission for his government, would be refused entry to the United States and to the territories of a large majority of the members of the United Nations. Though that does not excuse the fantastic pictures of foreign countries which Russian propaganda composes for the millions who have no means of correcting their inadequacies, it is in part offset by the determined effort of anti-communist counter-propaganda to penetrate the 'iron curtain', and in part by the fact that there must be, by now, many hundred thousand Russians who, mostly as soldiers, but often as scientists, business men, and journalists, have seen enough of the outside

167

world to supply a discreet corrective to the effect of the Russian propaganda machine. It must also be remembered that one of the Russian passions is for endless discussion; and the large correspondence even of a foreign paper of limited circulation like *British Ally* is evidence that not even the strictest censorship can prevent curiosity from seeking to pass beyond the limits it attempts to impose. I shall long remember a pathetic appeal to the editor of *British Ally* to continue his subscription to it from an old man in the area of Archangel who spoke of the interest it provided for himself and his blind wife when he read it to her in the long winter evenings of the North, and the request from a scientific institute to be allowed to subscribe for a second copy since the first was almost in fragments by the time it had been passed round from one member of the institute to another.

Yet none of these habits of the government is defensible; all one can do is to seek their explanation. That lies, I am confident, in the deep conviction of the Russian rulers that they are still surrounded by enemies on all sides, and that, just as Hitler's invasion justified their precautions before 1941, so the 'cold war' justifies their precautions after the victory of 1945. They are not prepared to believe that the offers of friendship are genuine in the light of the interpretation they place upon the 'cold war'. If it is argued to them that the 'cold war' is, at least in part, the inevitable outcome of the use to which they put Communist parties in other countries, and the unrelenting hold they keep over their immediate neighbours, Czechoslovakia, for instance, or Hungary, their reply is that they are not less entitled to a Monroe doctrine than is the United States, and that their patronage of Communist domination of the satellite régimes is only another form of that control America assures itself indirectly by the extension of financial aid which, however complex be the forms beneath which it hides, nevertheless brings the countries assisted into the orbit of American influence in all important issues of international policy. Not the most solemn affirmations of political leaders either in Washington or in London will persuade them that the Atlantic Security Pact, Marshall Aid, and the creation of a Western Germany likely, in a comparatively short time, to become a member of the European Consultative Assembly, are intended

168

merely to resist the danger of aggressive attack, are able to convince the Russian leaders that the affirmations are true.

'The nation was not conceived of as a democracy,' wrote 'A.E.' of Ireland in 1916, 'freely discussing its laws, but as a secret society with political chiefs meeting in the dark and issuing orders. No doubt our politicial chieftains loved their country, but love has many degrees of expression from the basest to the highest. The basest love will wreck everything, even the life of the beloved, to gratify ignoble desires. The highest love conspires with the imaginative reason to bring about every beautiful circumstance around the beloved which will permit of the highest development of its life. There is no real love apart from this intellectual brooding . . . Our civilisation must depend on the quality of thought engendered in the national being.'[1] The weakness of contemporary Russia is that its chiefs still consider it as a secret society in which orders are issued to the masses from the dark recesses of the Kremlin. It still lacks that refreshing vigour which comes from allowing the winds of freedom to blow as they will across its vast spaces. It still does not trust its people. Its government is still guided less by its hopes than by its fears. It still lacks faith in the strength and creativeness of what it has accomplished over the years.

Yet what it has accomplished is certainly more revolutionary of the values of mankind than anything elsewhere accomplished since the French Revolution. It has ended the exploitation of the many in the interest of a few. It has given to manual labour a dignity and a recognition which, in the normal process of industrialisation, only a small oligarchy of highly skilled craftsmen have been able successfully to attain. It has organised opportunities for innumerable numbers of those who earn their living by manual toil to find in their leisure a self-respect and a fulfilment on a scale elsewhere unknown. It has brought emancipation to literally millions of women who, before 1917, had little effective place in the boundaries of civilised life. It has gone far to breaking down that barrier between the worker by hand and the worker by brain which has so often left the 'intellectuals' of a society dependent upon the patronage of a narrow oligarchy of birth or wealth. It has broken down all the major barriers of colour and of creed so that the many

[1] *The National Being* (Dublin, 1916) pp. 7-8.

nationalities within its border have an important and increasing sense that they share in the equal consideration given to the nationalities that were either their masters like the Great Russians, or the policemen of their masters like the Cossacks. There is, moreover, important evidence to show that, outside the realm of politics, in the world of everyday offences, the Russians have made more interesting experiments in penal reform than have been made elsewhere in the last fifty years.

Immense claims have been made for Russian science since 1917; and there is no room for doubt that compared with any earlier period, the Russian Government has endowed scientific and technological research on an ample scale, and that it has made great efforts, also, to assure a wide interest throughout the society it rules in the importance of scientific mindedness. Not only is an interest in the achievements of science an integral part of education, but the effort to make its appreciation a fundamental element in popular consciousness is a genuine one. Like all such efforts it has its crudities, and there is a desire to claim priority for Russian men of science in discovery—in aeronautics, for example, or in penicillin—which is a rather pathetic mixture of hybris and nationalism. Yet, despite this, the evidence goes to show that the social significance of science is more widely appreciated in Russia than in any country in the world except the United States. It is, no doubt, true that Russian technology is still far behind American; it takes more than a generation to establish the 'know-how' of machines in any country where, previously, literacy and the machine alike were unknown to the vast majority of the population. But, given peace, by the end of another twenty years there is every reason to suppose that the significance of the scientist and the technician will be more deeply rooted in Russia even than it is in the United States; for while, in the United States, the machine brings with it, as the mechanical cotton picker is bringing to the South, serious fears about the unemployment it may cause, in Russia the fear of unemployment is a shadow which now no longer broods over men and women. Only the coming of war and the fantastic devastation it brings in its new forms can ever throw Russia back to the poverty which the revolutionary generation had to bear. Its grandchildren have the confidence that they will go forward,
170

and they have that confidence while the economic destiny of every other people hangs in the balance.

I assume that this is probable if we are able to avoid war; and I assume it despite all that is evil and childish in the Russian régime. For I am bound to regard as evil the reckless disregard of the worth of individual human life that is typical of Russia and its satellites, just as I am bound to regard as childish the deification of Stalin, the pretence that Russia is a democracy, and the insistence that the standards of the creative arts and letters are higher and more free than they are in Western Europe and America. The 'cold war' which Moscow wages against the Tito government in Yugoslavia is 'as indefensible as the 'cold war' waged against Russia by the United States. The bleak hostility to all criticism of Russian action is not merely sensitiveness; it is the making of a myth of infallibility as dangerous to those responsible for its manufacture as it is to those upon whom it is imposed. It has the unhappy effect of depriving Soviet Russia of the support of those who think it essential to achieve a balanced judgment between extravagant claims on any side. It prevents Soviet Russia from appearing to the outside world what it represents itself to be for the simple reason that, save in rare cases, it refuses to permit the examination of its claims to any save those who are already committed to its support.

Yet no comment upon the problem of freedom in Russia would be either just or complete which did not take account of hope as well as of immediate actuality. All freedom means the power of men to choose in the area from which necessity has been pushed further back. It is not a matter only of hostility between men, of coercion of subjects by their rulers, of workers by their employers, of unequal laws, of the conflict between convention and novelty in ideas. Freedom also depends upon the devotion of human energy to liberate men and women from the unnecessary limitations of physical nature. A high death rate, preventable disease, starvation where food is available, the burden of toil so great that it makes thought a luxury, that enervating poverty which drives those who suffer from it to the point when they have lost all sense of self-respect, that unending succession of children which makes so many millions of women old and careworn before their time, all of these are

171

elements in the achievement of freedom without which the sense of the power continuously to initiate action which seems to the doer worthwhile is secondary in character. Ideal ends only become significant to the multitude when its members have experienced ideal ends. Until but little more than a generation ago, the overwhelming majority of Russians were peasants to whom natural catastrophe, a bad harvest, or a flood, a pest which destroyed cattle, were far more important than appreciation of Pushkin's poetry or the doctrinal conflict between the Bolsheviks and the Mensheviks.

I do not think it is unjust to claim, as the rulers of Russia have claimed, that, in the midst of poverty within and aggression from without, they have begun to push back the frontiers of necessity for millions of men and women who never knew before even that they could be driven back. To most Americans or Englishmen or Frenchmen, what they were seeking to do seemed to involve harshness and cruelty quite outside any experience the former had known. It would be more accurate to say that the harshness and the cruelty were outside the experience because the sufferers lacked the means, sometimes the right, to make themselves articulate. For it is to deprive words of their meaning to speak of freedom, in the inter-war years, of the shipworker in Jarrow, of the miner in South Wales, of the sharecropper in Arkansas. In her book on Jarrow, Miss Ellen Wilkinson gave an example of what depression in Jarrow meant. 'A.K. was a hewer until Hebburn colliery closed, when he got work at the Jarrow shipyard,' she wrote.[1] 'He is forty-seven years old . . . which means sentence of economic death on Tyneside if you are once "out" at that age. He hates enforced idleness, and is continually trying for work. He has three children, a boy aged sixteen getting 8/- a week "sick pay", a boy of fourteen, chronically rheumatic, and a child of eight. The wife is ailing and bloodless, and gets 2/6 a week extra sick allowance from the Unemployment Assistance Board. The eldest boy went to work as an errand lad at 6/- a week. He became ill simply because he was not getting enough food to stick the long hours and carry the weights required. The unemployment allowance of the family is 35/6. Doctor's notes have to be sent in periodically, for the mother

[1] *The Town That Was Murdered* (London, 1939) p 216.

and the sick boys. What is really wrong with all of them is the effect of a long period of semi-starvation. The doctor says so. The 2/6 extra allowance for the mother is conscientiously spent by the father in milk, eggs, and two ounces of fresh butter for her each week. When it does what it is given for and improves the mother's health, then it will be stopped, and cannot be given again until the doctor again has to say that the woman is suffering from malnutrition.' Miss Wilkinson notes that A.K. is among 'the men [who are] intelligent citizens taking an interest in their town's affairs'. She quotes the remark of one of her friends in Jarrow : 'If they are going to keep us poor, they ought to keep us ignorant. Perhaps it hurts less when you don't know.'[1] Alongside this may be put the carefully drawn picture of a Southern sharecropper. 'The tenant,' write Raper and Reid,[2] "lives on fat tack, corn bread, sorghum, molasses, 'taters in season. A can of sardines or salmon is a delicacy in many cotton cabins. The resulting pellagra, rickets, low vitality, and unnecessary sickness mean "lazy" adults, and "puny" children and short graves . . . The field tools used by the typical tenant farmer would not seem strange to Moses and Hammurabi. There is nothing very modern about one-horse gears, single-stock plows, long-handled hoes, double-blade axes, and a long sack to drag through the field at picking time. The tenant farmers of the South, with few exceptions, still live and move in a slow and simple world. The plantation tenant women have none of the modern conveniences. They do the family wash over tubs, heat their flat iron before open fires, "tote" in the wood, carry water from well or spring, and bathe the children in washpans. But they bear yet heavier burdens; they work along with their men in the field during the rush seasons in spring and fall, and bear more children than any group of women in America, except the women of Southern Appalachia and Ozarkia. The tenant's low plane of living is enforced by his small income, below sixty-five cents per day on an average . . . (after interest charges are paid to landlord and merchant) . . . the tenant family's income of two hundred dollars is actually worth much less than in cash . . . The typical

[1] *Ibid.* p. 217.
[2] *Sharecroppers All* by Arthur F. Raper & Ira De A. Reid (Chapel Hill, 1941) p. 21 f. esp. p. 25-7.

farm tenant has only overalls and denim jacket, often patched
. . . in education the children of tenant families are handicapped in several ways. Scant clothing keeps many from school
even in mild weather, while on rainy or cold days, they are
almost compelled to stay about home fires . . . too often
attendance turns upon the demands of the cotton fields and the
whims of parents. Moreover, the typical tenant farmer, whether
white or negro, moves from one cabin to another every year or
so, thus further interrupting school attendance. Generally
speaking, farm tenants and wage hands do not participate in
community affairs. They are the inarticulate benefactors (bene-
ficiaries? H.L.) or victims of the public policy and private
practices of those who control the life of the community. Few
farm tenants and wage hands vote . . . The administration of
justice and public services also reflect the domination of the
plantation owners, and the defenceless role of the landless
families.'

Anyone who considers the lives of men and women like
those of Jarrow or of the deep South in the United States can,
I think, easily understand why, after long centuries of mis-
government, the defeat of 1917, which even the aristocracy in
large part found the natural outcome of corruption and ineffi-
ciency, should have been in Russia the signal for revolution.
What, I suggest, is significant is that once the machinery of
government broke down, it was not to the parties which promised freedom of speech or freedom of association which won
the support of the masses; it was to the leadership of the party
which promised peace, bread, and the land to the millions that
those millions turned. In the confusion of competing ideals
Lenin applied the insight he had wrested from reflection upon
long and passionately felt experience. He saw that the old
traditions had broken down, and that the opportunity was there
to create relations of production in which freedom could be
defined anew. He made his appeal victorious by associating
the new ideal of freedom with the wants felt most keenly by the
overwhelming majority of the population. He recognised that,
to make freedom effective in the sense that an aristocracy or a
successful bourgeois have defined freedom, he must first create
the conditions in which ideal ends like freedom of the press or
constitutional freedom should mean something real and vivid
174

to those who could rarely read or write, and to whom the principles of constitutional government lay outside any experience with which they had become acquainted. To the private in the Russian Army freedom meant the right to go home, away from the barbaric horrors and humiliations of the battlefield. To the peasant it meant access to the land and freedom from the power of the landlord. To the urban worker it meant freedom from the exploitation of the manufacturer. No other appeal was so widely and so deeply rooted in ordinary experience as that made by Lenin. It created a situation in which the supreme coercive power of the society fell into the hands of the party he led, and no other rival party ever became strong enough to wrest it from them. It thus became the function of the Bolshevik party, if it could, to organise the conditions in which Russia could pass from the realm of necessity into the realm of freedom.

CHAPTER X

I DO not think anyone could argue with objective honesty that the Russian Revolution has fulfilled all the high hopes formed of its future by its friends. It has, as I have said, immense achievements to its credit; but the Russian people and the rest of the world have paid a heavy price for them. Some part of that price, no doubt, must be attributed to the Russians themselves. All revolutions relax the inhibitions of civilised living; and a people like the Russians, historically disciplined to the brutal ways of tyranny, careless of the value of human life, mingling a friendly good nature with sudden gusts of savage cruelty, were not squeamish in their treatment of opposition in the process of consolidating the new form of power. And since in politics, as in nature, action and reaction are equal, it is perfectly intelligible that to the dictatorships of the old régime, there should have succeeded the dictatorship of the new; had Lenin and his colleagues not acted as a Committee of Public Safety, the Wrangels and the Kolchaks and the Denikins would have dealt with them as ruthlessly as Thiers and Gallifet dealt with the Communards in 1871. Something, too, must be allowed for the fact that, as Lenin himself said, all successful revolutions, like war, bring out men who find satisfaction in the infliction of cruelty, men like Stavrogin's 'ape', Peter Verkhavinsky, whom we know to have been modelled by Dostoievsky on the Nihilist, Nechayev. There are not only the 'underground men'; there are also the demoniac types, the men who have passed beyond good and evil, Stavrogin himself, the murdered father Karamazov, Svidrigailov, those of whom, in the suppressed chapters of *Stavrogin's Confession* Dostoievski makes Father Tikhon say: 'There are truly ugly crimes, crimes whatever they may be which, the more bloody, the more horrible, the more awesome become, so to speak, more dramatic. But there are crimes, too, so full of shame and disgrace, so past the limits of horror, that they cease to belong to art.' We must not underrate the part this element has played, not least when arbitrary power has been put in its hands in an organised way, as in the G.P.U. and its successors. Where we are dealing with the results of authority so exercised, whether in Russia, or anywhere else, the process of repression grows in barbarity by what it feeds on; in our own lives we have seen this in Germany and Italy, in Spain and in Japan.

Nor must we underrate the price exacted from the Russian people by internecine strife within the confines of the Party dictatorship itself. This seems to be an inevitable feature of revolution. We can see it happening quite early in the English Civil Wars, perhaps most clearly in the famous interchange between the Earl of Manchester and Cromwell at the close of 1644.[1] It emerges almost at once in 1789, when the French States-General became the National Assembly; it deepens as the attitude between classes become more sharply defined; and, when the Girondins embark upon war to limit social advance at home, it blazes into the conflict between Girondins and Jacobins which makes terror a permanent instrument of policy until Thermidor. It is the central theme round which is built the revolution in Paris both of 1830 and of 1848; few things, indeed, are more illuminating than to see the emergence of the first conflict of the June days in 1848 out of what in February had been the hope of unity, or to read the impact of that evolution in the minds and writings of men so different as Tocqueville and Guizot, Thiers and Louis Blanc. The development of the February Revolution in the Russia of 1917 into the social tempest of October follows a similar rhythm; the difference between Paris in 1848 and Moscow in 1917 is the architectonic genius with which the Bolshevik Party, under Lenin's astonishing leadership, fitted the pattern of its movement to his view of Marxist principles. To maintain their hold internally, the Bolsheviks had no alternative but to break their enemies or to be broken by them. The major problem which arises comes when, in the last year of Lenin's life, the foundations of the new society were beginning to assume both clarity and firmness of outline, and the Bolsheviks had to decide upon the next step they would take.

The conflict between Stalin and Trotsky began before the

[1] Sir Charles Firth, *Oliver Cromwell* (London, ed. of 1938) p. 114.

178

death of Lenin, and passionate as was the desire of both to succeed to the inheritance Lenin left, it would, I think, be mistaken to regard it as nothing more than the incompatibility of two such different personalities. That their deep dislike of each other was an important element in the outcome is as clear as that Conservative dislike of Mr. Winston Churchill, so amply shared by Mr. Ramsay MacDonald, which kept Mr. Churchill out of office from 1931 to the very eve of war in 1939. But behind that dislike I think there were also important doctrinal differences. Trotsky, with all his immense doctrinal gifts, was always the proponent of permanent revolution, the theorist who set Bolshevism in the context of a necessary world-revolution in which the great results of the Russian effort were only, as it were, the first act of a far mightier drama in which the working classes of Europe put the final seal of their approval upon a Russian victory that was bound to be ultimately doubtful until the rest of Europe at least rallied to its support. Stalin was the supreme organiser of the party-machine, interested in the world outside Russia as a secondary matter, convinced that, granted the conditions of 1924, the devastation, the fatigue of the workers, the proof that the capitalist societies of the West had shot their bolt, it was urgent, at any cost, to build socialism in a single country. Given his massive control of the party apparatus, given, also, the careless disrespect in which the pride of Trotsky drove him to underestimate such matters, it is not very difficult to understand why Stalin won. He was not conducting a free debate. He was fighting to subordinate the world revolutionary movement to the needs of the Russia which, in his view, could not be subordinated to a dubious world movement which had failed Russia from 1917 to 1924 without danger to its own stability. Trotsky made the enormous error of thinking of Stalin as a 'gray and colourless machine'. He underestimated from 1924 to his expulsion from Russia, the power of this 'machine' and its leader to build against him an alliance against which, in the absence of mutual esteem and confidence, the *émigrés* of the past were largely powerless. Lunarcharski has rightly said that the best side of Trotsky was apparent only where the sheer size of historic events made personality unimportant; he had no gift, with his

179

air of imperative command, his passionate desire to leave for himself the rôle of the great historic revolutionary leader, his willingness even in 1914, to launch bitter attacks against Lenin for 'factionalism', to descend from the heights of philosophic principles to wage serious battle with a man who, like Stalin, finds no organisational detail too small if its outcome is to safeguard his position against all rivals. When the final dispute came, the principals might hurl text and counter-text from Lenin at each other's heads; and, step by step, though without acknowledgment, and usually with fantastic vituperation, Stalin would adopt the ideas of Trotsky—by then in an exile from which he would never return—as though they were the outcome of his spontaneous insight. But what is significant in these troubled years is that, man by man, and group by group, Stalin had utterly destroyed the men who knew what he owed by way of debt to his great rival; and from the first Five Year Plan, in 1928, to the outbreak of world-war in 1941, he had made himself, for the overwhelming mass of Russians in Russia, the natural residuary legatee of Lenin, worshipped and safeguarded as the modesty of his predecessor had never dreamed of as possible. The 'democratic centralism', of which Lenin was the author, had been turned by him into a social theory in which invariably his last word was the undiscussable word. The exiles, the treason trials, the massacres, the collectivisation of the peasantry, the war against Hitler, had left him with a supremacy so far beyond challenge that it did not occur to any member of a foreign Communist Party after 1941 to doubt that in him had become summarised the natural and inevitable historical outcome of the ideas which Marx and Engels and Lenin had so brilliantly expounded before his advent to power. It was the supreme embodiment of infallibility in modern times. Not even the Pope could rival the grasp of universal knowledge and foresight that some cryptic half-sentence of the Russian Prime Minister offered, not only to his own people, but even to Mr. Roosevelt and Mr. Churchill as the inevitable doctrine to which they must adjust themselves.

It was at a high price that he purchased this eminence. The liquidation or imprisonment of virtually all his opponents among the historic figures in the Bolshevik Party, after trials

180

in which they made fantastic confessions of being linked, through Trotsky, with fascist plots, the purpose of which was, they avowed, the surrender of vital Russian territory to its enemies, and the complete disruption of its developing economy; the admission by an eminent physician in one trial that, while attending Maxim Gorki in a medical capacity, he took advantage of his position to murder the most distinguished Russian man of letters then alive; the sudden trial of the head of the secret police, Yagoda, who had been responsible for the first great purge of Stalin's opponents, and was now driven to admit that he himself was deeply involved in a plot to over-throw the Stalin régime; the decision, which Stalin himself admitted to have been carried out at excessive cost, to liquidate the Kulaks and collectivise agriculture—a proposal which, long before, Trotsky had urged was a vital condition of socialist success in Russia, in the face of fierce opposition from Stalin—probably a decision which cost the lives or the imprisonment of many hundred thousand peasants, and the destruction of at least more than a third of Russia's livestock; the sudden large-scale purge of Marshal Tukhachevski and many other members of the general staff, some of them among the best known soldiers in the Russian army; the temporary release from the fear of Hitlerism, first by the Russo-German Pact of August 23, 1939—a pact which made world war inevitable—then the seizure of Eastern Poland, and the three Baltic Republics which, in 1918, had been given a somewhat shadowy inde-pendence, on the basis of Lenin's determined support of the principle of national self-determination; the swift swoop on Finland, in the last weeks of 1939, in defiance of treaty obliga-tions, and regardless of the grave possibility that it might easily have led to a Franco-British attack on Russia in the spring of 1940, which would have meant irreparable disaster to the whole world; the mean and sordid assassination of Trotsky in his Mexican exile by an agent of the Russian secret police; and, finally, the decision deliberately to create the lamentable myth that Russia won the war alone, Anglo-American aid being dis-missed as a factor of hardly relevant importance; and the gradual strain in relations since the Potsdam Conference of June-July, 1945, out of which the 'cold war' and the rebirth of

181

the old Comintern in its renovated and limited character of the Cominform—all these are part of that price. They are inherent in the dynamic of the Politbureau, once the first 'Troika' decided, on Lenin's death, to exclude Trotsky, and, therefore, the policies of which he was sponsor, from any place in, or influence upon, the direction of Russian affairs.

I must say at once, and with emphasis, three things. First of all, it is obvious that no one outside the inner circle of the Communist Party of Russia can speak with any certainty about the truth or untruth of charges the Politbureau has made, or about the wisdom or the unwisdom of the decisions it has taken, because of the form given to the communist dynamic as the result of the struggle between Stalin and Trotsky which ended, three years after Lenin's death, in Trotsky's utter defeat and the exile which terminated only with his assassination. The published trials of the leaders who were purged, despite the scale upon which they were reported, give us no satisfactory clue to the justice of the Court's findings. There is a moment when one is tempted to feel that the narrative of the well-known journalist, Karl Radek, who was sentenced to two years' imprisonment, is a coherent and lucid explanation; but that involves not only accepting the guilt of Trotsky—the evidence against which is massive—but also belief in the confession of that previously supposed trustworthy Bolshevik, Serebreakov, the Deputy Commissar of Transport, who admitted to what is obviously a physical impossibility, the organisation of thousands of train wrecks daily for practically a decade. It means believing that Rakovski—whom many of us knew for long years with a respect and admiration that increasing intimacy only made deeper — was a blackguardly brigand whose whole life, after Lenin's death, was one gigantic lie; I find it impossible to take such a belief seriously. The murder of Maxim Gorki seems to have served no purpose in any degree proportionate to the crime. The trial of Yagoda and his confession must obviously throw grave doubts on the validity of all the purges previous to the discovery of his own iniquities. And if, at the time of Kirov's assassination in Leningrad in 1934, Stalin could order the execution as an act of revenge and terror of more than one hundred 'deviationists', none of whom had been
182

tried, it becomes by no means easy to understand why, in the utter indifference to public opinion this act implies, it was deemed necessary to stage these grisly dramas the outcome of which seems to have been agreed upon, before the curtain went up, between the accused and Vishinsky, then the Public Prosecutor. In none of these cases have we the material which would enable us to understand the outcome; how baffling they are can, I think, be seen from the fact that—in my judgment, quite mistakenly—so experienced an observer of the Russian scene before the Second World War as my friend, Mr. Louis Fischer, has advanced the theory that, in return for agreeing to confess, none of the accused was executed, and that all of them were merely sent to distant exile. I think it is highly probable—though the evidence is not available—that Marshal Tukhachevski and his colleagues were, at the least, intriguing with foreign Powers against their government; and I think that is shown partly by the fact that the trial, conducted by their military equals, obviously convinced the Court, and that their execution did not destroy the morale of the officer-corps when war came. If there had been any serious doubt of guilt in the mind of the Court, I do not think it possible that Stalin would have received such whole-hearted loyalty from the remarkable group of great commanders who led the Russian armies so superbly against Hitler. I can see no possible justification for the assassination of Trotsky, a major responsibility for which must rest upon Stalin's shoulders. For, even if it be true that Stalin never directly ordered his murder, the M.V.D. must have been fully conscious that the death of Trotsky would, at the least, be an immense relief to the Generalissimo, not least at the particular moment at which it occurred, and organised their plans accordingly. To put it no higher, Stalin's relation to the murder is akin to that of Henry II to the murder of Thomas à Becket; the knights who struck Becket down in Canterbury Cathedral to satisfy Henry's expressed and angry desire that someone 'should rid him of this turbulent priest', behind whom there were organised vital forces with which Henry was at war, were very like the agents of the M.V.D. who, in ridding Stalin of the omnipresent shadow of Trotsky's criticism, rid him of the most influential and able ghost by

183

whom the propaganda of the Communist Parties shows him to have been haunted.

The agricultural collectivisation stands on an entirely different footing. It has never been denied by the Russian government that this policy was carried out with ruthless brutality. Many thousands of peasants were executed, probably some millions were forcibly exiled, and, in revenge, the peasants may well have destroyed something near half the livestock and draught animals, as well as murdered a considerable number of communist officials carrying out the government's orders. But it must be remembered that, by 1928, there was an agrarian crisis of immense proportions. The acreage sown had declined; production was going down, and the peasants were withholding food and raw materials from the market with the dual result of hampering industry and threatening the towns with starvation. Had the government yielded to the peasants' insistence on their right to expand their individual ownership of the land and to produce for the market on an ordinary capitalist basis, there would have been an end to any prospect of socialism in Russia. Sooner or later, the whole experiment would have collapsed, and Russia would have become an overwhelmingly peasant country, incapable of defending itself against the Nazi onslaught which came finally in 1941. Hitler would have been able to detach the Ukraine from the Soviet Union, and, as its defeat in war would have been mainly due to inadequate industrialisation, it is at least highly probable that the decision to collectivise agriculture saved Russia from territorial disintegration.

There was, therefore, no real alternative before the Soviet Government except to choose between collectivising agriculture and abdicating. Once it chose the former, it had to act swiftly, and, given the psychological mood of the peasants, swift action meant compulsion, and compulsion meant what may be fairly described as virtually a civil war. Granted all the brutalities, it is nevertheless evident that, by the end of the third five-year plan, the government's victory in that war brought great benefit to Russia. It not only greatly increased agricultural production. It banished from Russian life the small peasant proprietor, with his narrow petty bourgeois outlook, scratching a bare living from the soil, and only too often, as, notably, the experience of American depression made plain, becoming, through insufficient capital, or a bad harvest or soil erosion, the victim of the moneylender or the merchant. There is a measurable improvement in technique, mechanisation has begun to interest the peasant in adapting himself to the possibilities of scientific agriculture, and the collective farm, geared to the provision of a small but significant place for the individual initiative of the peasant, has given the latter a sense of economic security, has made the communication of scientific knowledge much simpler, and has gone a long way towards solving the relation between the city market and dairy produce. If the experience of the Second World War is any index to the future, it looks as though the collective farm has come to stay, and that the government and the peasantry will find ways and means to an accommodation which, though it will be slow in coming, will accept collectivisation as the datum line, increase the place of the machine in farming, seek to relate a remuneration of individual effort within the collective, and make possible, through contact with scientific agriculture, a new breadth of outlook in the peasant mind. It looks, I say, as though this is the probable evolution. The alternative would be the revival of conflict between the government and the peasant, and the reappearance of the historic antagonism between town and country. In that alternative, of course, there is the possibility of another and dangerous civil war which might not only prevent swift recovery from the Nazi invasion, but jeopardise the whole Revolution itself. That is why I think it likely that experiments in accommodation will be built around the collective farms; for they alone offer the prospect of a continually advancing standard of life for the peasant in which his relation to the government solves problems for him that he has neither the capital nor the power, nor the knowledge, to solve alone. A basis for agrarian progress has been found; what matters now is that the superstructure built upon it should be developed with common sense and imagination.

If it is legitimate, for the purpose of clarity, to separate what are, in fact, the two sides of a single force, the internal dynamic of a government's policy from the dynamic that is the outcome

of external pressures, the examples I have just discussed illustrate the elements out of which the internal dynamic of the Russian government's activities were compounded. The external dynamic is more complex in character; and to make its meaning appear in direct perspective, it is important briefly to look back to the October Revolution and its consequences. It is fundamental to remember that Lenin led that revolution in a defeated and devastated country, with the enemy knocking at its gates, his own people hungry and fatigued and divided, with an industrial machine hardly less broken than the administrative apparatus, and at a stage in the First World War where the initiative still seemed to lie pretty fully in German hands. He saw the success of the Bolsheviks as the prelude to a European Revolution, and he assumed that this European Revolution was the condition for the survival of Bolshevik authority. His calculation was a mistaken one. He had not only to force upon his colleagues agreement to sign with Germany the humiliating treaty of Brest-Litovsk; with them, he had to face five years of grim civil war, in which no quarter was given or taken, and his major opponents were supported by the anti-German forces; with them, also, he had to face direct intervention in the North by Great Britain, on the Pacific by Japan and the United States, and in the Caucasus by Great Britain and France, which came fairly near to detaching Georgia from the Soviet Union. His Government had no place, after German defeat, at the peace conference at Versailles. When the newly-formed Polish Republic attacked Russia, it was saved from defeat by Allied aid, and he was compelled to agree to Polish boundaries which even Lord Curzon believed to be without justification. He saw the brief revolts of his sympathisers in Hungary and Bavaria crushed by the threat of starvation in the first instance, and by the collaboration of the Weimar Government with the traditional German general staff in the second. If his government received some vocal sympathy from small sections of European Labour, in the first five years of his Government the only effective aid he secured was the insistence in Great Britain by the socialist and trade union Councils of Action in 1920 that Mr. Churchill's patronage of intervention should cease, and the relief to miti-
186

gate the horrors of famine and disease which came from the United States and from the nobly unforgettable humanitarian effort of that great European, the explorer Nansen. Immense claims from foreign nationals upon the newborn Russian state were supported by their governments. He could not secure even the beginning of commercial relations with Great Britain until 1921; *de jure* recognition was not offered until the last few weeks of the first Labour Government in 1924. The Rapallo Conference, indeed, gave him the chance to make a far-reaching agreement in 1922 with Walther Rathenau on behalf of the unstable and half-dead Weimar Republic. From the United States, Russia was to receive *de jure* recognition only in the second year of Franklin Roosevelt's first term, when Hitler had already arrived at power. There were no international loans available, either through the League of Nations or from private bankers, for a revolutionary state in whose permanence few statesmen believed, and of whose evil character and danger to democracy most of them, not least two of the most outstanding men in the British Labour Party, Mr. Ramsay MacDonald and Mr. Philip (later Viscount) Snowden, were profoundly convinced. It is not an exaggeration to say that, from the October Revolution until it joined the League of Nations in 1934, Russia survived less by its own strength than by the inability of its enemies to agree upon how it should be destroyed, and that, while aid and flattery were lavished upon fascist régimes like those of Mussolini and Horthy, a broken Russia had to proceed to rebuild its shattered foundations without sympathy or goodwill from any foreign power.

The impact of this situation upon its economic position was inevitably profound. That Russia has become a great industrial power was made clear by the war. But it is also obvious that there is a very large wastage of manpower, above all of skilled manpower, and that this wastage makes the level of output per worker still seriously less than in the older industrial civilisation. Lenin never failed to insist that 'in the long run', as he put it, 'the productivity of labour is the supreme factor in assuring the triumph of a social order'. If this criterion is applied to the Russian position, it is not possible to deny that the workers in the Soviet Union have not yet become effectively

187

adapted to the technique of the machine, and that despite the control of discipline by manager and foreman, despite piece-rates and bonus-systems, despite severe punishment for absenteeism and late arrival at work. Even the so-called Stakhanovite movement, despite its many outstanding personal achievements, may well have done more harm than good. It widely increased production norms, and it brought to many workers an excitement in the technique of their jobs, a wider understanding of the relatedness of all the different factors of workshop organisation, but it was not sufficiently an expression of total organisation in an industry. It was sometimes recklessly individualist. The passion for production records often means the uneconomic use of machines, an increase in accidents through the pace of work, injury to the health of the workers through the reckless determination to rival Alexey Stakhanov's fame. The new productive norms were too rarely the outcome of scientific study and too much the result of an individual passion for fame and reward, like that of a great tennis player or of a golf champion. It is possible also that Stakhanovism drove too deep a wedge between an aristocracy of 'champion' workers, and the rank and file who saw a new craft aristocracy able to attain a wage thirty to one hundred times as much as the average worker. It may even be said that Stakhanovism injured the general factory discipline by its tendency to make the extraordinary the measure of the normal, and thus to drive the worker by fear instead of co-operation. It centralised far too much authority in the industrial leaders and managers; it left an important contradiction by announcing reliance upon the social initiative of the worker on the one hand, and upon the penalties imposed for violation of factory rules on the other. The Politbureau itself recognised this. At the Eighteenth Congress of the Russian Communist Party, one of its secretaries, Malenkov, vigorously attacked 'the big and the little factory dictators'; he spoke of 'Soviet ignoramuses, who preen themselves on their proletarian origin'. He lashed the 'party tongue-waggers' who announced large targets the fulfilment of which they did not know how to organise.[1] But he did not say how much this outcome was the consequence of a factory pendulum

[1] Speech at the Eighteenth Party Congress. February 15-20, 1941.

188

which vacillated violently between production as a great competitive game, and production as a half-integrated system of relations in which the workers at the basis of the pyramid were often ruthlessly punished because they were slow in adjusting themselves to a new and sudden pace of effort.

The overall picture of Russian industrial development is, I suggest, one of immense achievement and immense waste. The achievement is seen partly in the sheer volume of production in post-war Russia as compared with pre-war Russia, the wide opportunities of technical training which the government has created, the remarkable eagerness, both in young and old, for knowledge, both scientific and cultural, the awakening of backward peoples to a level of patriotic effort which has enabled them to throw off the frustrating inhibitions of centuries. But all this is set in the context of quantity rather than quality, of dictatorship rather than democracy, of fear rather than of consent. There are many great scientists in Russia; there are far too many the basis of whose work shows inadequate training marked by narrowness and the lack of profound perspective. The passionate thirst for understanding often dries up because it finds by grim experience that it must drink only from the fountains which the government has provided. There are rich endowments for science and technology, but there is an imposed and harsh orthodoxy which has a quite inadequate appreciation of that restless and spontaneous curiosity which lies at the heart of vital discovery. A great culture, with its pervasive influence, cannot be the outcome of minds not free to roam where the spirit takes them.

Nor must it be forgotten how few of the dominant generation in Russia to-day have a first-hand acquaintance with the revolutionary dynamic of the October glory. The trade unions have been compelled by the party to exchange that exciting dynamic for complete subordination to the decisions of the Politbureau in all matters of fundamental concern. True and important as it is to recognise that he no longer faces a private employer with the power to exploit him for gain, the worker may often face a bureaucratic-minded manager whose fear of being held a failure by those above him, drives him into unnecessary rigour to those below. Even when one has granted

189

the vast opportunity that is given the Soviet citizen to point out this or that small weakness in the operation of the social and economic system, he is given no effective opportunity to express his views on the foundations of the régime. He moves amid a ceaseless stream of propaganda which exhorts him, at all costs, to safeguard the Revolution from its enemies outside, to trust his leaders without limit, to recognise the vast superiority of his way of life to that of foreign nations outside the boundaries of Russia. His thinking is swept down avenues with high walls over which he seeks to look at his peril.

The dictatorship of Stalin and his colleagues has enabled great strides to be taken in the economic evolution of Russia. It is easy to see that, without dictatorship, order could not have been wrested from the chaos left by war and revolution. It is easy even to see that the large-scale industrialisation of Russia could not have been attempted, much less achieved, by the leisurely processes of democratic discussion in a peasant society to the members of which the new machine-technology was a second revolution. It is again easy to see that the industrialised economy could only have been made to serve the needs of national defence by making the fulfilment of these a priority far more important than the provision of an abundance of consumer goods. But to the degree that the Russian economic order has become a socialist order, and in proportion to its advance to high levels, the relaxation of the dictatorship was fundamental if there was not to emerge a contradiction between the economic and the political ways of Russian life. For when the foundations of Soviet industrialism had been firmly laid, there was no real relaxation of the dictatorship on its political side. The Soviet citizen remained politically immature, and the leaders of the Communist Party were, so to say, convinced of the need to perpetuate their own authority as a dictatorship. They were convinced by their own propaganda that it would be a threat to the safety of Russia to release the initiative of ordinary citizens from the omnipresent shadow of repression and to branch out into large-scale democratic experiment.

By taking this view, the Russian leaders not only strengthened, both in industry and politics, the very forces of that bureaucracy they professed to be ardent to curb, but they

190

weakened the forces which, culturally and psychologically, would have enabled them to move, with relative ease and swiftness, to the plane where the Soviet citizen demonstrated the power of a socialist economic order to issue into that régime of democracy and freedom which ought to have been the result of the defeat of Hitler and Mussolini. The Russian victory, that is to say, ought to have involved the democratisation of the political system. The new life ought to have begun as a call to freedom. That it failed to have this character is a tragedy the responsibility of which must rest very heavily upon the Western Powers. Their statesmen do not answer this charge by counter-charges of Russian suspicion and obstruction, of Russian ambitions for expansion, of an obstinate Russian refusal to respond to offers of treaties which reciprocally guaranteed peace. For, first of all, the Russian leaders approach the whole problem in the background of their massive experience of Western hostility before 1939 and the contrast with the aid given to fascist dictators and the unhappy combination of appeasement and excuses offered for Japan and Hitler down to the very eve of the outbreak of the Second World War. Secondly, the Russians are bound to contrast the attitude of the Western Powers to the Italo-Abyssinian War, on the one hand, and to the Russo-Finnish War, on the other. Thirdly, they are bound to remember the deep general conviction, both in London and in Washington, that, in familiar phrase, the German Army would sweep through Russia like a knife through butter. They are bound, in the fourth place, to note the long wrangle among the Western Powers about the establishment of a Second Front at a time when Russia's existence hung in the balance and to view that wrangle in the light of Mr. Churchill's own statement, made through Mr. Harold Macmillan to the European Consultative Assembly, that, as the heroic martyrdom of Stalingrad approached, he was constantly turning over in his mind ways and means of safeguarding Europe against what he termed 'Russian barbarism'. They must, further, weigh the significance of the immense post-war propaganda against Russia, the eager pressure for a preventive atomic war, the attempt even to thrust them into the position of men seeking expansion by aggression, the encouragement,

191

under the special patronage of the American Government of Mr. Churchill, and, to a large extent, the Labour Government in Great Britain, of a solid anti-Russian bloc, and the readiness of the United States to assist any people whose government will take an anti-Russian 'line'.

The very fact that it is the peoples, and not the governments, of Western Europe and America, which have prevented the British Foreign Office and the American State Department from recognising Franco Spain must seem hardly less significant in Moscow than the creation of a Western German state, with very much the character of the Weimar Republic in the two or three years before Hitler's advent to power. Nor is it possible for the Russian leaders not to note that the Vatican— the first organisation to conclude an accord with Hitler—has taken the offensive against Russia and its allies all over the world, and is seeking, with strong support from London and Washington, to give the protective colouration of a religious crusade to what is, in fact, a world counter-revolution in which, in the name of religious freedom, the Vatican seeks to persuade Roman Catholics to resist the secular authorities in spheres which it is very difficult to regard as ecclesiastical. It is striking to note how swiftly and eagerly the Western Powers have sought to protect Roman Catholic leaders in countries where Russian influence predominates, while they have felt themselves unable to protest against repression of socialists and communists in Spain and Greece—the Greek régime being a client government of Great Britain and America — on the ground that it is contrary to international usage to interfere in the affairs of a sovereign and independent state. And when, in Poland, Cardinal-Archbishop Hlond condoned the grave pogrom against the Jews at Kielce, it is notable that none of the Western Powers made public protest to the Vatican against the encouragement he thus gave to what had been one of the most ugly features in the national life of pre-war Poland. To this must be added a word or two about the situation in the Far East. All the major weight of American aid and influence has been thrown on the side of Chiang Kai-shek and the Nationalists. It continued even after the corruption and tyranny of Chiang's government was patent to the whole world. It continued even after it was obvious that much of the military

192

aid given to him was being sold by his own officials to the Chinese Communists against whom it was to be used. It did not cease until most of Nationalist China had fallen to the Communists, with whole armies deserting to them, with Chiang himself a half-fugitive in Formosa, and his wife, as well as other leading members of the Kung dynasty, in self-imposed exile. There were warnings, and to spare, of the character of Chiang's government, from General Stilwell, for example, before the surrender of Japan, and from General Marshall after it, as well as from nearly every responsible American correspondent who knew from within the vicious interests which dominated Chiang's policies. Mao Tse-tung and his followers were certainly Communist. But most observers bore witness to the two facts that, in the territory they won, they governed with honesty, and that they won the allegiance of its inhabitants by the depth of the effort they made to help the poor Chinese to help themselves. The Chinese Communists were, of course, profoundly attached to Moscow; but the Russian attitude to them was diplomatically beyond criticism until it became evident that the Civil War which broke out after the Japanese surrender was, in effect, made in Washington. Excuse after excuse was invented to enable Chiang to defeat the Communists; the only people deceived by the excuses were the Americans themselves. It is an American journalist, long resident in China and of deserved eminence, who has said that 'Asia to-day regards America as the last great bastion of reaction, a nation that speaks of freedom but, in the ultimate analysis, always aligns itself on the side of the *status quo*. Even for the most conservative of Americans a conservative foreign policy is unrealistic; as between stability and change, change must win . . . the peasant will believe that that system is best, and offers the most liberty, which gives him the quickest solution to the troubles of his daily life. He will vote for it, fight for it, die for it. If we move to halt this tide we are lost. Not all our powers can do more than preserve a brief and somewhat ignoble isolation'.[1]

After Japan's surrender, Russia made two immense blunders in China. The first was the Sino-Russian Treaty; the second was

[1] Theodore H. White and Annalee Jacoby, *Thunder Out Of China* (New York, 1946) p. 320.

the ruthless cruelty with which Manchuria was stripped of all its machinery which was transported for use to the Soviet Union. But Russia took no part in the post-war civil conflict, even though it was clear that the American support for Chiang Kai-shek was, in its basic purpose, a policy aimed at preventing China from falling under Russian influence and control. What adjustment, then, does America propose to make when Nationalist China is crumbling to pieces, and the bankruptcy of American policy has been admitted by the Secretary of State? We can answer that question only in a negative way. We know that no more aid is to be given to the Nationalists, despite interested pleas both from the military and from certain financial and commercial groups. We know that American diplomatic offices are being closed everywhere in China, and that American residents and their wives have been advised to return as quickly as they can to the United States. The ambassador of Nationalist China is still recognised in Washington as the representative of the whole Chinese people, and Nationalist China still has its seat, and, therefore, a veto power, in the Security Council of the United Nations. To Communist China, of course, no recognition is extended; and we have no light upon what is in the mind of the American Government save that its view of a Communist China will be determined by its relations to Russia. It is difficult to be certain what this means in so swiftly changing a situation. But it looks as though the United States regards China as an important instrument in the 'cold war'; and that this was the primary motive for the support of Chiang Kai-shek, and that accordingly, a Communist China which refused to accept this rôle would have the uncertain status, with all its difficulties, imposed upon Soviet Russia from 1917 to 1934 when the United States withheld diplomatic recognition from it. Whether this would be followed by an American veto upon the entrance of Communist China into the United Nations we have still no means of knowing. What does emerge is the fact that, if the Chinese Communists can become the effective government of the whole Chinese people, there will be an overwhelming adjustment in the relations of the great Powers in the Far East.

That adjustment will be emphasised by American policy in

194

Japan. Here, though an Allied Commission has had a formal existence, all the real control of Japan has been in the hands of General Douglas MacArthur whose responsibility is, through the American War Department, to the President of the United States. It is the General's view, in which he appears to have the support of the War Department,[1] that, in the four years that have passed since the surrender of Japan, he has succeeded in transforming it into the true image of a 'Christian democracy', and that it has recovered sufficiently from the evil habits of that fascist militarism which led it, not only into partnership with Hitler and Mussolini, but into the effort so carefully planned and so barbarously executed to establish a dominion over the Far East akin to that which Hitler sought to build in Europe. General MacArthur thinks that a treaty might now properly be concluded with it restoring it, of course upon conditions, to independent statehood once again; under his direction it already has had the benefit of free elections, which have given it a parliamentary system with an executive responsible to the legislature, under, for the present, the supervisory veto of General MacArthur. The attitude of the American Government to the General's work seems one of complete approval. The Under-Secretary for the Army, Mr. Tracey S. Voorhus, after a fortnight's inspection of Japan told the Press of his 'deep and abiding respect for the truly historic work General MacArthur has done, is doing, and will continue to do, in post-war Japan'. 'The success,' Mr. Voorhus continued, 'which the United States had achieved in Japan and Western Germany was due to the essentially humanitarian character of American occupation which was made possible by the inherent humanity of America.' 'Two great and civilised peoples,' he explained, 'had fallen into evil ways under despicable leadership. But the genius of the United States had seen that rather than punish them, it was necessary to restore, help, and re-educate them . . . The United States had no ulterior motive in doing this, but merely sought a peaceful world.'[2]

No reasonable person has the right to doubt the humanitarian character of American occupation either in Germany or in Japan; there is a magnanimity before suffering in the

[1] London *Times*, Sept. 12, 1949.
[2] London *Times*, Sept. 12, 1949, p. 3.

historic behaviour of the American people which is beyond praise. But to accept this view does not involve the conviction that General MacArthur is right in his judgment that Japan is now a 'Christian democracy' ready for a treaty which restores it to sovereign independence, or that Mr. Voorhus is right in assuming that Western Germany and Japan may be regarded as having been re-educated into the habits of democratic freedom by our defeating their 'despicable leaders', and helping them rather than punishing them for being misled. To many of us, the danger of a revival of chauvinism in Western Germany remains acute; and that is the expressed warning to the people of Western Germany by the British High Commissioner, General Sir Brian Robertson. There is much evidence to show that the denazification of Western Germany has failed to root it out; and that the elections of 1949 have put the political power into the hands of Right Wing parties which, while they are supported by many sincere democrats to whom the Hitler epoch was hateful, also shelter powerful forces which regard the one error of Germany between 1933 and 1945 to consist in its defeat; and to this must be added the vital fact that the ownership of industry in Western Germany, and particularly the massive potential of the Ruhr, remains in the same hands as before Hitler came to power, largely, that is to say, in the hands of the men who put Hitler into power, and gave him enthusiastic assistance in the fulfilment of his policies. Much the same is true of Japan. Once it began to recover from the shock of atomic devastation, of the blow to its prestige involved in unconditional surrender and the reduction of the Emperor's status from that of a god to that of an ordinary monarch, it is difficult to see that the foundations for any fundamental change have been laid by General MacArthur. It has, of course, no armed forces, and no means of direct access to the raw materials essential to their re-equipment if it had them. But the party structure of the country is very much what it was before Pearl Harbour, save that the militarist party has under the Occupation necessarily disappeared, and the Left Wing parties, though unwelcome to General MacArthur, are less frowned upon than in the days of General Tojo. The trade unions have an inferior position, with serious limitations both

196

upon their political activity and their freedom to strike. Japanese industry still remains in the hands of the two notorious empires which exploited it for their private advantage. There has been no large-scale agrarian reform. There has been no large-scale social reform. There is more freedom of speech than there was before the defeat; and General MacArthur is now a temporary divinity who has taken over the Emperor's functions and must, therefore, receive the incense which once was offered to Hirohito. Apart from the Supreme Commander and his admirers, no one knows what will emerge in Japan when the occupation ends. That its ruling class will be deferential and humble to their conquerors while they remain in Japan is naturally beyond all question. But there is really no serious evidence to suggest that the foundations of fundamental change have been made by General MacArthur. He established a conservative government in a tradition-ridden country, and placed behind it the strength of the armed forces at his disposal; and he devolved political power, subject to his veto, upon the industrialists and landowners who formerly shared in its exercise. Quite naturally they were grateful to him, and loud in his praises. But an outsider may be pardoned if he is unable, like the Supreme Commander, to detect in those flattering eulogies the authentic voice of a Christian democracy.

CHAPTER XI

I T would take me too far afield to discuss in separate detail each area of the Far East, and the American evaluation, sometimes the British also, of its meaning. What, above all, concerns me is to point out that each element in this evaluation is part of an overall stategic conception of that 'cold war' which is to contain Russia and so to prevent the spread of Communism over the ancient East, thus preserving, it is assumed, the vast Asiatic continent for the Western philosophy of freedom and democracy. The Americans are convinced that only force can prevent the Russian expansionism, and that its success means the subjugation of 'free' populations to dictator ship, as well as the loss of the chance to assist in the development of areas the resources of which are unknown, and may well be among the most potentially valuable in the world. Should Asia be driven or persuaded into Communism, it is obvious that the American or Western 'way of life' would lose, despite its present technological superiority, the chance of becoming the major factor in shaping the future of civilisation. It is assumed in Washington that there is profound reason to fear aggression and infiltration from Russia and its instruments unless there is always sufficient force at hand, capable of swift mobilisation, to arrest any effort on Russia's part to break through the circle which, mainly under American auspices, the Atlantic Powers have thrown round Russia to limit and to mitigate its influence.

It sounds, I know, absurd to suggest that the attitude of America to Communism and, above all, to Communism under Russian direction, is inspired by fear; yet it is increasingly difficult to interpret the postulates of American foreign policy in any other way. It is not only the vast scale of American rearmament; it is not only, either, the domestic suspicion in the United States of most liberal opinions as the outcome of inspiration secretly derived from Moscow; it is not even the increasingly urgent emphasis that is given to the importance of the stockpile of growingly more powerful atomic bombs. All these have a bearing on the ultimate content of the American attitude which the outsider is bound to regard as significant; the place of the Federal Bureau of Investigation in the American Government, the range of its activities, bear a startling resemblance to the habits of the police-state which Americans themselves denounce so angrily outside the borders of their own country. But the really startling strand in American foreign policy is its organisation of the Grand Alliance against Russia — inadequately camouflaged as alliance against 'aggression'—which persuades them not only to underwrite the North Atlantic Security Pact, but to invest strength, also, in the protection of Greece and Turkey as, so to say, frontier forces against Communism, and to toy with the possibility of an arrangement with Franco Spain, though it is impossible even for the most rabid of anti-Russians in the United States to regard these Mediterranean states as having even a remote relation to freedom and democracy. Any calm and detached American observer will agree that the spread of Communism cannot be effectively stayed by force of arms; and he can see, almost without argument, that were the 'cold war' to be transformed into a 'shooting war', whatever else it would destroy, one of its earliest, and most permanent victims would be that 'American way of life' which, either in Europe or Asia, it was intended to defend. The American Government is not now taking limited and calculated risks; it is moving remorselessly to risks it is impossible to measure. It has made the grave psychological error not only of preparing the mind of its own people for a third world war, but of creating the impression of a readiness to assist any foreign government which demonstrates its hostility to Communism.

I do not doubt at all that its attitude has been in a considerable degree governed by the follies and stupidities of the Russian Government itself. Beginning at least as early as its inept attempt to evade its treaty obligation to evacuate Iran at the end of the war, Russian foreign policy has been a crude, and often brutal, effort to build up strength for the Soviet Union against any attempt to push it back into the dangerous isolation it experienced between the two world wars. No one can honestly defend the wholesale looting of which it was
200

guilty in Manchuria. No one can honestly defend the ruthless use of allied Communist Parties to impose the dictatorships known as 'people's democracies' in Eastern Europe, least of all the way in which, once the allied Communist Party had seized the reins of power, there followed purges, treason trials, censorship of the Press, suppression of free thought in the universities, wholesale detention for long periods without trials, and the establishment of a compulsory one-party system as the alternative to the kind of uneasy coalition where, as in Hungary, other parties are permitted to exist on condition that they dance as puppets on a string held by the Communist leader who is temporarily in favour at Moscow. Nor does the Russian Government win respect from the outside world by the way in which it conducts the proceedings of the Cominform. It is clear that this organisation does not meet to discuss the common problems of its members on equal terms; it meets to work out the application of orders from Moscow by its members. The experience of Yugoslavia under Tito has made it obvious that Moscow regards the other Communist states as dependencies which must obey its will, and that their refusal to accept this position of subordination not merely results in a world-wide campaign of execration, but in the organisation, under the authority of Moscow, of conspiracy to overthrow a recalcitrant government from within by all the means it is possible to mobilise.

I do not attach the same significance to Russian obstruction in the United Nations as I do to the matter I have listed above. The veto power, against Russia's use of which vehement protest has been made, seems to me inherent in a body which is not intended to be a world-government; and I think Mr. Bevin was wholly right in saying that its use must be limited by the growth of conventions about its employment rather than by specific formulae written into the Charter. It is, no doubt, a matter of profound regret that agreement could not be reached about the use of atomic energy. But here I am bound to say that, in my own view, the case against the acceptance of the American plan made by the Russians is far stronger than they knew how to make it. There is, in fact, hardly an aspect of the American offer which does not contain important loopholes which would enable the United States to retain a monopoly of the atomic bomb until it was satisfied that the International Atomic Authority—upon which Russia would be in a minority without the power of veto—had fulfilled the conditions upon which the American Government would reveal its special knowledge and agree to hand over its stock of bombs. It is, moreover, clear that, under the American plan, the Russians would easily find themselves at a disadvantage in the disposition of atomic plants, and under a serious handicap if vested interests in capitalist states, like those of oil and coal, were influential in slowing down the pace of research into the use of atomic energy for industrial purposes. No doubt the Russians have used the platform of the United Nations, both in its primary organs and in its sub-committees, to engage bluntly and crudely in propaganda against the Western Powers, often with all too little excuse; I think it should be said that the representatives of the Western Powers have amply retorted in kind. In any case, what matters in the proceedings of the United Nations is of secondary importance in the sense that the differences which emerge there are the effect, and not the cause, of tension upon other planes to the roots of which it is essential to penetrate.

Here, I think, it is fundamental to bear in mind two things. The first is that just as fear of Communism has become an American obsession, so fear of capitalist attack on Russia led by the United States has become a Russian obsession. It is easy to see why. The Russian leaders have never forgotten capitalist intervention in the Soviet Union at the end of the First World War. All their fears were revived and deepened by Mr. Churchill's speech at Fulton, Missouri, in March, 1947, which, not unfairly, they related to his earlier anti-Bolshevism. Since that speech, Mr. Churchill has been the leader of a consistent campaign for an anti-Russian bloc, expressions of which may fairly be found in the North Atlantic Security bloc, in the establishment of Western Union, and in the decision to split Germany into two by the creation of a West German Republic, the first Chancellor of which announced, as he took office, that revision of the existing Eastern frontiers was a primary object of his policy. They see in the Truman Doctrine, and, indeed, in

202

the Marshall Plan, a deliberate effort by the United States to use its immense economic power to fight Communism all over the world, and, especially, of course, in the Soviet Union. They recognise the weakness implied in the massive losses they suffered during the war; probably twenty-five million people became homeless, more than half their livestock was destroyed, and at least half their agricultural machinery, as well as great cities like Kiev, Odessa, Stalingrad, and Kharkov, not to speak of millions of human beings, civilian as well as military. No one can know better than the Russian leaders that they have every-thing to gain by peace and everything to lose by war. They are convinced, however, that their safety is proportionate to their strength, and that, once they showed signs of weakness, they would be subject to aggressive attack. That belief has received what is, perhaps, its most important confirmation in the revela-tion that, in the autumn of 1942, when Mr. Churchill was praising, with enthusiasm the heroic achievements of the Russian Army, he was also thinking out ways and means of preventing what, even then, he called 'Russian barbarism' from being able to dominate Europe. Nor do the Russians see, in the offers of security they received—Mr. James Byrnes's forty-year treaty, or Mr. Bevin's offer of a fifty-year pact—anything sufficiently specific in content to offset the inferences they draw from the persistent growth in the intensity of the 'cold war'.

So long as these fears, on both sides, lead to the anger and irritation by which the whole atmosphere is rendered dark, I see no prospect of any serious relaxation in the Russian dicta-torship. Stalin and his colleagues will take no chances of risking the creation in Russia of a discontent that may be fomented from outside by the modern techniques of propaganda. They will continue to be convinced that the activities of communist parties in capitalist democracies, even in capitalist democracies where a socialist government is in office, is not less a legitimate protection of their safety than the less direct methods by which the Western Powers safeguard themselves against communist permeation. They cannot help, moreover, watching with some eagerness the possibility that the trend of events, certainly in Italy, and perhaps in France also, may give them new allies whose impact may well change the whole international scene.

They may well suspect that, in the creation of a West German Republic, the United States, Great Britain and France, have created an instrument intended to be the base of hostility against Russia, to throw overboard both Yalta and Potsdam, and to be, not only a constant source of friction in the separated Russian zone of Germany, but also both a means of increasing the industrial potential which can be organised against the Cominform states, and an additional insurance against the danger that 'free enterprise' may have to give way to socialism in a Europe which cannot otherwise find an effective pattern of either economic or political unity. The West German Republic has no more than a formal democratic appearance. All its major characteristics bear a painful resemblance to Weimar Germany just before Brüning gave way to Von Papen who in his turn opened the road to Hitler. There is a solid Social Democratic Party; but it is mainly a middle-aged party, and the best weapons it might have hoped to possess were withheld from it when the British Government failed to alter the structure of economic relations, especially in the Ruhr, and despite its pledge to socialise the heavy industries there. There is a deep chauvinism in the first government of Western Germany. Revision of frontiers is already openly demanded. The constitutional forms adopted at Bonn give no more promise of stability than those adopted at Weimar; there is, indeed, an unhappy, because profound, resemblance between them. Even after over four years' effort, neither the passionate drama of Nuremberg, nor the punishment of the horde of lesser Nazi gangsters has made any deep impression upon the mass of the population. Denazification has not been a seriously measurable success. Anti-semitism persists. The immense effort put into the re-education of the Germans has not been very satisfactory; the best evidence we have suggests that, especially among the younger generation, the main outlook is a pessimistic nihilism which is more easily accessible to extremist doctrines, especially on the right, than to doctrines which seek to domesticate liberal ideas in Germany. It is notable, too, that the recognition of German responsibility for the Second World War is superficial compared to the depth of German conviction that the country's post-war sufferings more than wipe out that responsibility. A

204

great deal of Nazism remains, and many of those who occupied important positions under the Hitler régime retain, especially in industry, a great influence and even authority. The hatred of Russia is profound; the hatred of Poland is profound also, and perhaps more dangerous because it is deeply permeated by contempt. An unarmed West German Republic, denied full independence, unable to secure the restoration of full German unity even within the provisional frontiers agreed upon at Potsdam, is bound to remain in large degree a pathological community, denied the fulfilment of its supreme ambitions. An armed West German Republic is like a battery of heavy guns pointed directly to the East. The German policy of the Western Powers only serves, in fact, to deepen the Russian fears that the grand coalition is being prepared step by step against the communist states under the guidance and with the resources of the United States. It only intensifies the deep suspicions which have broken the prospect of mutual confidence between the two great groups of Powers. Every step in Russian policy must be interpreted in terms of a fear which haunts the whole world like a demon which we grimly lack the power to exorcise.

A world beset by fear is a world afraid of freedom. This realisation is fundamental to the grasp of the Russian position. We are dealing with a people which has passed from one dictatorship to another without the experience of constitutional government. We are dealing with the aftermath of a century's conspiratorial effort. Not least, we are dealing with a political philosophy which has the power and tenacity, the compulsion and the passion of a religion to those who profess it. It is in the profoundly religious character of Russian Communism that there lies, I think, the secret of its tremendous dynamic. Therein lies its capacity to evoke a total response from all who are devoted to its service. That is why they can accept the writings of its leaders as a scripture to be dogmatically expounded. That is why also we find in the ranks of Communism the martyrs, the heretics, the mixture of compassion and cruelty, of complex suspicion and simplicity of faith, of conviction that the gospel must be spread, and of insistence that those who hold it are a race apart, with an insight of exceptional profundity the

205

possession of which is the condition of salvation. No one who has watched the evolution of Russian Communism over the last thirty years can avoid the conviction that all the phenomena it has revealed bear the closest resemblance to the phenomena of Christianity. I would only add three things. The first is the need for the outsider to realise that the rationalism of the Communist, like that of St. Thomas Aquinas or of Cardinal Newman, begins only at the point where the creed has been accepted, and it has become the purpose of the believer to draw correct inferences from given axioms and postulates; the one thing that is barred is his right to examine their validity. In this sense I suggest that a book like Newman's *Grammar of Assent* expounds not less the approach of the Communist than of the Roman Catholic to the faith he holds. Given the acceptance of the creed, there is no escape from the conclusions it emphasises; *extra ecclesiam nulla salus* holds equally for Moscow as for Rome. That is why, in his final spiritual crisis, the convicted heretic seeks salvation by the admission that his errors are sins. He confesses lest he tempt others into the damnation of his heresy.

The second point is the totalitarian character of the creed. We who are the heirs of the Renaissance and the Reformation, who have inferred from the experience they embody the wisdom not only of toleration, but also of a certain scepticism about the permanent and ultimate validity of the values we hold, do not easily accept the rise of a new church, which, like the Roman Catholic Church in the middle ages, declines to accept the claim to autonomy of any realm of thought or conduct. Just as mediaeval science was set in the context of the Roman Catholic Church, as were also philosophy and art and politics, so likewise the Communist Church insists that what, outside its authority, men have come to see as secular and independent realms, must be reduced to its unified sovereignty. So art and music and literature, science and technology, every aspect of life, it is not too much to say, are ordered to conform to a pattern prescribed for them by the governing body of a Communist Church, the Central Committee of the Russian Communist Party. It is, of course, strange to us; we find it difficult to conceive that, for example, Mr. Herbert Morrison,

206

as Lord President of the Council, should tell the Royal Society what line it must follow in its biological researches, or insist to the Universities that they must discontinue the recommendation of certain familiar text-books to their students; and we should, I think, grow very angry if Sir Stafford Cripps, as Chancellor of the Exchequer, insisted upon the closing, say, of the Cavendish Laboratory at Cambridge, or the Biometrical Laboratory in the University of London on the ground that, since the validity of democratic socialism was beyond discussion, these institutions were failing to translate its principles into their work. Certainly, we should be overwhelmed with surprise if the workers in the Cavendish Laboratory, or the Director of the Biometrical Laboratory suddenly began to beat their breasts, to confess to abominable ideological sins, and to promise, amid roars of applause, to mend their ways in future.

But none of this behaviour would be surprising in the Roman Catholic Church. We do not need to go further back than Galileo to see it operative in the realm of science, or to the Vatican Council of 1870 to see it operative in that realm where the boundaries of church and state touch one another, or to the well-known Encyclical of Leo XIII on economic questions, or to the vigorous attack, in the first years of this century, which Pius X launched on philosophies of which he was advised by his councillors to disapprove. It is a little startling to see an historian as eminent as Duchesne admit frankly that there are areas where the facts must be adjusted to the requirements of the Vatican. No detached observer can examine the Church's treatment of Döllinger, or Loisy, or of Tyrell, without recognising the baneful spirit of the mediaeval Inquisition. Nor must we forget that, so long as the Papacy exerted temporal power, or was given a specially privileged position by the Government of a community like Spain, or Naples, it enforced until well on into the nineteenth century, conformity in belief and behaviour over the whole realm of life, that it searched out refusal to conform by an elaborate system of espionage, and that, directly or undirectly, it imposed sanctions to compel obedience which were ruthless in conception and ruthless in operation. At least from its adoption by Constantine, the Roman Catholic Church moved steadily towards totalitarianism; in its conviction that it possessed the secret of salvation, it had no hesitation

207

in persecuting, not merely its opponents, but even those whose attachment to its doctrines was passionately sincere the moment their interpretation of its doctrines did not commend itself to the rulers of the Church at any given time. And, even after the Reformation, and the movement it involved towards a secular state, the Church has never ceased to fight a rearguard action against the attempt to narrow its authority. Nor has anything been more notable than its willingness to ally itself with any force from whose action it could secure the protection it deemed desirable. The Vatican's concordat with Mussolini was obviously a source of immense strength to an evil régime; and this generation ought not to be allowed to forget that the Pope recognised Hitler with a swiftness that outpaced the action of any other sovereign. And to all this, moreover, must be added the important fact, so remarkably exhibited in the exquisite art of Newman's *Apologia,* that members of the Church have been able to discover the secret of freedom in the very depth of their submission to its authority.

There are two other aspects in the likeness of ecclesiastical totalitarianism, as exemplified in Rome and in Moscow, which deserve at least brief annotation. The Church's triad, sin, confession, penance, with forgiveness as the outcome when that cycle is completed, finds its exact parallel in the Communist Party even though in the latter the process, generally, has a more public character save where the offence has arisen from an embrace, conscious or unconscious, of heresy. Anyone who has seen a party 'cleansing' in Russia would find it difficult to believe that he is not observing in operation the ritual of an ecclesiastical organisation. The second aspect is the fascinating combination of absolutism and democracy in a single organisation alike in the Roman Church and the Communist Party. The centralisation of ultimate power in the Papacy has the closest possible resemblance to the centralisation of ultimate power in the Politbureau. The humblest parish priest in Italy has risen from obscurity to the overwhelming dignity of the Supreme Pontiff's position; but the vastness of the road so opened is no more remarkable than the width of the opportunity which transforms the son of a poor Georgian shoemaker into the Premier of the Soviet Union whose simplest utterances are accepted with adoring veneration by the members of Communist Parties all over the world. It is, indeed, tempting to suggest that, just as the overwhelming body of Roman Catholics find no invasion of their freedom in the compulsion to conform to doctrines which are, in fact, remarkable for the elasticity with which they are adapted to each special environment they encounter, so no Communist feels unfree when a pronouncement from Moscow compels him to unsay on one day what he had proclaimed with ardour the day before. The effort spent by each in the eager adjustment of mind and heart to the new directive he is bidden to follow is not only a remarkable exercise in loyalty, but also, I venture to think, a proof that, for millions of minds, the will to obey makes the fusion of totalitarianism and democracy not a contradiction, as it seems to the outsider, but a fulfilment in which the believer finds an intense satisfaction. I will not pursue the parallel further than to say that it would be easy to find in the pronouncements of the Comintern, and of its successor, the Cominform, ordinances which reproduce the exact spirit of a Papal Bull like *Unum Sanctum,* and that an ecstatic defence of the Papal power such as the fourteenth century treatise, the *De Potestate Papae* of Augustinus Triumphus, has its exact analogy in the official defences of the power of the hierarchy in Moscow over the parties which recognise the duties of obedience to its authority. A loyal Communist in 1949 writes of the deviations of Marshal Tito in the same angry passion as that in which Father Parsons, in the sixteenth century, called upon the faithful to renounce their allegiance to the heretic Elizabeth of England who dared to match her strength against the majesty of Rome.

The third point I am anxious to emphasise is the dual standard of behaviour to which the Communists believe themselves to be entitled.[1] It is important to understand the basis upon which this duality is defended, since there is no aspect of Russian action which has aroused such furious anger. From their angle, there is no prospect of either a democracy or a freedom that is real, except in the classless society to which socialism alone can give birth. In the absence of a classless society, there is a state of permanent war between bourgeois

[1] I have dealt with this problem at length in its strategic aspects in a Labour Party pamphlet, *The Secret Battalion* (London, 1946).

and proletarian; and the war can end only when, with the victory of the proletarian revolution, men pass from the realm of necessity into the realm of freedom. Their journey there is, of course, only complete when the victory has been fully consolidated and there is no possible threat, internal or external, to the revolution. To further that revolution, and to speed its coming being the highest obligation incumbent upon Communists, it follows that for them moral action is action which serves the revolutionary cause. And since decisions upon such action are taken by the Party leadership, it follows that a Communist acts morally when he obeys the orders of that leadership; this obedience has priority over all other obligations. Values in ethics, therefore, are not the outcome of arguments which have resulted in the acceptance of good and bad, right and wrong, in terms of a theory which the philosopher seeks to make persuasive by its logical consistency. The values which generally prevail in any given society are the outcome of a class conflict which can only be explained in terms of historical sociology. For the values of bourgeois ethics are an ideology in the sense of Engel's famous remark that 'ideology is a process accomplished by the so-called thinker consciously, indeed, but with a false consciousness. The real motives impelling him remain unknown to him, otherwise it would not be an ideological process at all.'

CHAPTER XII

THERE is far more truth in this view than appears on the surface; and it is difficult not to agree with Marx that ethical theories abound where there are deep antagonisms in a society; that is why he called the 'goddesses of justice, freedom, equality' a 'modern mythology'. For, overwhelmingly, our notions of good and bad, right and wrong, are conditioned, in a class society, by the place we occupy in it. The slave-owner who argues that slavery is good, and that it is therefore right for him to own slaves, is trying to enforce obedience to a system about which he has an emotion of approval, either because he was brought up in a slave-owning family, and regards the condition of a slave as 'natural', or because his success in life is marked by the fact that he has come to be an owner of slaves. A capitalist who insists, when an industry in which he has invested is nationalised without compensation, that it is a moral outrage thus to expropriate his property is, no doubt, convinced that he is putting his view in moral terms which are the outcome of an objectively rational logic; but his conviction is an example of that 'false consciousness' of which Engels spoke. And it is a similar 'false consciousness' that made the owners of the cotton mills in England oppose the early Factory Acts on the ground that all their profit was made in the last hour of the day. The Church which argues that the disappearance of belief in its principles would open the flood gates of immorality adopts the same attitude; it is seeking to preserve itself against attack by creating the feeling that its opponents are careless about the need for 'good' behaviour as a vital element in social welfare. The objectification of our private judgments or of the judgments made by some body like a government or a church or a political party, whose lead we follow is, above all, an effort, under conditions of conflict in a society, to impute moral guilt to those who oppose them. When Mr. G. E. Moore justifies 'the common legal rules for the protection of property' by saying that 'the desire for property is so universal and so strong that it would be impossible to remove it', and therefore regards the broad character of the present social system as built on the ethics of common sense, he really means that the traditional attitude to private ownership of a very eminent Cambridge don has the status of a universal moral law, about which there can be no valid difference of opinion; indeed, he goes even further when he affirms that 'it seems doubtful whether Ethics can establish the utility of any rules other than those generally practised'.[1]

Here Moore is really saying that moral analysis pronounces the *status quo* to be good, from which, of course, it follows that an analysis which pronounces the *status quo* to be evil must originate in an invalid ethical theory. It is evident at once that this is simply a method by which he can safeguard the kind of social order in England which he finds attractive. But the very fact that he is hostile to a change in that social order means that his values are being challenged, and that his 'realistic' ethics is a way of attacking both the logic and the morals of those who urge the necessity of change. Not less revealing is the unsuspected 'false consciousness' of the Cambridge Hegelian philosopher, McTaggart; that has been made clear by his biographer, Lowes Dickinson, in some pages of exquisite irony in which he explains how, without knowing it, the beauty of Cambridge, and the glamour of its traditions, transformed him from a young and ardent radical into a passionate conservative with a special dislike for trade unions.[2]

In the light of this approach, it is extraordinarily interesting to compare the impact of an ethic like that of G. E. Moore upon two of the most perceptive and distinguished minds of the generation which, roughly speaking, reached the maximum of its influence at the period when Hitler was striding relentlessly to power. R. G. Collingwood was an Oxford historian and philosopher. In his remarkable *Autobiography,* published, significantly enough, in the days of unhappy disillusion which followed Neville Chamberlain's visit to Munich, he says bluntly and boldly that the effect of the realistic ethics of G. E. Moore was, whatever the intention of Mr. Moore and his

[1] G. E. Moore, *Principia Ethica* (Cambridge, 1903) p. 335.

[2] G. L. Dickinson, J. M. E. McTaggart (Cambridge, 1931) p. 112. On all this there is a brilliant article by L. S. Fauer, in *Science and Society* (N.Y., 1942) Vol. VI. No. 3, p. 242.

disciples, to prepare men's minds for receptivity to fascist doctrines. They cut themselves off from the world, and, in their dark cave of contemplation, sought to attain states of mind which gave them direct experience of beauty and truth and love in complete independence of the outside world, and in the conviction that social action interfered with the achievement of those states of mind in which beauty and truth and love could be experienced by each at its highest level. Collingwood notes that, on a visit to Spain during the horror of the civil war he learned at first hand what was involved by retirement to the dark cave. 'Henceforth,' he wrote, in a mood of high public passion, 'I fight in the daylight.'[1]

The significance of Collingwood's outlook is, I think, seen in revealing perspective if it is set alongside a remarkable memoir by Lord Keynes, which he read to a group of Cambridge friends in 1938, just before the visit to Munich.[2] He explains how, in 1902-3, he and they fell under the spell of G. E. Moore, and how, in a broad way, he remained a believer in Moore's ethical philosophy. 'I see no reason,' he said,[3] 'to shift from the fundamental intuitions of *Principia Ethica;* though they are much too few and too narrow to fit actual experience which provides a richer and more various content. That they furnish a justification of experience wholly independent of outside events has become an added comfort, even though one cannot live to-day secure in the undisturbed individualism which was the extraordinary achievement of the early Edwardian days, not for our little lot only, but for everyone else, too.' Here, obviously, Keynes does not regard his experience as part of, or conditioned by, the world about him; and the 'undisturbed individualism' which everyone enjoyed in the 'early Edwardian days' raises interesting questions of what Keynes meant by 'everyone'. It could not have been the miners or the dockers, or the railwaymen, for they were on the threshold of what was to become a passionate discontent, and if any, or all of them, lived by 'experience wholly independent of outside events', this extraordinary phenomenon went unnoticed by any of their contemporaries.

[1] *An Autobiography* (Oxford, 1939) p.
[2] *Two Memoirs* (London, 1949); the second memoir 'My Early Beliefs' beginning on p. 78.
[3] *Ibid.* p. 94.

But Keynes went even further. 'We lived,' he continues,[1] " . . . entirely in present experience, since social action as an end in itself and not merely as a lugubrious duty has dropped out of our Ideal, and, not only social action, but the life of action generally.' In practice, of course, he tells us, he did not forget the world outside, 'but I am recalling what our Ideal was in those early days when the life of passionate contemplation and communion was supposed to oust all other purposes whatever.' Keynes thought it was 'a big advantage for us to have escaped from the Benthamist tradition . . . I now do regard that as the worm which has been gnawing at the insides of modern civilisation and is responsible for its present moral decay.' There then follow two remarkable passages. 'It was this escape from Bentham,' he wrote, 'joined with the unsurpassable individualism of our philosophy, which has served to protect the whole lot of us from the final *reductio ad absurdum* of Benthamism known as Marxism. We have completely failed, indeed, to provide a substitute for these economic bogus-faiths capable of protecting or satisfying our successors. But we ourselves have remained . . . altogether immune from the virus, as safe in the citadel of our ultimate faith as the Pope of Rome in his.' To what criteria of social behaviour did this 'escape from Bentham' lead? 'We entirely repudiated a personal liability on us to obey general rules. We claimed the right to judge every individual case on its merits, and the wisdom, experience and self-control to do so successfully. This was a very important part of our faith, violently and aggressively held, and for the outer world it was our most obvious and dangerous characteristic . . . We recognised no moral obligation on us, no inner sanction, to conform or to obey. Before heaven we claimed to be our own judge in our own case.'[2]

Keynes then goes on to explain the deep rationalism of himself and his friends. They accepted the idea of a 'continuing moral progress by virtue of which the human race already consists of reliable, rational, decent people, influenced by truth and objective standards, who can be safely released from the outward restraints of convention and traditional standards, and inflexible rules of conduct, and left, from now onwards, to

[1] *Ibid.* p. 96.
[2] *Ibid.* pp. 97-8.

214

their own sensible devices, pure motives, and reliable intuitions of the good.' He admits that this ethical philosophy 'was flimsily based, as I now think, on an *a priori* view of what human nature is like, both other people's and our own, which was disastrously mistaken'. He reminds his friends that 'we repudiated all versions of the doctrine of original sin, of there being insane and irrational springs of wickedness in most men. We were not aware that civilisation was a thin and precarious crust erected by the personality and the will of a very few, and only maintained by rules and conventions skilfully put across and guilefully preserved.'[1] He concluded that 'we used in old days to get round the rich variety of experience by expanding illegitimately the field of aesthetic appreciation (we would deal, for example, with all branches of the tragic emotion under this head), classifying as aesthetic experience what is human experience and somehow sterilising it by this misclassification'. So Keynes concludes that 'there may have been just a grain of truth' in the passionate denunciation in a letter written—it is a significant date—on April 19, 1915, by the poet and novelist D. H. Lawrence: 'You must,' he wrote, 'leave these friends . . . [they] are done for forever.'[2]

No one who knew Lord Keynes will need to be told that few men of his generation combined the love of beauty and the zeal for the pursuit of intellectual truth with a selfless and courageous devotion to public well-being; his writings are there to testify to this remarkable union. That makes the 'false consciousness' of this illuminating self-examination all the more revealing. Under the sharp probing of Mr. G. E. Moore's keen scalpel, he becomes an individualist *à outrance*, interested only in disconnected flashes of vivid aesthetic experience; the world outside, with its ugliness, and hunger, and evil, is uninteresting and insignificant except as a 'tragic emotion', also to be 'aesthetically experienced'. When, a generation later, he reflects upon his outlook, at a time when there has already been one World War, and the second is almost at hand, while still grateful for a training which enabled him to 'escape from Benthamism', and, thereby, from Marxism as its *reductio ad absurdum*', as preserving the 'unsurpassable individualism'

[1] *Ibid.* p. 99.

[2] *Ibid.* p. 103. The letter from D. H. Lawrence is printed on p. 77.

of his philosophy, his power to safeguard himself against attaching too much importance to the economic motive, he yet came to see that there was evil irrationalism in man's nature, an irrationalism which went deep, and that civilisation was only preserved by what may fairly be termed an aristocracy imposing, by a mixture of guile and determination, a respect for the inherited tradition, the accepted conventions of behaviour, upon the barbarous many.

What is unmistakable here is the fact that the influence of G. E. Moore was still the decisive factor in Keynes' outlook as late as 1938. He was still the 'unsurpassable individualist', separated from the rest of society by the conviction that only his personal experience could give birth to valid 'states of mind' which formed the real savour of life. He still thought Marxism—how the view would have astonished Marx!— merely an extreme form of Benthamism in which economic factors were given an excessive importance; but he had come to realise the fragility of civilisation, to see that it was only preserved by the efforts of a few whose stratagems preserved among the many a veneration for the inherited ways of behaviour. This, we must remember, is the Keynes who had been through the profound disillusion of the Versailles Peace Conference in 1919, who, in one of the most brilliant pamphlets of our time,[1] had predicted with angry accuracy the tragic consequences, all of them economic in their foundation, which were bound to result, and did in fact result, from Mr. Churchill's decisions about the exchange-rate between the pound and the dollar in 1925, and was working at a revision of classic economic theory which, apart from the work of Marx himself, may justly be regarded as perhaps the most formidable attack its exponents had encountered since Jevons and his contemporaries had sought to turn the flank of socialism by making marginal utility—itself a theory rooted in hedonism— instead of the labour theory of value the keystone of the arch of economic philosophy. When Keynes, morever, wrote this illuminating essay, his economic theories had already become the main clue to the nature of the New Deal of Franklin Roosevelt in the United States.

It is, I think, clear beyond dispute that it was the influence

[1] *Essays in Persuasion* (London, 1931) p. 244.

216

of G. E. Moore which not only led Keynes to the rejection of Marxism, but to a rejection the more complete because it dissuaded his keen and powerful mind from taking the trouble seriously to understand Marxist philosophy. He did, indeed, visit Soviet Russia, and recognised in the values its leaders were seeking to establish a formidable challenge to capitalist society, so often 'a mere *congeries* of pursuers and pursued'.[1] It is significant indeed that Keynes should never have attempted any serious revision of his moral philosophy; and that he remained, to the end of a life full of devoted public service and high intellectual accomplishment, the neo-Platonic aristocrat, not only contemptuous of the ordinary people of whom, in any serious and organised way, he had no direct knowledge, and convinced that civilisation would be destroyed were it not for the artifice — Plato's 'noble lie' — of the 'very few' who persuaded the multitude to venerate inherited tradition and convention. It was only late in life that he came to respect what he called the 'extraordinary accomplishment of our predecessors in the ordering of life . . . or the elaborate framework which they had devised to protect this order'. He even quotes with approval the famous suggestion of Plato in the *Laws* forbidding the young man to enquire which laws are right or wrong, and limiting the discussion of defects to old men who, when the young are absent, may remark upon them to another old man, or to one of the rulers of the state. He laughs at his own 'impulse to *protest*'; 'I behave,' he wrote,[2] 'as if there really existed some authority or standard to which I can successfully appeal if I shout loud enough—perhaps it is some hereditary vestige of a belief in the efficacy of prayer'.

What may seem to be a digression is, in fact, fundamental to the argument I am putting forward. With exceptions that I shall note presently, the 'false consciousness' implicit in Moore's ethical theory, and, through the influence of Moore, permeating so deeply the mind of Keynes, is itself a form of the dual morality which characterises so much of Communist behaviour. We are told that, with Communists, the end justifies the means, that they raise expediency to the level of an ultimate principle, that they treat their fellow-Communists by one standard of

[1] *Essays in Persuasion*, p. 307.
[2] *Two Memoirs*, p. 100.

truth, and non-Communists, even if they are allies, by another standard. But there is an important sense in which 'false consciousness', and related modes of behaviour, have, if with far more sophistication, very much the same effect. All Mr. G. E. Moore's immense dialectical skill, for example, is used to persuade his readers that ethical philosophy makes it an obligation to defend the private ownership of the means of production; and this result is achieved not by the examination of the results of that private ownership upon all but a very small minority of the population, but by the searching investigation of the logical consequences of a system of postulates which are, in fact, given to Mr. Moore by intuition drawn by him from his private (and very limited) experience, and then translated into universal values by being affirmed with massive emphasis so that his readers are overawed. A system of values like that of Mr. Moore, which does not examine the historical origins of his experience, nor seek to measure the results of the intuition to which it gives rise upon other people, is surely, with all its skill, special pleading for the kind of world and the kind of values which Mr. Moore has found satisfactory; interesting though it is psychologically, it is essentially autobiography rather than social philosophy. It tells us what Mr. Moore finds good in this world, but it gives us no reason at all why his scheme of values should be binding upon anyone else. It is a wholly individualist ethic the authority of which over other people is dependent upon their being conditioned, by legal and other means, to conduct which makes them in fact subordinate instruments to Mr. Moore's tastes. Since, such conditioning apart, every other person is in the same position as Mr. Moore, the logical result of his conclusions is an anarchy which is only kept in check because the coercive forces of society are, in most communities, on the side of Mr. Moore, or of those who take a position analogous to his.

The attitude of Lord Keynes is even more significant, above all because he saw the inner working of governments at first hand, and knew with intimacy what is involved in the arts of political leadership in, for example, modern capitalist democracy. Basically, Keynes accepted Moore's approach. But as the Second World War approached, he added certain special conclusions of his own. The first was that civilised life was the creation of a special minority which made provision for its protection in each age; the second was the need to use 'guile' upon the multitude, if this protection was to be effective; and the third was the need to venerate the past lest, by reckless irreverence, the whole structure of civilised living be brought crashing down by people untrained to appreciate the exquisite, if temporary, states of mind from which he and his friends derived their supreme moments of happiness. He still thought that states of mind alone matter, 'provided we agree to take account of the pattern of life through time'.[1] To take account of that pattern meant reverence for the ways in which by 'guile and skill' the aristocracy had preserved civilisation. The masses, as Edmund Burke put it, should be led 'to venerate when they are unable presently to comprehend' by the 'noble lies' of their leaders. That set a limit to the individualism it was permissible to practice by those who could penetrate the veil behind which rules and conventions which would not stand up to rational analysis enabled the fragile structure of civilisation to be preserved. By insisting that the order and pattern of society should inspire mysterious emotions which no reason should seek to reduce to a rational state of mind interstitially experienced, men like Keynes could avoid the insistence of D. H. Lawrence that they were 'done for forever'.

The 'false consciousness' of G. E. Moore and Keynes was, in each of their cases, something of which neither was aware; they developed their doctrines with deep sincerity, without being able to recognise the very limited experience upon which they were built. That is not, of course, true of other men, or, still more, of other organisations. The motives behind the revealed motives with such political leaders as Mussolini and Hitler, in our own day, of Bismarck and Cavour in an earlier generation, can be documented with a fullness that leaves no doubt of the dual morality upon which they were based. Hitler, for example, certainly persuaded Mr. Neville Chamberlain at Munich that he was eager to co-operate in making firm the foundations of world peace even while he was preparing to satisfy appetites which made war an imperative necessity if they were to be satisfied. Mr. Churchill's praise of Russian heroism set the tone

[1] *Op. cit.* p. 102.

of British public opinion about the future of Anglo-Russian relations; only an intimate circle around him was aware that, during the four years from June 22, 1941, his praise was always subject to the limitations, never fully revealed to the public until his Fulton speech of 1946, that he was prepared by force, if necessary, to prevent the expansion of Communist ideas under Russian leadership. In the same kind of way, more than sixteen hundred years ago, the biographer of the Emperor Constantine, Eusebius of Caesarea, presented his subject as 'a thrice-blessed soul, united with God, and free from all dross of mortals', when few could have known better than he that Constantine was, in fact, a crafty and cruel politician, greedy of power, nicely calculating the balances of forces in the complex struggle he had to wage for supremacy, and offering his protection to the Christians, still in a minority in the Empire, largely because the more important elements among the Pagan majority were convinced that further persecution would destroy civic life, have baneful economic consequences, and perpetuate the zeal of the mob for bloodthirsty massacre. What Eusebius represents to us as a decision divinely inspired by miraculous occurrences was, in sober fact, a shrewdly calculated stroke in an intricate battle for power. Eusebius' own highly decorative account is nothing more than propaganda on behalf of the ecclesiastical hierarchy, an attempt to strengthen its position, especially the wide influence won by the return of its properties lost under the persecution of Diocletian, by placing its new authority under the direct protection of Heaven, with Constantine in the part of an inspired instrument converted to that rôle by a miracle of overwhelming force.

This duality, of course, is far more clear in the case of bodies like churches, governments, political parties. The contrast between the gospel Christianity which the Roman Catholic Church affected to preach, especially where property and the right to human dignity are concerned, and its combination of savage persecution and unlimited greed as it moved to the position where it could claim, and seek to enforce, its sovereignty over princes is literally overwhelming. So, too, is the massive deception practised by all the members of the Non-Intervention Committee during the tragic years of the Spanish

Civil War; even Mr. Eden did not shrink on occasion from insisting to the House of Commons that he had no knowledge of German and Italian activities in Spain, intelligence reports about which must have been lying on the table at the very moment when he was affirming his ignorance of the events they described. Nor can there be any doubt that, in the last months of 1941, the Japanese Government was preparing that attack upon Pearl Harbour which the presence of its envoys at Washington was intended to obscure until the blow itself had been struck. No one believes that the air-lift became necessary in Berlin in 1948 because the means of land communication through the Russian zone required large-scale technical repairs; but the Russians insisted on acting as though this myth was fact in order to throw on the Western Powers the responsibility for a policy which might easily have led to war. It is always worth remembering that Pope Paul IV, in 1557, put Machiavelli's *Prince* upon the Index, without that preventing its use as the main source of the Roman Catholic defence of the massacre perpetrated in ninety more years of bloody religious wars against the heretics which the Church abominated.

The moral dualism of the levels upon which political parties work is too well known to need elaborate documentation. At almost the birth of the party system in England, their habits led the great Trimmer, Lord Halifax, to coin his famous saying that 'ignorance maketh a man enter into a party, and shame preventeth him from leaving it'. Anyone who compares the purposes for which Mussolini and his Blackshirts marched on Rome with the ends he sought to achieve when he was in possession of power will wonder that he was able to secure not only enthusiastic support from an able philosopher like Gentile, who was, after all, himself an Italian, but, even more, a tribute from Mr. Winston Churchill in 1927 which had in it something of the glow of conviction that he put into his ardent eulogies of President Roosevelt and Generalissimo Stalin in the course of the Second World War. Anyone, too, who compares the original programme of the Nazi Party, which was declared irrevocable in the 'twenties, and won for itself the support of hundreds of thousands of little shopkeepers and insignificant

221

school teachers, with what Hitler did in his years of power, not least his contemptuous dismissal of the programme about the same time as his massacre of Röhm and the latter's supporters, as well as others like General Schleicher who might have been obstacles in his path, will find it hard not to argue that parties which refuse to be cynical have little hope of life. Mr. Stanley Baldwin has frankly confessed that he pledged the Conservative Party in Great Britain to disarmament and the full use of the League of Nations— though he had no intention of respecting either pledge—because he was convinced that a bellicose attitude would have lost his party the general election of 1935; there is very little evidence to suggest that his confession that he had no such intention in policy injured his standing with the party he led, or made any profound impact on the nation as a whole. So, too, at Blackpool in 1945, the Labour Party, at the instance of its own Executive Committee, resolved unanimously that it would make Palestine into a Jewish state, and its representative, who within a few weeks was to be Chancellor of the Exchequer, spoke with eloquent fervour of its unbreakable determination to act in this way. Yet it had hardly taken office before it embarked, under the leadership of its Foreign Secretary, Mr. Ernest Bevin, upon a policy directly antithetic to its announced resolve; and it carried out the changed purposes with a relentless ferocity which, had it not been for the angry criticism of other nations, especially the United States, and the waging of what was virtually an undeclared war between the British Foreign Office and the Jews in Palestine, might easily have led Mr. Bevin to fill with the victims of his angry fury the graves that Hitler had left empty by his defeat. Yet Mr. Bevin, despite a record that is, in most aspects of Palestinian policy, both mean and shameful, never lost the confidence of an immense majority among the members of the Parliamentary Labour Party.

It is in the background of behaviour such as this that we must approach the dual morality of the Russian Communist Party and its satellite parties beyond the Soviet Union. We must note, first, that it is not only a revolutionary party, but one founded on underground conspiracy which endured for many years, watched and permeated by the secret police not merely in Tsarist Russia, but wherever its members were in exile; and we must remember also that for many years a large number of its important members paid for their activities by death or imprisonment or the haunted and hunted life of the political refugee, against whom the secret police of no small part of Europe were in league. And, after 1918, we must remember the risks attendant upon membership of many of the satellite parties; the treatment of Dimitrov in Bulgaria, of Rakosi in Hungary, are only two among innumerable examples of the dangers attendant upon Communist activity in most European states. Even in Great Britain, where the tradition of political toleration has always been strong, there were, in the inter-war years, some ugly prosecutions of British Communists whose treatment by the authorities, and especially by the Metropolitan Police, is in singular contrast to the leniency extended to British Fascists. And, after 1945, the angry suspicion with which Communists were treated, their exclusion by statute from a number of vocations, the scale, as in the United States, of the witch-hunt against them relentlessly pursued by the fantastic Un-American Activities Committee of Congress, and by the Federal Bureau of Investigation, were all calculated to create something like a pathological state of mind amongst them. We must remember that even suspicion of sympathy with Communism was sufficient, in the United States, to cost many people their jobs, and that the process of 'screening' in the Federal Civil Service, even where the official involved was wholly innocent, might easily mean the investigation of some two hundred of his friends and colleagues, the questioning of his servants and neighbours, the use of the journals he read and the books he possessed as one of the criteria of his trustworthiness, and even, on occasion, the hint to his wife of marital infidelity in the hope that this might induce her to reveal facts to the Federal agents which she might otherwise refuse to divulge.[1] There were instances in which, in a 'loyalty' test, the suspected official would not be permitted either to know the charges made against him, nor even to see, much less to have competent legal examination of, the secret service agents whose testimony resulted in the unknown

[1] This is the summary of an actual case within my own knowledge. H.J.L.

charges. A number of people, some of them former members of, or sympathisers with, communist parties, became self-appointed 'delators' of Communism and its adherents. The campaign of innuendo, suggestion, 'smear-tactics', as it came to be called, assumed amazing proportions as professional journalists began to discover that there was an income to be made by writing and broadcasting on the 'communist danger'. Even a statesman of Mr. Churchill's eminence was willing, as in his election broadcasts of 1945, to lend the authority of his great reputation to confuse the public mind over the issues raised by communist activity; and his example was, of course, followed by a host of lesser political figures. It is worth while remembering that when the famous negro singer, Mr. Paul Robeson, who is a Communist, gave a concert at Peekskill, New York, which American ex-soldiers attempted to break up, not only did the twelve hundred state police present refrain from controlling the disorders thus started but the Governor of New York, the Republican candidate for the Presidency of the United States in 1944 and 1948, ordered a special Grand Jury to investigate the violence, with terms of reference to the Grand Jury which indicated that the disorders were provoked by the violence of those who had come to hear Mr. Robeson sing, and he asked it to discover whether the concert was organised as 'part of the communist strategy to foment racial and religious hatred', and whether the 'communist-led guard forces' could be held to constitute a 'quasi-military force'. Mr. Dewey's action, no doubt, is an extreme example of calculated and dishonourable bad faith; but it is important to note that, on the anti-communist side, it is simply an instance of the strategy for provoking hysteria in the records of which Göring's burning of the German Reichstag in 1933 retains its loathsome pre-eminence.

It is in this background that the dual morality of the Communist has to be explained. The Communist Party is essentially a Church militant surrounded, as it thinks, by enemies on every side. It is organised like an army, or, better, there is a good deal of resemblance between its structure and that of the Society of Jesus Each level in its hierarchical structure must give unquestioning obedience to the level above itself. There is provision for discussion of plans, but at the stage where the appropriate authority transforms the plans into orders, these must be obeyed without hesitation even where there is the right of appeal to the sovereign body in Moscow. On a formal view, the Communist International has been dissolved; but it still remains the case that exceptional power belongs to Moscow whose decisions are binding upon all members. That is well illustrated by the expulsion of Yugoslavia from the Cominform, and the consequential large-scale effort to overthrow, by internal and external measures, Marshal Tito's régime there. The Marshal insisted upon his independent right to follow a policy of which Moscow disapproved, and he thus found himself in the position, as it were, of the great German theologian, Döllinger, after the Vatican Council. There had been debate, in which he had put his point of view, but though the decision went against him, Marshal Tito persisted in his heresy. Discipline, therefore, required his excommunication, and the degree in which he refused to accept the obligation to renounce his heresy measured the degree in which the Church from which he had been expelled was bound to attempt the imposition of sanctions against him. The passionate anger with which he has been attacked is, indeed, an index to the importance of defection by a man who had been an outstanding figure in the Communist Church. It became necessary, as with Trotsky twenty years ago, to attack a dangerous heresy at its roots, lest it triumph over the announced orthodoxy of the Church.

CHAPTER XIII

THE Communists are not only a militant church, but a proselytising church. Working, outside of Russia, either among unbelievers ready to persecute them, or, as in the satellite states, as a minority controlling the state-power, but with the knowledge that they are poised upon the edge of a precipice, three clear principles of policy are fundamental. The first is that, wherever they may find themselves, their canons of belief and of behaviour are set by the commands of Moscow; allegiance to Soviet Russia takes precedence over any other allegiance they may hold; even if this is a principle without legal validity, the moral obligation it creates goes far deeper in its hold upon character than the compulsion of any legal form can hope to achieve. That is well illustrated by the way in which the British Communist Party denounced Hitler as a 'Fascist beast' on the outbreak of war on September 3rd, 1939, and a month later, on October 7th, in accordance with the changed attitude of Soviet Russia, swung round to the insistence that Great Britain was the aggressor in a new imperialist war—a view it threw completely overboard when Hitler attacked Russia on June 22nd, 1941, a change which at once made all Communists devote all their energies not only to the ardent support of the Churchill Government in Great Britain, but also to the enthusiastic acceptance of a leading rôle in resistance movements in all countries occupied by the Axis Powers. It is vital to the grasp of communist behaviour to realise that it follows the leadership of Russia, whatever direction this leadership may take.

The second principle is the obligation, in communities where the Communist Party is in a minority, and unlikely to attain a position where it can seize the state-power, to infiltrate into other organisations, especially working-class organisations, preferably by affiliation as a whole, but, if need be, by individual penetration and, if necessary, concealing the communist character of those who are accepted into membership. In all such cases, Communists must act together as a unit, pushing forward the normal communist policy on every possible occasion, running their own candidates for the key positions in the particular body, using it, in fact, so far as they can, as a para-communist organisation. These have been the bases upon which Communists have sought to permeate the British Labour Party. Some have joined as individual members of the Party with permission from the Communist Party to conceal the fact that they are Communists. The Communist Party itself has frequently applied for the right, as a body, to affiliate to the Labour Party, insisting that it will be loyal to the principles and to the constitution of the Labour Party, even when its activities outside have offered the clearest possible proof that it could be loyal to neither. It has denounced the Labour Party as consisting of 'lackeys of capitalism', or 'lackeys of' imperialism', or 'social fascists', or of men who betray the working-class movement at the very time when it has been seeking to secure affiliation to it on the ground that there is assurance of its loyal devotion. There is no leader of the Labour Party since 1920 whom the Communists have not slandered and vilified as an enemy of the working class. Lenin's famous sentence—'I embrace Arthur Henderson as the rope embraces the man who is about to be hanged'—expresses to perfection the communist appearance of good will behind which is the reality of a determination to wreck the Labour Party and become its residuary legatee when the work of destruction is complete.

The history in Great Britain of communist relations with the trade unions and the trades councils is analogous in character. It is the record of a consistent and untiring effort to use organisations in which communist membership is small as an instrument of communist purposes. That effort has been accompanied by campaigns of trickery, falsehood, and vilification which have not been compensated for by the zeal and devotion that the Communists have brought to its service. I do not think it is generally true to say that the Communists in the trade unions have been responsible for strikes which violated the discipline of the unions; I think it is generally true to say that they have always used strikes, and especially unofficial strikes, to sow discord and distrust between the rank and file in the trade unions and their leaders. And it is beyond doubt that, in many disputes below the national level, the activity of the Communists is built on obedience to the instructions of their own Party leaders rather than to the objective facts of the concrete situation they confronted. I do not believe that such activity is the result of 'instructions from Moscow'; but I do believe that the Central Committee of the British Communist Party follows a general line, communicated to its members in trade unions, which is related to a directive given to them from Moscow. Nor, on the evidence, can I doubt the willingness of members of the Communist Party to exploit every situation in which they can get involved for the purposes of the Party and not for the purposes of the union. They may regard themselves as Marx urged them to be, as the 'vanguard of the working class'. But they use that position, wherever they can, on behalf of a social philosophy which, whatever its merits, has so far failed even to approach the possibility of winning support from a majority of the unions.

Nor does the story stop there. Alongside the effort to infiltrate the Labour Party and the trade unions, the Communist Party has built, or is concerned in, a large number of parapolitical organisations in which they appear merely to cooperate with other bodies, but which are, in fact, pretty completely dominated by the members to whom they assign the task of controlling them. Akin to these are the special conferences they summon from time to time, on subjects of interest and importance in which the agenda; the membership of the resolutions committee, the list of those who are to be called upon to speak, have been settled by them long before the conference has ever met. There are many people, who are not Communists at all but desire to promote friendship and understanding with Russia who are led by that desire to join one or other of the societies the Communist Party sponsors for this purpose. Almost invariably, they find that its policy simply reflects what the Communists desire to be British policy towards Russia, that they are led into denunciation of any action towards Russia of which the Communist Party disapproves, that they have no chance of criticising Russian policy, and that though, as British citizens, they can seek to improve British relations with Russia, there is no parallel Russian society the function of which is to create a climate of opinion which will persuade the Russian Government to seek more friendly relation with Great Britain. They lend themselves, in short, to a complex propaganda-machine the purpose of which is, quite simply, to prove that Russia is always right, and that those who hesitate to admit the infallibility of its government are either the enemies of the Soviet Union, or on the way to that condition, and this makes them either the enemies of freedom and democracy, or, what is worse, the active agents of counter-revolution.

This, broadly speaking, is typical of a situation where, as in Great Britain, the Communist Party has little prospect of governmental power for a considerable period. It is worth while to consider briefly the position in those 'people's democracies' in Europe which have been achieved either by the fusion of Social Democratic Parties with the Communists, or, as in Czechoslovakia, by a *coup d'état* planned by the Communist Party. In all of them, with the partial exception of Hungary, it has resulted in the emergence of the one-party state; more especially, what was to have been an alliance between equal partners, the Social Democratic Party and the Communist Party, has been transformed into a fusion of both into one, with the swift emergence of the Communists into all leading positions, both in the Government and in the Party. Those who were not at one with the new régime were dismissed from their posts, or condemned to forced labour, or driven to take the risks of exile. A strict censorship is imposed on books and newspapers, and the freedom of the foreign journalist is severely handicapped. Broadcasting becomes the instrument of government propaganda wholly; and the line followed is strictly that laid down by Moscow. If the contemporary Communist leader, Gottwald, or Anna Pauker or Rakosi, becomes the embodiment of the past national tradition, he shares his new honour with Generalissimo Stalin, who becomes, so to speak, the supreme patron and protector of the new social order, the invariable recipient of flattering testimonies as the great guide through whose wise direction the change was made possible. Relations with the Western nations, not least cultural relations, begin swiftly to diminish; and any close contact with their diplomats becomes very close to a dangerous adventure, unless it is officially undertaken at the instance of the new governors. The security police become a major and outstanding sign that the safety of the people's democracy has become a higher law than the classic safeguards of liberty of the individual person. There is often 'protective arrest'; there are many instances of long and close detention before some suspect is brought to trial; and, where a major offender is arraigned, like Rajk in Hungary, it is pretty certain, as in the great treason trials in Russia, he will make a dramatic confession of guilt in court, emphasise the enormity of his crimes, and, even if he pleads for mercy, he is likely to admit that whatever sentence may be imposed upon him is no more than what he deserves.

In nations like France and Italy, where the Communist Party has held, at least since 1945, a position of great authority, its habits have followed, so far as possible, those that are characteristic of the new 'people's democracies'. When efforts at a fusion with the Socialists have failed, the latter have been treated with a hostility which has usually been ever more profound than that exhibited towards the parties of the Right. In France, after the Liberation, the Communists joined a coalition government under the leadership of General de Gaulle, and there was a brief honeymoon between them and the Gaullistes in which almost fulsome compliments were exchanged. When the General's reactionary authoritarianism brought his coalition to an end, the Communists were prepared to stay in the new government; but an alliance with them proved impossible since, apart from their representatives in the Cabinet, they insisted on the right of their deputies to give or to withhold their support in the Chamber as they thought fit. This insistence resulted in their expulsion from the government. Since they went into opposition, their effort has been twofold in character. On the political side, they have bitterly attacked all French policies which sought to integrate France's relation to the Western Powers, notably over Marshall Aid, and the North Atlantic Security Pact; and they have combined such attacks with a flood of personal invective against the French socialist leaders, especially Léon Blum, which has to be read to be believed. Certainly, it is not an exaggeration to say that,

231

whatever the intention of communist policy in France and Italy, it has gone far towards making irreparable the breach with the Socialists, and that it has pinned so much of its hopes of economic breakdown in both countries as to be driven into a position where it is practically compelled to exploit every difficulty that occurs, even to the point of representing obvious economic failures as important successes. Able, therefore, as is communist leadership in both countries, and feeble as has been the Socialist leadership in each, thus far both French and Italian Communists have done more to strengthen the forces of reaction in their respective countries, to drive them into the orbit of American influence than they have to put themselves in a position where they figure as the natural residuary legatees of Conservative breakdown. Had they set their outlook in a frame of French or Italian reference; or had they, in the famous phrase of Keynes, made it clear that they were 'good Europeans', their psychological hold upon the great mass of unattached citizens might have gone far deeper. But the methods of action and of thought that they have chosen, the swift, and too often inexplicable changes of view which have characterised their action, make them appear far more missionaries *in partibus infidelium*, than the exponents of ideas which have arisen and developed in the background of French or Italian needs. They give the appearance, first, of borrowing the values they hold, and then trying to provide them with an attractive and appealing national pedigree, than to have been driven to adopt them out of circumstances which left them no alternative choice. Nothing shows this as clearly as the communist attitude to philosophy and history in France; for there, the journals of opinion in which they express their views while, often enough, showing that special French *flair* for clarity of positive exposition, in the realm of critical analysis abandon all pretence of standards of judgment which command respect as soon as they handle an official Russian book, especially if it appears under the name of an important Russian leader. Their attitude becomes one of meaningless genuflection, in which they are obviously more concerned with the quality of their orthodoxy than with the quality of their thought. What is in their mind is far less the light they can throw upon the subject, than their anxiety to win

232

confidence and approval in Moscow. Whatever be the road to intellectual understanding, it certainly does not lie in so futile an abandonment of independent and original analysis such as this way of thought implies.

There is one example of concern for the quality of orthodoxy which will, perhaps, serve as a general illustration of what I have in mind. The Czechoslovak Republic decided in the spring of 1949 that all books and periodicals and sheet-music shall in the future be published at the instance of Central Publishing Council of the Ministry of Information and Public Culture.[1] This change, it is explained, is to prevent their appropriation by 'capitalist speculators' who held, with some honourable exceptions, both men of letters and musicians at their mercy, and created a situation both on the production and distribution sides which was 'quite insupportable'. It provided 'the most fertile ground for the flowering of capitalist licence and anarchy'.[2] Individual publishing is therefore abolished. Czech and Slovak books, musical publications and reproductions are, therefore, nationalised that they may be more fully at the service of the whole people. All such cultural productions will cease to be published by a private publisher, or at the author's expense, but will appear under the auspices of a number of associations whose proposals are approved by the Central Publishing Council. There will be no restriction upon the freedom of expression, since Act 94 is to be read in conjunction with Section 20 of the Constitution of May 9th, 1944, which guarantees that freedom 'subject only to the public interest, and the cultural needs of the people'.[3]

The rapporteur of the measure in the National Assembly, Professor Julius Dolansky, of the Charles University in Prague, was emphatic upon the advantages it offered. 'We shall suppress and destroy only literary trash,' he said,[4] 'pseudo-art of all varieties . . . If here and there perplexed voices may be heard calling for allowing the publication of books at the

[1] Act 94 of March 24, 1949. I use a very illuminating pamphlet published by the Ministry of Information and Culture in English in May, 1949, and printed in Prague by Orbis. H.J.L.

[2] *Op. cit.* p. 10.

[3] *Op. cit.* p. 12.

[4] *Op. cit.* p. 13 f.

author's expense, it should be realised that this is as perverse and dubious as if someone were to demand in the era of the people's democracy and of Socialism the right to establish a private factory or other capitalist enterprises. The privileges of wealthy individuals will never return . . . Everything that is valuable, creative, and vital, everything that is of significance for the community and society, will live in the socialist culture, live more fully and more finely than even before. Is not the miraculous flowering of Soviet culture, in a country where there are neither private publishers nor private booksellers, nor traders in art, a brilliant example and model, even in this respect?' His view was strongly supported by Mr. Vaclav Kopecky, the energetic Minister of Information, who urged that the publication and distribution of books 'should become the care of the state, and should be directed by the state, *with a view towards cultural needs,* with a view towards the cultural needs of the people, with a view towards higher educational interests'.[1] Mr. Kopecky explains that, under the system of private publishing, the real aim of the publishers was 'to protect their reactionary ideological position at all cost[s] . . . to open the market for tendencious foreign matter, more particularly for *Western productions of the notorious Memoir type.* We particularly regret the profligate expenditure of so much precious paper, of which we stand in great need to-day, on the publication of worthless, superfluous books, of harmful productions of foreign Western origin, while our authors and the works of the national classics were being generally neglected'.[2] 'There can be no doubt,' Mr. Kopecky continues,[3] '. . . . that we are making sure that publishing will, in future, serve higher interests than those of profit, that it will serve the interests of ideas, political enlightenment, culture, education, and so forth.' Mr. Kopecky then explains how, on the basis of the proposal of the Publishing Council, the Ministry would either give leave to publish or 'in necessary cases, it will be possible to re-examine the decision made'.[4] He denies that the new system will injure authors. *'Our Constitution,'* he told the

[1] *Ibid.* pp. 15-16.
[2] *Ibid.* p. 16. Italics in the original.
[3] *Ibid.* p. 18. Italics in the original.
[4] *Ibid.* p. 21.

Assembly.[1] *'explicitly guarantees the freedom of creative mental work.* We want our literary artists to feel in their work as free as possible, and to create new works as abundantly as possible. *In equal measure, however, we recognise the freedom of criticism, and the freedom of the selection, as regards the fruits of creative activity.* Surely we cannot interpret the notion of creative freedom in the absurd sense that everything that is produced, be it ever so feeble or reactionary, should be printed. We are concerned that creative freedom should in the most profitable manner aid our cause, the cause of the people's democracy, and the cause of Socialism.' 'All our publishing activity,' Mr. Kopecky concludes,[2] *'will be directed towards a progressive, revolutionary, people's democratic literature, towards a socialist literature.* And just as we shall support our own literature, we shall spread the works of the great literature of the Soviet Union, the literature of the people's democratic countries, and progressive literary works from other countries, works which are in harmony with what we feel, and which are capable of showing us the working people of other countries struggling for what we have already achieved.' Mr. Kopecky ended his vivid defence of the new Act[3] by telling the Assembly that 'on this road a blazing example is set to us by the great Soviet Union, *led by Generalissimo Stalin.* On this road we are guided to a fair and happy future by our beloved President, *President of the Republic, Comrade Klement Gottwald'.*[4]

One other aspect of this decision deserves annotation. The chairman of the Union of Czechoslovak authors, Mr. Jan Drda, also explained to the National Assembly the immense benefits of the new system. After explaining that the old régime gave a full opportunity for 'reactionary forces' to 'sabotage' the culture of the nation, and how 'foreign cultural workers' visiting Czechoslovakia could take home with them 'a graphic lesson of the way in which the people's democratic order aiming at Socialism liberates, supports and organises its creative forces in the cultural no less than in other spheres'.[5] Mr. Drda pro-

[1] *Ibid.* p. 23. Italics in the original.
[2] *Ibid.* p. 24. Italics in the original.
[3] *Ibid.* p. 28.
[4] Italics in the original.
[5] *Op. cit.* p. 30.

235

phesies with enthusiasm that the Act of 1949 will 'ring the death-knell of literary scrap and . . . remove the reactionary rot and mildew so often secretly vegetating on the printed page'. It will enable a vital exchange to be made between Czechoslovak culture and the 'glorious Soviet culture' as well as a 'deepened relation and recognition of all progressive authors and works in the rest of the world'. It will prevent the spread of 'pseudo-scientific, idealist, and other reactionary ideas, anti-Soviet, anti-Marxist, and anti-democratic polemics' which, too often, appeared 'under the guise of scientific and documentary interest'.[1] 'In the planning of our culture,' Dr. Drda says with enthusiasm, 'we shall set against the stupid, false and wily cosmopolitanism represented by American blood-and-thunder thrillers, and ready-made pornographic rags or by the existentialism of M. Sartre, the combatant and active internationalism of that literature which struggles for a better morrow for men and the world.' Soviet literature in particular 'remains the brightest aim not only for the Czech and Slovak reader, but for all our writing'.

I have illustrated, at some length, the approach of the People's Democracy in Czechoslovakia to the establishment of new values in literature. I might, not less easily, have used the Russian approach to the creation of new values in music, when Zhdanov on behalf of the Central Committee of the Communist Party explained to composers of the distinction of Shostakovich and Prokoviev the 'line' they ought to follow in their future work; they were especially warned against the temptation to bourgeois formalism by a political leader who, if he was not a professional musician, did at least know three hundred folk-songs and strongly favoured 'tuneful' music. It is almost as tempting to discuss the same Zhdanov's famous attack, in 1946—he was evidently a specialist on literature, too—on the satirist Zoschenko, and the poetess Anna Akhmatova, or the argument of Alexander Fadeyev, at the Wroclaw Congress of Intellectuals, in August, 1948, that 'if hyenas could use fountain pens, and jackals could use typewriters, they would write like T. S. Eliot'—a specially interesting conclusion from a novelist to whom English is an unknown

[1] *Op. cit.* p. 32.

236

tongue. But the Czechoslovak legislation is of exceptional interest, both because the law itself, and the arguments by which it was supported were made by men who were deliberately emulating the methods of a régime which they knew from first-hand experience had attained little success in the area of policy they decided to impose upon their own people.

No doubt there is much to be said for the criticisms they levelled at the system they suppressed. Far too much capital and paper was wasted in the production of worthless books. A number of writers of real distinction found it extraordinarily hard, before they won their reputation, even to get their books seriously considered. There was always an excessive volume of detective stories and 'thrillers' and books that tread delicately around the frontiers of pornography. No one, indeed, could look at a good deal of the immense amount of foreign literature in translation in a Czech bookshop without a sense of sheer bewilderment at the taste of the publisher who bought the rights of translation and the habits of the bookseller who decided to stock it. I think, too, that it is probable that the waste of capital upon much of this literature stood in the way of publishing a number of important works of scholarship, and that one of the effects of the ceaseless flow of futile novels, like the machine-made 'American Westerns' referred to in the debate in the National Assembly was to drug their addicts into a condition of civic slumber that led them into a continuous mood of irresponsibility. There is probably no librarian in England or America who could not tell countless stories of readers to whom almost any book, especially impossibly romantic fiction and futile biographies or memoirs, are ways of escape from reality.

This is to say that a large number of bad books are published every year by men whose knowledge of the market assures them that they will profit from the transaction, and that there are readers in abundance who find in them satisfaction; there is in some sort, almost a Gresham's law in the publishing world. But this is surely a smaller danger than to give a Ministry, even with the check of consultative organs, the right to decide what shall be published in terms of a political directive than transforms both books and music into forms of pamphleteering which achieve success only by making its first canon of substance the orthodoxy which the officials of the Ministry will require. The experience of Russia itself has made plain that orthodoxy is not a static thing. John Reed's *Ten Days that Shook the World*, which had almost classic status in the time of Lenin is no longer permitted reading; nor is the Webbs' *Soviet Communism* which was hailed, for some years after its publication, as a work of extraordinary value. There is, of course, a prohibition against the circulation of all that Trotsky ever wrote, except to readers in an especially privileged position, so that his remarkable pamphlet, *Literature and Revolution*, by all odds the best Marxist defence written to defend the position taken by Zhdanov, his illuminating *Autobiography*, and, above all, his superb *History of the Russian Revolution*, remain unknown to, and undiscussed by, Russian critics and historians. Anyone, moreover, who compares the first collected edition of Lenin's works with the last edition, will see not only significant changes in the text, but fantastic alterations in the attached explanatory notes which can only have been made to eulogise the part played by Generalissimo Stalin at the expense of his defeated rival by a sycophant unfit to be trusted with the annotation of any important documents. And anyone who compares the successive histories of the Russian Communist Party written by Zinoviev, Yaroslavsky, Popov, and the Party's historical section under, we are told, the watchful eye of Generalissimo Stalin himself, who is also part-author, will feel tempted to feel that Mr. Justice Holmes was right when he criticised those authors to whom all facts are born free and equal.

One would like, further, to know just how far the censor's grip will reach. Will it allow the unimpeded circulation, for example, of T. G. Masaryk's *Autobiography,* or that of Eduard Benes, both of which defend values no longer acceptable to the Gottwald régime; what view will it take of T. G. Masaryk's *Spirit of Russia* which, despite its obvious weaknesses, has an insight into its subject that has rarely been surpassed? And, particular books apart, it is important to know with some precision what the Czechoslovak Government means by its pledge to follow the example of the Soviet Government in the publications it authorises. No doubt there has been a number of highly distinguished figures in that literature—a great novelist

238

like Sholokhov, for example. But few honest critics would be willing to put second-rate hack-work, written to a formula as unreal to an artist's conscience as the official hagiography of the Roman Catholic Church, Ilya Ehrenburg's *The Fall of Paris,* for example, or his *Storm,* or Fadeyev's *Young Guard,* or even Gladkov's *Cement,* against the work of Tolstoy and Dostoievsky, Turgenev and Chekov. The official criteria for literature and music and painting deprive them of the imaginative individuality which marks the great artist. If in every novel and play we can always be sure that the hero will be a good Communist, and the villain almost certainly in the pay of the American Federal Bureau of Investigation, or of the British M.I.5, if, in the histories, it is always Lenin's supreme good fortune to follow the right 'line' because Stalin stands lovingly on guard by his side to protect him against the danger of mistaken decisions, if the musical composer is to think first of all the tuneful melodies that the grocer's boy can begin to whistle as he goes out from the concert-hall into the street, if no painter or sculptor has really arrived until he has a portrait or a bust of Lenin and Stalin to his credit upon which there is stamped the seal of official approval, not least, if all philosophy and economics are merely to confirm inferences from Marx and Engels and Lenin which the Politbureau regards as safe, there will be a sterilisation of culture in Czechoslovakia as demoralising as that which has taken place in Soviet Russia itself over the last ten years and more. None of the creative arts can march meekly behind a commander whose position depends not upon the inspiration he can communicate, but upon the official authority he can impose. It is surely significant that most poets achieve the eminence of the laureateship either because the power of spontaneous song has gone out of them or because they never sought to stray beyond those bounds of discretion which made their work intelligible to minds like those of George III or Queen Victoria. No one ever expects that a Shelley or a Byron or a Walt Whitman will arouse the enthusiasm of courtiers whether at Windsor or at the Kremlin. That is why Zdhanov thought the poetry of Akhmatova 'pretty poor stuff'. That is why, also, Queen Victoria and the Prince Consort were anxious to persuade Disraeli that Martin Tupper deserved a baronetcy.

I do not deny for one moment that the place of the arts in any civilisation presents a series of problems of the first import-ance. I am confident that William Morris was right in his insistence that it is both an evil and a dangerous condition in any society when the artist is divorced from the people. I am confident, too, that all great art has a social function to perform, that there is, for example, a permanent and profound truth in Shelley's great aphorism that poets are the legislators of the world. But that does not mean that the artist must be an officially directed propagandist always concerned so to write or to compose or to paint as to appeal to the largest possible number of the people and encourage them to hasten the advent of the new socialist civilisation. It means, indeed, that all art should seek to escape from the narrow walls of a coterie, that it should refuse to regard pecuniary success as the test of its importance, that it should be fearless and independent, report with fidelity to truth as it sees it, and be determined to com-municate the exceptional insight which it is its glory to possess. Decadent art is not, as the Russians seem to think, art that refuses to accept the ideology of Socialism as the framework of its effort. Decadent art is rather obsequious art, whether it makes its genuflexion to power or to money or to popularity, or takes pride in its unintelligibility to the masses as proof of its greatness, thus insisting that there is a beauty of emotion or of understanding they can never hope to penetrate.

A proposal, therefore, like the Czechoslovak law I have dis-cussed above is reactionary for the same reason that similar laws now in operation are reactionary; it is a deliberate attempt to fetter the artist's spirit to principles he may not examine, to compel him to accept insights he has not achieved for himself. This is what I have called obsequious art, and obsequious art very rapidly ceases to be art at all. Experience may make a greatly gifted artist into a Communist; but it will only do so if the artist is free to accept Communism or to reject it. It is, indeed, as Lenin wrote to Maxim Gorki forty years ago, folly not to see that great art, and, therefore, the great artist, cannot be manufactured by the authoritarian imposition of a philo-sophy to the axioms and postulates of which conformity is exacted. It is, indeed, bad Marxism to maintain that the position of the artist, like a sheep in a flock, is to be nothing more than a unit in a vast, undifferentiated mass, no longer entitled to discover for himself the independent personality which is the inner essence of his quality as an artist, and from discovery to move to a self-expression that frees him to develop his insights as he will; the primitive character of the society at once reveals itself, for the very nature of a primitive society is to subdue its members to a common discipline in which they serve a purpose they dare not seek to question. At bottom, that purpose is always the defence of the society from attack, the aggression of some other society, the anger of the Gods, the niggardliness of nature, the mysterious punishments the unpropitiated dead may threaten against the living who have failed to fulfil their fixed and rigid obligation to those who have passed into a life beyond this life. The taboos of a primitive society must never be broken; on the contrary they are its sheet-anchors, and the man who breaks them is obviously bringing the whole society into the gravest possible danger. Those taboos still persist. There are many who believe that those outside the true faith will be eternally damned; and they are prepared to punish the insistent heretic even with death, in part, perhaps, for his own salvation, but, above all, lest his heresy contaminate the society and thus lead it to destruction.

But this belief that heresies are crimes to be punished is true of politics as well as of religion; and it is especially true when the society concerned is anxious about its future. A sense of urgent danger in any community acts at once as a demand for uniformity of ideas and of behaviour. It develops a need for reassurance, almost a ritual of appeasement, a desire to expel the elements of nonconformity which are held to threaten the power of the society to stand firm and united against its enemies. Most characteristics of Russian history are of a kind only too likely to reinforce this outlook. There is no constitutional tradition which could have made the right of opposition almost part of the process of government. Literacy is so new that it is easy to understand the quick susceptibility of the population to propaganda built round the two themes that the old Russian world was evil and that the external enemies of Russia seek to restore that old world. The mental climate of the 'cold war' emphasises in the memory of Russians over thirty the hard days of the Revolution and civil war—the latter

241

so much encouraged by external enemies—and to those under thirty it keeps alive, vividly and fearfully, the barbarous cruelties of Hitler's invasion, keeps them alive, indeed, more painfully by the visible fact that most Germans still hate the Russians, and that the Atlantic Powers, under the leadership of the United States, think of Russia's future in terms of a readiness to use the Western Germany they have called into being as the basis of the attack by which they hope to destroy a way of life they know to be ultimately incompatible with their own.

'We may prate of democracy,' wrote Sir Arthur Quiller-Couch, 'but actually, a poor child in England has little more hope than had the son of a Athenian slave to be emancipated into that intellectual freedom of which great writings are born.' There may be some degree of exaggeration in that judgment, but there is also a profound truth in its severity. In an important sense the Russian Revolution has evoked a hatred which, even after more than thirty years, has not yet begun to exhaust itself. It is a hatred which goes far deeper than anything evoked by the French Revolution. The great events in France brought the middle class to power, but, in a fundamental way, its conquest of political power merely gave formal recognition to a change that had been in the making in the economic sphere for more than two hundred years. To the social outcome of that change the churches had no difficulty in adapting themselves, with the result that the sanctions in their armoury continued for many years to be an invaluable addition to the discipline imposed by the combined strength of the state-power and the market economy. The Christian churches seemed to give unreserved support to the necessary operative principles of capitalist civilisation; and the appearance of continuous economic expansion, at least up to 1914, and, psychologically, even up to 1939, both in Europe and in America always seemed to mean that, with intelligence and goodwill, what were regarded as temporary difficulties could be overcome if changes were made in the proper spirit of national give-and-take. Compromise, as we have always been reminded, is the whole art of successful politics.

I do not think it is difficult to understand why, for almost a century after the Chartist Movement failed, that outlook carried such overwhelming weight in a country like Great Britain.

242

It had an unbroken constitutional tradition of more than two hundred and fifty years. Up to the outbreak of the First World War, it seemed to possess not only remarkable economic security, but wealth enough to enable its upper and middle classes always to offer to its workers sufficient concessions to persuade them not to risk endangering the foundations of its social system. The persuasion, indeed, went so far that a majority of the leaders in the socialist movement, alike on its parliamentary and its trade union side, were deeply anxious to avoid discussion of the real nature and function of the state-power, the meaning, or the reality of the class struggle, or the degree to which reason would persuade a ruling class to accept the necessity for a wholesale change in the special privileges its legal title to rule enabled it to enjoy. Revolutions were events which occurred in unhappy countries where despotism begat misery, like Russia, and revolutionists were mostly poor and excitable exiles who, after some failure to seize power in their own country, found a refuge here in which they delighted to spend their days in the British Museum, a place which most Labour leaders knew as a place like the Zoo in Regent's Park, or Madame Tussaud's, where the strange exhibits might interest the children on a wet bank-holiday. Nothing illustrates more profoundly, I think, the completeness of the British sense of security in the years before the First World War was over than the fact that Philip Snowden, already a national figure, was a bitter critic of Sir Edward Grey's foreign policy, especially the alliance with Tsarist Russia that it involved after 1907, while he admitted, almost a generation later, in his *Autobiography*, that in 1917 he had never heard of Lenin, and that, had he done so, he did not think he would have wished to meet him. Philip Snowden built his socialist faith on a body of abstract ethical principles which, as a whole, amounted to a still more abstract conception called 'justice', which became concrete by the straightforward process of eventually winning a socialist majority in the House of Commons, and proceeding, by appropriate legislative changes, to use that majority to transform private into public ownership of the means of production, distribution and exchange.

It is hard to know how early it dawned upon the leaders of the Labour Party in Great Britain that the October Revolution

243

in Russia was, like 1789 in France, one of those immense historical upheavals which would inevitably alter the outlook of every man and woman not only among those who could lead, but also among those who could follow. It was an upheaval so profound that for literally scores of millions of human beings it called into question the validity of values which few of them had ever thought of questioning until its vast shadows began to brood ominously over the world. It involved, above all for the politicians who performed with such distinction the historic minuet of Westminster and Washington two great difficulties that disturbed them greatly. The Russian Revolution, first, while it could be explained, could not be explained away; and dissatisfied people everywhere, not least in the ancient East, began, almost to their own surprise, to suspect that patterns of power which they had been taught to think of as eternal, were in truth as liable to change as the pattern of Tsarist power. The growth of this suspicion, moreover, coincided with the growing public perception that the axis of economic supremacy was shifting rapidly after 1919, had, indeed, already in considerable degree shifted, from Europe generally, and from Great Britain in particular, to the American continent, where its character was largely moulded by the unique combination inherent in the material resources, the technology and the productive relations of the United States. The suspicion, further, coincided with the development of an economic depression at once so far-reaching and so profound as to offer convincing proof of the central thesis upon which the Bolsheviks had made the October Revolution—the thesis that the maintenance of the productive relations called for by capitalism was incompatible with the realisation of the dignity of man.

How grimly the inter-war years drove home that lesson can be found in a mass of quite decisive experience — in the paralysis of the American business man in 1933 until the three or four months were over during which, almost prayerfully, he watched the efforts of President Roosevelt to restore confidence in the United States, in the distressed areas of Great Britain where continuous unemployment ate away self-respect and hope in thousands, and where in 1939 the outbreak of war offered to large numbers of young people the first chance of a paid job offered to them since they had left school at fourteen, in that swift decay of French patriotism, above all among those with large incomes, which made the step from enthusiasm for the neo-Fascism of La Roque a bridge over which they passed to the acceptance of that Vichyisme which meant the end of their country's independence, or in the nightmare years of Hitler's barbarism so ugly in its methods that to innumerable decent minds the declaration of war against him in 1939 brought to them something like a sense of peace. There are a hundred similar instances to illustrate the incompatibility of a capitalist society, even if its political form were democratic, with a life that was gracious and dignified not for some fragment of mankind especially favoured by birth or wealth or the chance possession of acquisitive skill, but for all men and women prepared to earn their bread by the sweat of their brows.

Even in those inter-war years, the immense efforts of the Russian people to consolidate the gains of the October Revolution and assure security for their development encountered, from almost every quarter, the selfish fanaticism of a plutocracy in retreat. That is, I think, shown above all by two things. There was not a Foreign Office in the whole of Europe which ever had the desire, much less the will, to make the system of collective security to which their governments were pledged work with a genuine degree of effectiveness; that is shown clearly enough by the sacrifice of Abyssinia to Italy, the hollow mockery of non-intervention in Spain, and the pitiless aquiescence in Hitler's destruction of independent Austria and independent Czechoslovakia, and, further, had not both Mussolini and Hitler possessed ambitions which cut across the lifelines of the other capitalist powers in Europe and the Middle East, with Japan in a similar frame of mind in the Far East, it would not have been impossible in the years between the two world wars to have staged a gigantic counter-revolution at the expense of Russia the cost of which would have been borne by the workers all over the world. That is, after all, the secret which underlay Mr. Neville Chamberlain's passionate search for appeasement; he was driven to the humiliation of Munich by his conviction that its alternative was a war of which, as he said, he believed that Soviet Russia would be the residuary legatee. Hitler apart, Mr. Churchill's approach was not in

245

principle very different. He was for Franco in Spain, for Mussolini in Italy, for King George and Metaxas in Greece, and his determination to destroy Hitlerism, so superbly displayed in the supreme hours of danger, was entirely compatible, as he has himself made plain, with thinking out ways and means, even at the moment when the Germans were fighting in the streets of Stalingrad, by which the idea of the Russian Revolution—to his mind simply "barbarism"—could be contained within the historic frontiers of Russia. It is not, I think, excessive to say that well before the victory over Hitlerism in Europe Mr. Churchill had thought out all the implications of what later came to be known as the 'Truman Doctrine', and that the main source of his anger at his defeat in 1945 was that he did not remain in a position to carry it out with the immense authority in his hands that would have come to him with a new period of five years as the Prime Minister of Great Britain. He found only a diminished comfort in expanding the immense reputation he had justly won as a war-time leader in the effort to speed the organisation of the challenge to the Russian Revolution he had failed to complete at the end of the First World War.

This is in fact to say that for over thirty years capitalist interests have waged a world-wide campaign to destroy the new values which the October Revolution was seeking to affirm. The campaign had the same effect as similar campaigns during the Cromwellian Revolution in seventeenth-century England or that of 1789 in France. It drove the men who made the Revolution into securing its survival by means of a ruthless dictatorship which sought, for its own safety, to exploit every source of discontent they could discover outside the boundaries of Russia; and it drove the enemies of Russia not only to intensify their effort to break the revolutionary impetus inside Russia, but to break also the effort to communicate its dynamic beyond. They failed in both. They failed inside Russia because the leaders of the Revolution were relentless in their repression of any threat to their authority. They failed outside Russia because they were never willing to pay the price of creating a dynamic of their own. By 1937, for example, the New Deal of President Roosevelt lost its major driving power in the economic field through what can only be termed the sullen and angry

246

sabotage of the great corporations. British policy, under Mr. Neville Chamberlain, still clung to that historic orthodoxy of the Treasury which accepted the equilibrium created by the market economy as a limit beyond which adventure was dangerous; in the result there were never less than a million unemployed until the inescapable imperatives of the war made its demands on manpower the equivalent of a public works programme. In France neither the Socialists nor the Socialist Radicals could ever gather strength enough to make changes of sufficient importance to convince the mass of the workers of their faith in their own formal ideals; and, where they did reform, as in the shorter working week, and the institution of holidays with pay, they reduced production in the very areas where the worsening international situation should have impelled them to increase it. Nor did they show in their foreign policy the *élan* and the decisiveness which might have given new inspiration to the French workers. They accepted, usually without regret, the lead of Mr. Chamberlain towards appeasement; after the assassination of M. Barthou in 1934, the only initiative French Governments displayed was exhibited in the efforts of Laval and Bonnet, supported by a host of lesser figures, to outdo Mr. Chamberlain in his search for accommodation with Mussolini and Hitler. When M. Daladier acquiesced in the assassination of Czechoslovakia at Munich, he entered upon the path that led straight to Vichy; he threw away not only the goodwill of his main foreign allies, but which was worse he broke the spirit of his own fellow-citizens by enabling what was in fact organised treason to clothe itself in the garments of peace at any price. He enabled corruption to pose as patriotism, and the enemies of French democracy to attack its freedom on the pretence that by seeking an alliance with Hitler and renouncing the false friendship of Great Britain, they were finding the sources of new greatness in France through the sufferings of Nazi occupation.

The years from 1918 to 1939 are haunted years. They led from a bad peace to an unnecessary war. The governments of France and Great Britain as well as, in large degree, the governments of the United States, reserved for their enemies the support and enthusiasm they refused to offer to their friends. There was a number of occasions before 1933 when help to the

Weimar Republic would have destroyed the Hitler Movement; not only did they never give that help, but they were never willing to recognise the menace of Hitlerism, even after his advent to power, when his overthrow would have been an easy adventure. Until the Italo-Abyssinian War, they encouraged and supported Mussolini; their refusal to impose real sanctions upon him not only broke the League of Nations, but was a deliberate encouragement to the dark forces everywhere in the world. It was the same story in the Far East. When he was Foreign Secretary at the time of the first large-scale threat by Japan against Chinese unity and independence, Sir John (now Viscount) Simon not only refused to co-operate with the American Secretary of State, Mr. Henry L. Stimson, who proposed an Anglo-American initiative against this aggression; he was the principal advocate in defence of the Japanese Government even though it was everywhere known that the aggression was merely the first step in a policy intended to reduce China virtually to the position of a colony dependent upon Japan. An eminent Conservative politician, Mr. L. S. Amery, actually urged upon the British Government the duty of inaction on the ground that the Japanese were doing in China no more than we ourselves had done in the acquisition of India; and he argued quite simply that Japan should be left unimpeded because there was no other way in which an empire could be won. It is ironical indeed, as one looks back, to realise that the consequence of leaving Japan to continue its effort to eat up China as though it was an artichoke had the results, first, of enabling Japanese militarism to mobilise all the raw materials necessary to enable it to play its monstrous part in the Second World War, second, to destroy thereby the greater part of the prestige of the colonial empires in the Orient, and, third, to encourage Hitler by offering to him, in the critical years, one more demonstration that aggression evoked not punishment but an appeasement out of which important gains could be secured. And in the years between 1931 and 1945 the hatred of Communism was so basic an element in the thinking of most political leaders in Europe and America that few of them had any serious notion, when Japan was finally defeated, either of the intense hold that nationalism, with its inherent demands for independence, had gained upon the peoples of the East, or

248

how far the idea of national independence was tied to a vision of social liberation as well. That blindness wrecked American policy in China; the speed of the Chinese Communists' ability to wreck the régime of Chiang Kai-shek despite the vast aid he received from Washington was mainly due to the contrast between his social policy and that of Mao-Tse-tung and to the recognition that such Chinese reformers who supported Chiang were totally devoid of serious influence. It was obvious not only to the common people of China, but also to Chiang's own armies and their leaders, that the Generalissimo had become the instrument of a vast horde of commercial and agrarian gangsters to whom victory over Japan merely meant the hope of relentless and unimpeded exploitation. American policy in China disintegrated. But even more foolish were the efforts of the Dutch and the French to retain colonial empires the foundations of which were ruined beyond hope. The one bright fact in the whole Far Eastern picture was the wise decision of the Labour Government in Britain — a decision for which the main credit belongs to its Prime Minister, Mr. Attlee —to recognise that they had neither the physical power nor the ethical right to impose their sovereignty upon Burma and India and Ceylon, and to pretend that peoples were the partners of Great Britain whose main objective was to rid themselves of its yoke, if need be by the unleashing of what would have been a guerilla war as ugly as it would have been ruinous. By accepting the inevitable in a friendly spirit, Mr. Attlee probably saved more in material wealth and moral prestige for his country than any other policy could have achieved. It is only regrettable that his Cabinet did not insist upon an equal wisdom in his Foreign Secretary's fantastic policies in the Middle East, and especially in Palestine, and those of his Colonial Secretary in Malaya. An ideological approach to the problems of empire which begins with the assumption that all Communists are bandits, and all bandits Communists, is not likely to formulate with any approach to adequacy the nature of the problems which a Minister has to solve, least of all when these problems are made a hundred times more intricate by the psychological results of a revolutionary upheaval. That, certainly, is the perspective in which the British Government must set the issue it has to decide about the future of Hong Kong.

CHAPTER XIV

THE more closely, in fact, we examine Russian policy, the more clearly do two major tendencies emerge. On the one hand, the outlook of its government is deeply permeated by fear. It is afraid of the immense productive potential of the United States; it will be many years before it can compete with that potential were the 'cold war' to be transformed into a shooting war. It is afraid of the implications of the vast alliance of powers which has been built up around the strength of the United States, since, strategically, only the instant conquest of the West European Powers, and of the Middle East, as well as the bases in the Pacific taken over by Washington, could give it effective protection against large-scale bombing, including the atomic bombing of important Russian cities which are now being painfully rebuilt. It is afraid of the new West German state, so obviously now itself an American base, and eager to win back the occupied Eastern Zone and be in a position to revise the provisional Oder-Neisse frontier laid down at Potsdam. It cannot be sure that, in another war, the immense pressure it has been compelled for so long to impose upon its own peoples will evoke the same remarkable response as it did from 1941 to 1945, it knows that the masses are fatigued, and the scars of the devastation wrought by the wanton brutality of the Nazi invaders has gone too deep, both physically and psychologically, to be healed rapidly; that is one of the major reasons why its propaganda is so earnest in its loud insistence that the Western Powers are bent on Russia's destruction. That it fears the possibility that, in a new world war, the Red Army might develop into a position where its standing might develop into quasi-independence of the Party, and even rivalry with it for leadership, is suggested by the speed with which the Politbureau pushed the remarkable military leaders of the struggle against Germany into a background which, for most of them, has almost become oblivion. Nor is it possible to doubt that the immense energy devoted to preventing any normal contacts

251

between the Russian people, so endowed by nature with the genius for friendship, is, first of all, the fear that a wider knowledge of Western achievement might stir up discontent among millions whose standard of life is still low compared with that of Western countries, and, second, make it far more difficult to impose the tightness of control which the M.V.D. is still able to persuade the Politbureau in Moscow to regard as an urgent necessity. Generalissimo Stalin is well aware that, given a period of peaceful development sufficient to let the masses be offered ease instead of hardship, there will arise in Russia the demand for both a personal and a political freedom which no Russian Government could deny; but he and his colleagues in the party leadership are convinced that the time has not yet come for any relaxation of the immense police-power—still an *imperium in imperio*—upon which they believe the security of their régime continues to depend. For them, both personal and political freedoms are luxuries born of security; and it is obvious from the aggressive obstinacy both of Molotov and of Vishinsky that they feel no assurance that they have yet attained that security. They remain convinced that, under American leadership, a conspiracy is maturing for the over-throw of Russia; and even in the offers of friendship that have been made to them, they find proposals and propositions intended, in their view, to work to their grave detriment. In no sphere, of course, is this attitude more important than in that of the control of atomic energy—perhaps the most disturbing area of conflict in international relationships to-day. For though the Lilienthal - Acheson plan seems an outstanding act of generosity to most Americans, what disturbs the Russians is that, if they accepted it, the pace of peaceful development in this supreme field of research would be mainly in capitalist hands, or in that of governments unable to free themselves from capitalist pressure; and the very important fact that their own counter-proposals, which go a very long way to meeting the central problem, have never been examined with anything like reasonable consideration since they were first put forward. Nor have they failed to note that the Truman - Attlee announce-ment that atom bombs have been successfully exploded in Russia evoked from the Western Powers, not the realisation that new discussions had become imperative, but the determination to enlarge the atomic programme, and especially the American, so that the original American lead could be maintained. The whole episode, from the day when President Truman announced at Potsdam to Generalissimo Stalin the forthcoming explosion of the first bomb over Hiroshima has been bedevilled by the insistence of the Pentagon in Washington that the problems of atomic energy must be set first in a military and only second—and a long way behind—in a civil context. So liberal-minded an administrator as Mr. Lilienthal as head of the American Atomic Authority has not been able to conceal the fact that he works in an atmosphere in which both the Pentagon and a large part of American public opinion think of atomic energy in terms of its military potential, with a far slighter interest in the immense possibilities of its civilian use.

It is fear, also, which is the governing factor both in the creation, and in the functioning, of the powers which, under the tutelage of Russia, make up the Cominform. Nothing demonstrates this fact so well as the expulsion of Tito's Yugoslavia from its membership' and the consequential campaign waged against him. It is notable, first, that from the moment of victory, the Russians were anxious to 'cushion' their Western frontiers by a barrier of 'friendly' governments. It is notable, second, that, as Russian relations with the Western Powers deteriorated, the Russian government began to define a 'friendly' government as one in which the vital posts were held by Communists. There then came a third stage in which non-Communist Ministers, who were deemed 'unreliable', capable, that is, of putting obstacles in the way of Russia's conception of policy, were driven out of coalition governments; examples of this are Nagy in Hungary, and Mikolajczyk in Poland. The fact that both fled to the United States, where they were warmly received, and began, almost at once, to publish attacks on Russia, convinced the Kremlin that this expulsion of the 'unreliable' was a vital necessity. The next stage arose out of the Marshall Plan which was regarded in Moscow in part as a method of bringing the states to be aided under the economic domination of America, and in part as making that economic domination lead directly to political dependence. Russia, therefore, refused to join in the plan, and compelled the Eastern

253

allies to refuse to join also; it is decisive in significance to note here that Czechoslovakia, then under Benes and Masaryk, which signalised its desire to join, was compelled to reverse its view; and it is not, I think, improper to infer that this sign of 'unreliability' was a weighty element in the decision to establish the Czechoslovak Communist régime in February, 1948.

I think it must be added that, mingled with this fear, there was a real hope, uncertain but not the less important for that, that the misery and devastation caused by the war might well lead, under suitable direction to an important expansion of Communist influence. I do not myself see how, otherwise, it is possible adequately to explain the ruthless Communist attitude to the satellite states of Russia, the unmistakable reliance upon the outcome of a postulated increasing misery in the capitalist world, or to the use of propaganda which was bound by its very nature to risk the danger that the 'cold war' would cease to be mainly economic and ideological in character. It is not, I think, an exaggeration to say that from some such period as the Stuttgart speech of Mr. James Byrnes, then the American Secretary of State, in the autumn of 1946, the directive of the Politbureau in Moscow was mainly hostile to the kind of effort which would lead to any real *modus vivendi* between Russia and its allies, on the one hand, and to the United States and its allies, on the other.

It was, indeed, a ruthlessness wholly certain of itself. That is shown by the elbow-room given to the well-known economist, Eugene Varga, to argue, in the face of overwhelming expert opinion in Russia, that there would not be a rapid degeneration of economic conditions in the United States, and that any policy built upon its expectation was bound to fail. In the normal way, Varga's persistence in a minority view would have led to a decision to reduce him to silence, accompanied, on his part, by a humble recantation. No such result followed; and it seems natural to infer from the tenderness with which his dissent was received, that his arguments had at least sown doubts in the minds of the political leaders. But it is equally reasonable to infer that the full-scale attack upon any breath of independence among the members of the Cominform, above all the savage repudiation of Tito's 'national Communism', and, only in a less degree, trials like those of Rajk and his co-defendants in

Hungary, were the expression of a determination on the part of Moscow to break all possibility of any hope of independence in the satellite states. It is, moreover, hard to avoid the conclusion that the Russian treatment of the Eastern Zone in Germany, as well as the harsh demands which were the main barrier to the conclusion of a peace-treaty with Austria, were, in both cases, a deliberate bid for delay made in the hope of a breakdown in the Western economy which would have given Communism a right of entry which it would otherwise have been unable to obtain. Certainly the pretended technical difficulties in Berlin transport are part of a history which is inexplicable unless one assumes that the Russian purpose was to drive the Western Powers out of Berlin, and thus to secure a prestige which would have resounded throughout the world. Even though I believe it to be true that the major purpose of Anglo-American policy in the Western Zones was at once to thwart the danger of any gain there in Russian influence, and, as a result of that overriding purpose, to close their eyes to the re-conquest of power in Western Germany by so many of the men, and the influences, who were basically chauvinist, and, therefore, pro-Nazi from 1933 until Hitler's overthrow in 1945, Russian policy, from Potsdam onwards, has assumed more and more a character which makes the possibility of the renewal of the Russo-German alliance of 1939 likelier than the creation of a unified Germany in which, to the common interest of the world, one could detect some real prospect of the dawn of democracy and the acceptance of peace. If the mistakes of Anglo American policy in Germany—the refusal, for instance, to establish socialised ownership and control in the heavy industries of the Ruhr— were of Himalayan magnitude, the Russian preparation of the Eastern Zone to be one of its new dependencies was bound to bring the *bona fides* of its policy into doubt even with those most anxious to be its friends.

To all this, moreover, there must be added the painful impression produced both by Russian policy and by Russian propaganda in other areas of activity. It is easy to see why the proclamation of the 'Truman Doctrine' should have caused genuine alarm in Moscow; it is even easy to see why Marshall Aid should have looked there too like the price for acceptance of something akin to the 'Truman Doctrine', and thus a special

255

form of insurance against goodwill for Russia. But, surely, the one sure way of testing the character of the American offer was an agreement to explore its possibilities, and not to reject it out of hand. It may well be true that the American Government would either have withdrawn the offer of Marshall Aid if its ambit had included assistance to Russia, or would have laid down terms for the extension of its aid that it would have been impossible for Russia to accept while maintaining its self-respect. What arose from Molotov's curt refusal at Paris even to engage with other countries in exploratory discussions with Washington was the profound conviction that the rulers of Russia viewed with suspicion and alarm even the prospect of European recovery through American aid; and each step of their policy, thenceforward, had the ugly look of a conscious effort to block the hope of that recovery by splitting the European continent into two camps. It was not as though Russia made, or was, indeed, in a position to make, an offer of aid comparable in magnitude to the American offer; on the contrary, its attitude, first, was an implied suggestion to the Western Powers, and especially to Great Britain, to accept the risks of a catastrophic fall in their standards of life—which might easily have led, and may still lead, to the outbreak of large-scale civil war—and, second, to realise that economic relations between the East and West of Europe would, in the future, depend upon a calculation made in Moscow as to whether more or less trade would be of assistance to the ultimate purposes Moscow cherished.

For it is obvious that an acceptance of the Russian formula by Western Europe would have meant economic breakdown. That could not have been imposed by governments like those, for example, of France or Great Britain on any acceptable constitutional basis; it would, therefore, have meant either elections, at which they would have been beaten at the polls, or an attempt, of which the success would have been dubious at least, to govern by methods which overrode their constitutional traditions. In Great Britain, certainly, a general election upon this basis would have made certain the victory of reaction; and Mr. Churchill, as its leader, would have rejoiced at the opportunity thus afforded him to take the country into a complete alliance with the forces hostile to Russia all over the

256

world. He could then have claimed electoral support for his decision; and the Labour Opposition would have been politically helpless. No doubt his economic measures would have aroused strong trade union resistance; but the elementary lesson of 1926 is the unmistakable one that trade union resistance, under bad trade circumstances, invites hopeless defeat, unless it transforms itself into a conscious battle for the state-power. To no one is this better known than it is to the Russian leaders; for the conditions of revolutionary victory have been set out by Lenin with magistral clarity in one of the most famous of his pronouncements. And though this situation is true in France in a much less degree, since the hold there of the Communists on the trade unions was much stronger than in Great Britain, the general character of the analysis is, I think, valid there also.

The fact is that in 1945 Soviet Russia had an immense fund of goodwill at its disposal, a considerable part of which its own policies have thrown away. Mainly, I think, the loss of that goodwill has been due to activities born of its own fears, and for some of those fears there was substantial ground. But an important element in the loss is the attempt by Russia to exact an unquestioning obedience to its orders, and profound psychological irritation caused by the mixture of arrogance and invective in its negotiations, and the return to a profound hostility to democratic Socialism. The significance of this hostility must not be underestimated. It has led to a repetition of the tactics of the years after the October Revolution. Democratic Socialists have been ardently wooed all over Europe, above all in the name of working-class unity, against the common capitalist enemy. But whenever the wooing has been successful, democratic Socialism has been broken into fragments, as in Italy, or greatly reduced in power and influence, as in France, or has been swallowed up as a python swallows a rabbit, where the wooing has been unsuccessful. Notably in Great Britain, all Communist propaganda has virtually returned to that disastrous pre-war phase where the Labour Party was represented as social-fascist in character, and the attempt has been continuous, on the trade union side, to hamper the Labour Government's effort at economic recovery. The communist attempt to slow down economic recovery in Great Britain is of exceptional importance because it has led them to support policies in the

257

trade unions which, quite obviously, could only lead to the sheer disaster of inflation, and it has shown little or no power to recognise how urgent is the continuance of a Labour Government in office to safeguard the workers themselves against the dangers implicit in the attitude of the employers to the increasing impetus of socialist policy. So far from the advance of socialism in Great Britain having assisted closer Anglo-Russian relations, it seems, as far as Moscow is concerned, to have assisted in their deterioration.

I think, myself, that there are aspects of the Labour Government's policy which Russia is entitled to regard as hostile to the building up of a common purpose. That is true of Greece, where Great Britain, in concert with the United States, has virtually imposed a corrupt and fascist-minded régime on the Greek people, and aided it with troops, munitions, and finance. Most of the excuses put forward in defence of these activities do not conceal the fact that the Anglo-American object is the strategic one of preventing Communism from reaching the Mediterranean; and the attitude to Greece of the two Western governments does not differ in nature from that of the Russian Government to Rumania or Poland or Hungary, against which both Great Britain and the United States have so bitterly complained. The main direction of British policy in the Middle East, moreover, has been, Palestine apart, to support jointly with the United States, a number of obsolete and evil feudal systems in return for the control of their vast oil reserves, and so powerful a voice in their foreign policies as to make them virtually Anglo-American air bases in the event of war. The Kingdom of Transjordan, for example, like the now-decaying Arab League, is wholly the creation of the British Foreign Office. Its territory was carved out for it from Palestine as a consolation for the failure of the Emir Abdullah to realise higher ambitions; and it was transformed into an independent kingdom, in sinister circumstances, by a British unilateral act. Its army is trained by the British, by whose subsidies it is wholly maintained; and a treaty of mutual friendship puts both its foreign policy and its aerodromes in the keeping of Great Britain. Nowhere in the Middle East, has either Great Britain or the United States sought to influence any of the Arab rulers to think in terms of so modernising their governments as to offer the Arab peoples
258

the prospect of improved health, better education, agricultural advance, the application of the heavy royalties paid to these fantastic rulers to elevate their peoples from the conditions of abject and helpless poverty in which they live. From a different angle, much the same is true of the British and American attitudes to Turkey and to Iran; in both cases, they subsidise bad government for strategic purposes. What they could do there, were it not for their hostility to Communism, is shown by the contrast between Soviet Armenia, and Turkish Armenia, or between Soviet Azerbaijan, and the Iranian province of Azerbaijan. Anglo-American policy is built upon a vested interest in ignorance, disease, and poverty, which are preserved in the wholly mistaken belief that these protect that interest from the infiltrations of Communist ideas.

The short-sighted folly of the Anglo-American view has now been demonstrated on a massive scale by the Communist advance in China. It is obvious that a repressed nationalism which has suffered long exploitation, internal or external in origin, is far more likely to be influenced by Communism than by any rival idea now sponsored by either Great Britain or the United States. The problem then becomes the very grave one of the speed with which Communism, with all its lines of approach leading from the central pattern woven at Moscow, can be reconciled with the much slower dynamic of ideas which emanate from Washington, or London, or Paris. The problem, moreover, is intensified by the fact that, behind Russian ideology is the passion of a religious faith, which, despite its errors and its cruelties, sweeps away into the waste-paper bag of history so many of the obstacles to progress, whether they are the decadent rulers who make government no more than the maintenance of irrational and obsolete privilege, or those who use it to prevent the painful but necessary habituation of a people to the organisation and the skills required by modern technology. Russian ideology may break the fetters of the past with a ruthless, even a barbarian disregard for life and freedom and law. What is important is not only that the fetters of the past are broken, but that most of those who are thus led from one bondage to another nevertheless recognise in the new bondage a step, as it were, in a dark tunnel through which they move towards the light.

All this may seem far removed from the point I set out to discuss earlier — the difficulty of dealing with Communist powers and with individual Communists, because their operations are conducted on the basis of a dual morality. Their conception of ethical behaviour is based on the broad assumption that whatever serves the Communist Revolution is right conduct, and that Moscow is the best judge of what best serves the Communist Revolution. Once they accept that criterion, they associate with non-Communists on terms that the latter do not understand; and in so far as they do understand them, they distrust the association and fear its consequences. It is worth while remembering that the same problem emerged at the time of the French Revolution. The propagandist enthusiasm of its missionaries set out to undermine not merely the foundations of the *ancien régime* in France, but of all societies in which the third estate was excluded from its due share, as they conceived it, of power. As they sowed the seed of their doctrine, they were convinced that they were emancipating whole nations from dead and outworn doctrines; it was a source of amazement to them that they were attacked, instead of welcomed, in the famous pamphlets of Burke and Joseph de Maistre. How they appeared to those who did not share their views has been admirably put by the eminent French historian, Albert Sorel. 'They compare,' he wrote, 'the propagation of the new doctrines with the extension of French power, the emancipation of mankind with the greatness of the Republic, the rule of reason with that of France, the liberation of peoples with the conquest of states, the European revolution with the domination of the French Revolution over Europe.' And to this must be added the fact that hatred of or affection for 'Bonapartism' affected the earlier generation in much the same way as hatred of or affection for 'Stalinism' affects our own generation. Only the Roman Catholic Church and Soviet Russia consciously seek to propagate doctrines which each believes to be universally valid and the key to all future well-being. It is not the least interesting feature of both the Roman Church and Soviet Russia that they should exact from those who believe in them the duty of unconditional obedience, and that the main attack against them should come from the nation-state, the rights of which they regard as transcended by their own claims, and that the main ground of that attack should be, in both cases, that their members cannot give to the nation-state to which they belong, an allegiance which is unexcepted and entire.

It is important here, I think, to recognise two things. The first is that allegiance to Moscow, like allegiance to Rome, creates this *à priori* distrust of those who hold it in a large degree, because, since the breakdown of the mediaeval *respublica christiana*, we have not been accustomed to think seriously of a loyalty which can, by its very nature, transcend national boundaries, and seek to transform a national community by means which do not arise from within that community, and for purposes to which it may be violently opposed. This is largely because, during the last century and a half, religious passion, both in Europe and America, has been comparatively rare, and it is easy to tolerate beliefs which have still more rarely any influence upon social and political behaviour. When the passion religion could create began to become in large degree something personal and inward, it seemed to move to a plane where its public relevance seemed slight enough to be treated with indifference. It is nevertheless obvious that if religious passion were once again to seek social and external expression, it would rapidly make the question of tolerance a matter for angry debate in which the force of public opinion would make the government of a national community watch carefully the shape of events. It is not very difficult to see how swiftly a major blunder by Rome could awaken at once the fierce anti-clericalism deeply rooted in France. It certainly seems as though the widening claims of the Roman Catholic Church in the United States which, in the single realm of education, do not seem in harmony with the separation of Church and State which most Americans profoundly desire to maintain, might—I do not think it impossible—if they were too arrogantly made, easily arouse into flames the ashes of fierce controversies that have long seemed to be cold and dead. Nor must we forget the depth of feeling that has been aroused by the conflict in East European States since the war between the Roman Catholic Church and the governments of the new 'people's democracies'. It is an illuminating thing that a Cardinal-Archbishop should seem a martyr to millions when he admits illegal exchange activities, and confesses to steps the purpose of which was the overthrow

261

of a political system he hated with all his strength. Had he known the decision Cardinal Mindzenty might well have used the words spoken by Chief Justice Hughes in a well-known dissent: 'In the forum of conscience,' said the Chief Justice, 'duty to a moral power higher than the State has always been maintained. The reservation of that supreme obligation, as a matter of principle, would unquestionably be made by many of our conscientious and law-abiding citizens.'[1]

Chief Justice Hughes may well be right when tempers are cool, and no great interests are at stake. He is quite certainly wrong when tempers are hot, and men feel that fundamental things are in danger. That has a contemporary proof in the trial of Rajk and his associates in Budapest in the autumn of 1949. No one who reads the public evidence, least of all the confessions, can for a moment believe that they represent anything like the whole truth of the matter. The affair is an act in a vast drama, the purpose of which is to establish the supremacy of Stalin, just as the Popes struggled against men, the depth of whose Christianity is obvious to us, in order to establish the supremacy of Rome. When it can be accepted as evidence, on the testimony of one Brankov, that Tito was an ally of Mr. Churchill in a common effort to win the Balkans and Eastern Europe for Western imperialism, anything can be believed. The agreement is as persuasive as the insistence that Mr. Churchill and Generalissimo Stalin joined hands in the hope of overthrowing Soviet Russia, because the latter accepted with enthusiasm the British convoys that fought their way so bravely to Murmansk. The truth obviously is that Rajk had some relations with, perhaps some sympathy for, Marshal Tito's brand of 'national Communism', and thereby became a dangerous enemy in the eyes of Moscow. There is a notable resemblance between the attitude of the mediaeval Church to heresies like that of the Cathari, and their ruthless suppression by the Pope and the Inquisition, on the one side, and the feudal nobility in, for example, Languedoc, on the other, and that of Moscow and the Cominform, as the spiritual power defining what may be believed, and the governments of the satellite states enforcing

[1] U.S. v. Macintosh, 1930. 243 U.S. 405. The majority of the Court decided that a conscientious objection to military service is a bar to the naturalisation of an alien.

262

submission by death and imprisonment. Do not let us forget that the persecution of the Albigenses achieved the status of a Crusade; or the important fact that when the heretic was brought before the secular court, the man who defended him there was certain himself to be an orthodox believer, and that he would therefore not only denounce the faith of the defendant, but insist that the conduct to which it led might easily undermine, by its social implications, the very foundations of government. Nor is it without significance that the Albigensian heresy, like the long-related tradition which preceded it, is shot through with a nationalist spirit which is always, in some degree, an attempt to escape from that Papal supremacy which sought to transcend nationalism, and impose everywhere a uniform doctrine to which Rome alone retained the key.[1]

The point I am making has been put with incomparable force by Mr. Bernard Shaw in that superb scene in *Saint Joan*, where the Earl of Warwick discusses with Cauchon, the Bishop of Beauvais, the meaning of the cult of the Maid. 'What will the world be like,' says Cauchon, 'when The Church's accumulated wisdom and knowledge and experience, its councils of learned, venerable, pious men, are thrust into the kennel by every ignorant labourer or dairymaid whom the devil can puff up with the monstrous self-deceit of being directly inspired from Heaven? It will be a world of blood, of fury, of devastation, of each man striving for his own hand; in the end a world wrecked back into barbarism. For now you have only Mahomet and his dupes, and the Maid and her dupes; but what will it be when every girl thinks herself a Joan, and every man a Mahomet? I shudder to the very marrow of my bones when I think of it. I have fought it all my life; and I will fight it to the end. Let all this woman's sins be forgiven her except only this sin; for it is the sin against the Holy Ghost; and if she does not recant in the dust before the world, and submit herself to the last inch of her soul to her Church, to the fire she shall go, if she once falls into my hand.'[2]

Mr. Shaw has here, I think, with dramatic incisiveness, explained the *leitmotif* which obsesses the Russian Communist.

[1] Cf. the illuminating book by Steven Runciman: *The Medieval Manichee* (Cambridge, 1947).

[2] *Saint Joan*, Scene iv.

He knows that he is in possession of the truth. He is convinced that the application of the truth he possesses is, as it were, the central condition upon which the salvation of the world depends. He will, therefore, not only not admit that speculation outside the truth he knows can be valid; even more, he is fearful of entrusting the application to any hands but his own. The truth, to him, is so clear, moreover, that he finds it difficult to understand why others do not see it, as he sees it, in its splendid simplicity; and he can only attribute their failure to the persistence of old habits and obsolete traditions which sanctioned behaviour obviously obsolete as his truth became victorious. From this angle, therefore, the heretic's challenge is the most dangerous of all. For it not only permits a way of life he has forbidden; it puts that way under the protection of an alternative truth, which claims the right to compete with his own. It does not matter to him that the alternative truth may be sincerely held; the important thing about it, for him, is that it seeks to construct a different world from his, to challenge his authority, and, if it grow strong, to persecute him and those who share his view. Heresy has thus to be rooted out at the first moment of its discovery. It is like Satan offering to man all the kingdom of this world in exchange for the surrender of his own soul.

It thus becomes easy, I think, to see why the Russian Communists view with suspicion and dislike the attempt of the Western bourgeois world to break down the barriers which separate it from access to the Russian people. With infinite labour and sacrifice, the Party has been able to impose its way of life on all the millions of the Soviet Union. Its leaders are aware—how could they not be aware?—that there remain many among those millions who accept the way without enthusiasm, often with some scepticism, often through fear rather than conviction. Full relations with the Western bourgeois world is like admitting the enemy within the gates, to offer what the Party regards as a dead or dying past the chance of preventing, or, at least of delaying the emergence of the future. The Western bourgeoisie, with its growing scepticism, its smell of decay, which is seen in the breakdown of all its traditional values, its bitter hostility to whatever disturbs the hierarchical structure of privilege, to maintain which its whole power is devoted, could only operate so as to arrest the acceptance of the new life by men and women who, increasingly, have come to take it for granted as a natural human condition, self-confident, optimistic, powerful beyond all challenge, living by standards which set the individual in a context of social solidarity, instead of leaving him indifferent to the world, as long as he is free to discover himself. Soviet Russia cannot yet offer to most of its citizens the material advantages that are enjoyed by the more prosperous members of the Western bourgeoisie. Why, then, should its peoples be exposed to habits and temptations which could threaten the way of the new life?

It is, of course, an intolerant attitude to all who take the view that men and women should be free to choose their own truth, and the way of life it implies, and that the choice will be the better made the more full the opportunity that is open to them to discuss other conditions than those into which they were born. The historical fact is, of course, that the number of those in any period who would genuinely welcome tolerance of this order of magnitude has been in every society in every period pitifully small. After its adoption by Constantine, Christianity did not make its way by intellectual agreement with other religions; for all its missionary endeavour, its successes were won and consolidated by offering to the pagan the choice between conversion and penalties which often involved nothing less than wholesale massacre. The same has been true of Mahometanism right down to our own day. There are, no doubt, sects which have made the refusal to persecute a central principle of the faith they held—the Society of Friends, for example, and the English Baptists. But it is important that both of them were persecuted minority groups, and that both of them are closely related to other sects, the Fifth Monarchy Men in the seventeenth century civil wars, to take a single illustration, who were not only prepared to fight their way to power, but did not regard themselves as bound by any laws save those which they themselves made.

Nor is this determination to protect the group from the danger of permeation by alien ideas confined to the religious sphere. Quite obviously, Russian suspicion of the bourgeois West, is paralleled, if it is not equalled by, the suspicions of Communism entertained by the bourgeois West. The sheer

265

volume of anti-communist activity now carried on by the Federal and State governments in the United States has reached fantastic proportions; and to it must be added the kindred activity of groups like the American Legion, the Roman Catholic Church, the National Association of Manufacturers, and a host of other bodies. This anti-communist activity endangers the freedom of every official, every teacher, and the overwhelming majority of clergy, in the United States. It penalises most officials of trade unions. It results in loyalty purges, in trials, even in a number of mass trials, in the growth of a system of espionage, and dilation, the scale of which has to be examined closely in order to be realised. Anyone who reads the actual experiences of one victim of this system, Mr. William Remington, who was able, finally to clear himself,[1] will find himself in the same atmosphere as that which permeated the Russian trials in the 'thirties. Mr. Daniel Lang, who has investigated the Remington case in careful detail, tells us that in the two years since President Truman, in 1947, ordered a check to be made on the loyalty of all Federal officials, over two and one-third million people had been investigated; and the then Attorney-General, Mr. Justice Clark, had listed one hundred and fifty-nine organisations, membership in which was to be regarded as proof of disloyalty. 'The F.B.I. agents,' writes Mr. Lang, 'are usually unknown to the men they report on. And he rarely knows which of his friends, enemies, colleagues, neighbours, servants, grocers, haberdashers, and so on, supplied the agents with information. Even if he does, he may not confront his accusers at his hearing, unless they agree to appear.' The presidential directive creating the Loyalty Boards instructed them not to make any of their verdicts public. The government employee may do so, but the chances are that he won't. If he is found guilty, he is sure to keep silent; if he is declared innocent, he usually doesn't want it known that he was ever suspected. To this must be added the fact that men are asked to prove their loyalty, in the face of charges which are not even disclosed to them; and that the opening of letters and tapping of telephones—the latter a method of obtaining information which Mr. Justice Holmes long ago described as 'dirty business' —have become a regular feature in the life of any person upon

[1] *The New Yorker*, May 21st, 1939, p. 37.

whom, for whatever reason, suspicion may fall. Long interrogations by Federal agents, much in the manner of those so angrily denounced when they take place in Russia or its allies, are now fairly normal. The refusal of visas by the State Department to any foreign visitor who is either a Communist, or known to be sympathetic to an understanding with Communism, has become standard practice; an American, indeed, who marries someone who is, or has been, a member of the Communist Party and is an alien, will find that she cannot secure a visa to enter the United States. Just as the Russian Government will not allow women who marry foreigners to leave Russia, so the American Government will not allow the communist wives of Americans to enter the territory. The American practice, in relation to marriage, has simply become the Russian system in reverse.

It would, of course, be absurd even to suggest that witch-hunting in the United States has even the appearance of approximating to the scale upon which it is practised in Russia; and there are other countries in Western bourgeois civilisation. Franco Spain, for example, or the Argentine, where the record is infinitely more ugly. It is also important not to forget that there must have been some bad cases in Great Britain, and a good deal of disturbing evidence to suggest that, in the East End of London, the Metropolitan Police discriminate against Jews and Communists in the clashes which follow deliberately provocative utterances by Fascists at their meetings, as well as a tendency on the part of stipendiary magistrates in the London area to treat Communists or Jewish defendants accused, on such occasions, of a breach of the peace more severely than they treat Fascist defendants arrested on a similar charge. If we are honest, this is to say, with ourselves, we ought frankly to admit everywhere a grave deterioration in the habits of tolerance, a much swifter resort to measures of repression in the course of the last generation. The great difference between witch-hunting in the United States, and witch-hunting in Russia is the undoubted fact that, in Russia, as in the countries of the Cominform generally, there is far less regard for the sanctity of human life, and far less ability for any accused person either to be properly defended or to secure from public opinion the recognition that the government, in undertaking a prosecution, may be

267

guilty of grave error, or even of indefensible dishonesty. No one, to my knowledge, came forward when men like Bukharin, Rakovski, Kamenev, or Sokolnikov, were tried in Russia, to protest that an elaborate drama was being enacted, the real truth in which was deliberately being concealed from the public view; Dimitrov openly boasted that Petkov was executed because opinion outside Bulgaria intervened on his behalf as, fourteen years before, it had intervened to save Dimitrov himself from probable death in Hitlerite Germany; Rajk was hanged in Hungary without any voice there being raised to suggest that his death was probably a tactical move in the 'cold war' between Moscow and Belgrade. If one compares these examples with the relentless efforts of the Dreyfusards to establish the innocence of a man against whom the French War Office, vital members of the French General Staff, and some of the most eminent members of the Roman Catholic Church were united, the Russians come very badly out of the comparison. It is grim, indeed, that Mr. Remington should have had to undergo the experience he did; but, at least, he was vindicated and he found a body of faithful friends to support him along every inch of the painful road he was compelled to tread. Even in the fantastic case of Mr. Alger Hiss, not only did he defend himself with gallant and courageous pertinacity, but two Judges of the Supreme Court of the United States came forward to testify to their complete confidence in his personal integrity. I am, I think, right in saying that in none of the Russian trials, nor in those of the other Cominform states, has any testimony on behalf of the accused been proffered by his friends to the court; nor has there been, in any of the trials, a decisive retraction of the confession of guilt that is made, before ever the accused is brought into court. The very fact, indeed, of his appearance in court involves the assumption of his guilt before even the Public Prosecutor has made his opening speech; and the official press bays for his conviction every day that the trial continues.

[*At this point Prof. Laski's typescript stops at the end of a page; not even notes for the continuation have been found.—R.T.C.*]

INDEX

269

271